Just
Another
Soldier

Just
Another
Soldier

A Year on the Ground in Iraq

Jason Christopher Hartley

HARPER

NEW YORK • LONDON • TORONTO • SYDNEY

HARPER

Grateful acknowledgment is made for permission to reprint from the following:

"Institutionalized," written by Michael Muir, Amery Smith, and Louiche Mayorga; © 1984 Bug Music (BMI), American Lesion Music (BMI), and You'll Be Sorry Music (BMI); administered by Bug; all rights reserved; used by permission.

Background image on photograph spread (pages vi–vii) © Owen Franken/Corbis; all other photographs copyright Jason Christopher Hartley.

A hardcover edition of this book was published in 2005 by HarperCollins Publishers.

FIRST HARPER PAPERBACK PUBLISHED 2006.

Designed by Elliott Beard

The Library of Congress has catalogued the hardcover edition as follows:
Hartley, Jason Christopher.
    Just another soldier : a year on the ground in Iraq / Jason Christopher Hartley.
    p. cm.
    ISBN-10: 0-06-084366-7
    ISBN-13: 978-0-06-084366-3
    1. Iraq War, 2003—Personal narratives, American. 2. Hartley, Jason Christopher. 3. Soldiers—United States—Biography. I. Title.
DS79.76.H374 2005
965.7044'3'092—dc22
[B]   2005050313

ISBN-10: 0-06-084367-5 (pbk.)
ISBN-13: 978-0-06-084367-0 (pbk.)

07 08 09 10 ❖/RRD 10 9 8 7 6 5 4 3 2

For Keith Wood

From Camp UDAIRI I Love You

In Kuwait before leaving for Iraq

Between my bunk and Matt's bunk, sitting at my laptop, where I did all my writing

Burning a dead dog, a common place roadside bombs are hidden

Ray and Melissa overlooking Ad Dujayl

Iraqi girl,
from a family of
squatters

Wazina

Iraqi kids in Ad Dujayl

April 30, 2005

TRUE AMERICAN HERO

Getting dressed in my desert camouflage uniform is something I've done hundreds of times, but it felt weird to be putting it on again for the first time in four months. Since returning from Iraq, my National Guard unit hadn't had any drills yet. Typically a drill weekend for us consists of some sort of infantry training, but this one, taking place at Camp Smith, about an hour away from my apartment, was nothing more than taking care of some paperwork and attending an awards ceremony and a dinner. I was wearing one of the uniforms I'd worn in Iraq. It was well worn and comfortable; my boots fit my feet perfectly—they were the only pair I'd worn for the last year. My roommate Matt, one of my platoon mates, was in uniform too now, something I used to see daily in Iraq. But being dressed in my uniform in our apartment in New Paltz, New York, made me feel fake, like I should be going to a Halloween party.

I'm very proud of the fourteen years I've served in the Army National Guard, but since we'd returned, I hadn't felt very gung-ho about being a soldier. In fact, I'd done everything I could to be as unmilitary as possible. I hadn't cut my hair for the entire four months we'd been back until a few days ago. I looked ridiculous with my mop of hair,

1

like I should have been driving a Camaro and listening to an eight-track. My hair hadn't been that long in years; I just wanted to grow it as long as I could out of spite. I had also grown a goatee and a mustache that made me look more like a child molester than a hipster, two other things that had to be shorn before getting back into soldier mode.

Before I deployed to Iraq, I was part of an infantry company based out of Manhattan. There are a lot of infantry companies in the New York National Guard, but only a few are based out of New York City. Companies from the city are dramatically different in personality (and ethnicity) than companies based out of other parts of the state, creating rivalries based more on resentment than on competitiveness.

I was born and raised in Salt Lake City, Utah—yes, I was once Mormon—and spent nine years in the National Guard there, where 99 percent of soldiers were white suburbanites. When I moved to New York City in 2000, it took some adjustment to learn how to better interact with the personalities of soldiers who had grown up on the streets. I was one of only two white soldiers in my Manhattan unit, a company that was almost entirely Hispanic, with a handful of other minorities. The other white guy was this jovial, barrel-chested Irish cop from the Bronx named Willy, who quickly became one of the best friends I've ever had. After a few months in my new unit, I realized I preferred soldiers who grew up in the city to soldiers who grew up in the suburbs.

When my battalion was deployed to Iraq, different companies were combined in order to get us to full strength. My city company was merged with soldiers from other parts of the state, and the disparity was the source of a lot of friction that never got resolved, even after eleven months in combat together. Now I was on my way to drill, where I would see all these guys for the first time in months.

I had pulled my uniform out of the duffel bag where it had been stuffed since I'd gotten back from combat and put it on without ironing it. I'd cut my hair, but it was barely within military standards and nowhere near as short as infantrymen usually keep theirs. It was still long enough that my hat didn't fit because of it. My uniform carried no rank. For the past several years, I'd been a sergeant, but on the second-to-last day of our deployment I was demoted. On the last day of my tour of duty, while at Fort Drum, New York, before being released back into the wild as a civilian, I wore the rank of specialist. As I drove away from Fort Drum that day, I threw my pin-on rank out the window. I never bothered getting another set of pin-on rank or having them sewn on. The stories in this book, and their presence on the internet, were the reason I was demoted.

Matt and I weren't in any mood to take this upcoming drill seriously. Before getting on the highway we picked up a case of beer at a gas station and put the cans in a garbage bag full of ice in his backseat. We drank all the way to Camp Smith.

All the stories I've ever heard from vets about returning from combat are stuff like "You fight for the guy next to you" or "The friends you make in combat will be the best you ever make." Whatever. For the most part, I enjoyed my time in combat. I love being in the infantry. I served with a lot of good soldiers in Iraq, in a platoon with solid leaders. Fighting there was an incredible experience for me, the culmination of almost everything I've wanted to do as an infantryman, but the worst part was being surrounded by so many assholes. When we got to Camp Smith, it was good to see all the guys again, most of whom I cared for a great deal, but it also reminded me of how much I couldn't stand them as a group.

Since the company I was originally a part of in Manhattan had been disbanded while we were in Iraq, now, like it or not, I was permanently a part of this new company. I wanted to show my face, hug everyone, then ask to be transferred to another city-based unit again.

We spent only two hours at Camp Smith before being released for the night. All we did during those two hours was fill out a few forms with our addresses and signatures. It's amazing how many times I've written my address on something for the Army. I know my company knows my address. They send me crap in the mail all the time. All these forms are printed out with a word processor, and the National Guard could save millions of dollars each year in man-hours if they would just let my sixteen-year-old sister teach the administrative guys how to use the Mail Merge function in Microsoft Word. I didn't mind it so much this time though, because we had plenty of beer.

Once we were released for the evening, about a dozen guys came back up to New Paltz for a night of further drinking. These were guys who never normally hung out together, but drinking is a much more unifying experience than modern combat. The rest of us had changed back into civilian clothes, but Willy was still in uniform, which drew a lot of attention in the liberal town of New Paltz. The sun had already set on the New Paltz skyline, the most visible feature of which is a watchtower on a cliff, the same one Bob Dylan wrote about in "All Along the Watchtower." Woodstock is a stone's throw away.

Ray, one of our company's snipers, was there as well. I love Ray. If there is a list somewhere of ten traits, any seven of which you'd need to become a psycho killer, Ray has six of them. Were it not for an innate kind of commonsense Zen spirituality he quietly nurtures, he would be a true-life Travis Bickle. His comic timing and deadpan delivery of one-liners, along with his legendary marksmanship skills, made him a rock star in our company in Iraq.

Willy is also impossible not to love. He's loud, loving, and totally uncensored. I once made the mistake of telling my mother that as long as I was near him, I felt safe. Now sometimes I wonder if she loves him more than me. I could call her and say, "Mom, my Humvee was hit today by an improvised explosive device and my legs were blown off," and the first question she'd ask me would be "Is Willy okay?" Ray and Willy were both from my original company in Manhattan.

Matt and our other housemate, Sean, were both from the upstate company that merged with the one Ray and Willy and I had been part of. Matt and Sean had been close friends for years. Sean was the baby of the company for a long time, a charming and good-looking kid who was always treated like the favorite son. He could do no wrong, and fully deserved the nickname he was given by the Dominicans and Puerto Ricans from my company: Golden Boy. I had been a team leader for our deployment, which meant I was in charge of three guys, one of whom was Matt. He's smart, capable, and an experienced paramedic in real life, and he resented like hell that I was in charge of him. He made my job as a leader difficult and miserable. It wasn't until the final few months of our deployment that we started getting along. Now I'm so attached to Matt (and Sean) it's pathetic. For nineteen months (and counting) my bed has never been more than ten feet from Matt's and thirty feet from Sean's. If Sean, Matt, and I spend more than five days apart, the first thing that happens upon the return of the truant member of the triad is a conversation about how much we've missed each other. Post-traumatic stress disorder is not a concern of mine, but post-traumatic "does this mean I'm gay?" attachment disorder does.

We didn't have to be to the awards ceremony until noon the next day. This was a good thing, considering how hungover most of us were. The ceremony was held in a restaurant large enough to accommodate a few hundred soldiers and their guests. It was a pretty big production, complete with congresspeople and high-ranking officers, most of whom I didn't know. All the soldiers present were being awarded an encased flag, along with a few other trinkets like commemorative coins and lapel pins. I was looking forward to getting the flag. My grandfather was in the Navy, and when he died I was given the flag that was draped over his coffin. I thought it would be cool to put both flags on the wall in my room, until I found out the flag I was getting had a plaque on it that read: TO A TRUE AMERICAN HERO. All the flags had the plaque. In fact, the word "hero" appeared on the plaque in two places. I appreciated the gesture of being given a flag, but there's no way I can take seriously anything with the word "hero" on it.

The ceremony was pleasant and pretty much like any other I'd ever been to, but this one made me feel a strange combination of sadness, guilt, and pity. There were a lot of soldiers there, along with their loved ones, who were taking it seriously—as I should have, but I couldn't. Willy and I were late, and we had a hard time finding a table with open seats, so we sat at one of the few with available seats. A young soldier was seated there with his parents and girlfriend. They looked frightened when Willy and I sat next to them. We were both still giddy from the night before, and Willy can be incredibly loud in this state. I felt bad thinking that we were probably ruining this experience for them with our irreverence.

The ceremony started with an invocation and some opening words, then the process of handing out the flags and other items began. There was a reception line all the soldiers walked down, shaking hands with the politicians and officers, ending with our company commander and first sergeant. I hadn't seen my commander since he'd gotten me demoted. He'd been a nemesis of sorts of mine ever since. He was a superb commander, and I have always had the utmost respect for him, but he really put me through the wringer when he initiated my punishment. I had written about my deployment experiences in Iraq in an online journal I called *Just Another Soldier*. He was furious when he found out about it, citing with extreme displeasure how I portrayed the Army and my unit and accusing me of violating operational security. My journal (or "blog" as they're called) had been online for five months during my deployment training, and my commander found it shortly before we left for Iraq. He asked me then to take it down, and I did so reluctantly, but I continued to write while in Iraq, emailing my stories to a list of friends. At the end of my tour in Iraq, with less than two months to go before I was to return home, I put the blog back online, along with everything new I had written. When my commander was informed about the blog being back online, I was taken out of my platoon and banished to our headquarters platoon, forbidden from going on missions, where I rotted away while an investigation was conducted.

Now he was a few feet from me, and I was moving down the line toward him. I knew he wouldn't be any more thrilled to see me than I was to see him. I wondered who else here tonight thought that what I had done was wrong. Herd mentality is strong in the military, and it doesn't take much to convince a majority of an idea. I wish I could say that it didn't bother me what my comrades-in-arms thought of me, but it did.

One of the joys of being in the military is experiencing a sense of belonging. But it was impossible for me to feel much of that at this time. For example, was I still assigned to the headquarters platoon, or was I part of my regular platoon again? If I was still in headquarters, what was my job? Who was in charge of me now? And what rank was I supposed to be wearing?

The paperwork to formalize my demotion hadn't gone through yet, and I was still being paid as a sergeant. When the investigation began, a hold was put on a promotion to staff sergeant I was days away from receiving. I thought it would be funny if the paperwork for my promotion went through before my demotion, or better yet *after* my demotion. In all seriousness, it still could—paperwork is processed at a snail's pace in the Army.

I went through the line and shook the hands of everyone in it. One of the officers who shook my hand noticed that I wasn't wearing any rank. He asked me what my rank was, and I told him, "I just got made a specialist, sir, but I haven't pinned it on."

"Well, congratulations," he said.

My company commander doesn't do token gestures for the sake of politeness, nor does he give out insincere platitudes, and I was half expecting him to refuse to shake my hand. When I put my blog back online, he had taken it very personally, seeing it as a betrayal. But when I came to him while he stood in the line, he made solid eye contact with me, smiled broadly, and shook my hand.

"How ya doin', Hartley," he said.

As far as I could tell, he was being completely sincere. This meant a lot to me. It made it impossible for me to hate him.

When Willy and I were done shaking everyone's hands, we immediately went to his car and dumped our flag and commemorative trinkets. Neither of us was interested in hanging around for the awards ceremony. We went back inside for a few minutes and chatted with some of the guys before we left. While I stood outside at the front door smoking, one of the battalion medics came up to me and said, "I read your stuff on the internet. I really liked it. It was really . . . I . . . I didn't know you could do that, I didn't know you wrote. It was really . . . explicit." *Explicit.* Interesting choice of words. For years, every time this guy saw me he'd say, "Hey Nina!" in reference to the porn star Nina Hartley, as if it were the funniest joke ever. He never got tired of greeting me like this. I appreciated the compliment he'd just paid me; it felt good to finally register with him as more than a guy with the last name of a porn star.

Later that night, back at my apartment, one of the guys from my unit sent me an instant message. "Dude," he wrote, "you got like the best award given after you left."

I had been awarded a medal for valor. But I wouldn't actually get it until the paperwork was finished being processed.

Fort Drum

September 30, 2003

In July 2003, I was verbally informed that my National Guard unit had been put on alert to go to Iraq. In the second week of September, we were given a "warning order" that we would be activated on September 29. With little more than two weeks until a deployment date, soldiers were expected to get their lives in order and prepare to deploy without so much as a single official document to give to employers, family, etc., regarding this imminent departure. On September 23, another warning order came down that stated that we "will enter active federal status on a date in October, which has not yet been determined." Six days out from when we were supposed to leave, and suddenly the Army turns into an indecisive prom date? Everyone being deployed had quit their jobs, planned going away parties, etc., and now they were being told to sit tight until . . . whenever.

On Sunday, September 28, I get a phone call letting me know that the deployment date was Wednesday, October 1, at which time I should report to my armory. Well, they did say it would be a "date in October."

I feel like I'm an infant and the National Guard Bureau (or whoever is in charge of the dissemination of information) is some avuncular stranger playing peek-a-boo with me while my mother is taking me for a walk around the block in a stroller. One minute I'm playing with my toes, the next minute some guy has me half excited, half scared shitless saying "Peek-a-boo!" then covering his face. And just when I'm thinking, "Where'd he go?" he startles me again right at the very last moment with "PEEK-A-BOO!" I can't decide if I want to cheer ecstatically or cry hysterically from the sheer shock of this absurd and stupid man.

Before you start thinking I'm a whiner, I should mention something very important: bitching is the only truly inalienable right of the soldier. I love the Army and I love my country. But that doesn't mean I have to enjoy the taste of horseshit. There are many axiomatic truths I will share with you with regard to soldiering. The principle of bitching is an excellent one to start with.

October 1, 2003

Friday, September 26, was my going-away party. My parents, my youngest sister, and one of my friends flew in from Salt Lake City for the weekend. Two friends of mine in New Paltz were gracious enough to have the party in their home, and they did the lion's share of the cooking. My parents don't drink and are never around people who do, and I was worried they would be uncomfortable at the dinner party. Fortunately, things could not have gone better, and I think they enjoyed themselves very much. Almost everyone I had invited was able to make it, totaling about twenty people. The entire night was indescribably satisfying for me.

The following night, at another party, Willy broke his foot while horsing around. He then became the world's most crestfallen and despondent soldier ever. We assumed he'd be nondeployable. But sometimes bullshit situations where soldiers are sent on deployments at the last minute can also be advantageous; in his case he was kept on the battle roster. He was told the break would take about a month to heal, so he was put on light duty for six weeks. He doesn't even have to wear a cast. That's Willy for you. Crazy brave, and stupid strong.

So I had my last meal (a gluttonous amount of sushi) and said goodbye to all my friends in New Paltz. I have to admit that my anxiety level was a bit high. I had a dream that I was in Iraq and the serial number on my rifle didn't belong to me. The absolute worst dream a soldier can have is the "Where's my rifle!" dream. Mine was, I suppose, a derivative of that. At least I had a rifle.

October 4, 2003

It's basically been confirmed that we will be in Iraq for at least a year, this means the deployment will be at least a year and a half, with two years total a good possibility. In the Army's infinite wisdom, we will be training at Fort Drum, in upstate New York—the frozen version of hell on earth. This is ironic, seeing as how afterward we'll be sent to one of the hottest places on earth. Ray put it best: You always keep the steaks in the freezer before you put them on the grill.

October 7, 2003

We're at Fort Drum now, and today we had NBC (nuclear, biological, chemical) training, sans nuclear. There could be no teaching environment more adverse to learning than this one was. Two companies of soldiers in one huge auditorium watching hour after hour of mind-numbing PowerPoint presentations about how to inject yourself with nerve agent antidote and the like. Keep in mind that none of us has had more than four hours of sleep a night for seven days now. A "test" was then administered by the instructor, who asked, "After the first injection, you wait ten seconds before removing it, right?" You simply had to nod your head. Think Danny Kaye being knighted in *The Court Jester*:

KNIGHT
The candidate must climb a stone wall in full armor!

THE JESTER is thrown over the wall while wearing full knight's armor and comes crashing down on the other side.

KNIGHT
The candidate passes!

The best part was the gas chamber. We filed into a room full of CS gas (tear gas) while wearing our protective masks. We did some exercises for a few minutes, then volunteers were asked to take off their masks. (They can't make you take your mask off anymore, since this isn't in keeping with the new wussified Army that doesn't want to yell at or hurt the feelings of soldiers—but they have no problem injecting relatively untested and potentially dangerous vaccines in us.) I took off my mask, stowed it in my carrying case, got to the ground, and started doing pushups. A few other guys followed suit and took off their masks as well. After I'd had enough, I calmly walked to the door and tried to control the combination CS gas/veal dinner burps that were boiling up to my now-covered-in-tears-and-snot mouth. The stuff burns like hell. It's like breathing wasabi. After I got the snot and tears to stop pouring out of my face, I had a cigarette.

October 8, 2003

WILLY—THE AMAZING BROKEDICK STORY

Since Willy broke his foot the day before we deployed, it's been an incredibly emotional trauma ride for the poor guy. First, he's told he can't go, then he's told he *has* to go since it's too late to take his name off the list. After spending several days not knowing if he's gonna get axed, we go through the administrative process to deploy: make sure guys' teeth are okay (if not, they get pulled; one guy had thirteen teeth pulled), make sure no major medical conditions exist and that medical records are in order, make sure guys have wills and powers of attorney set up, get them new ID cards, and give them tons of shots—I got anthrax and smallpox, among others. I was surprised at how much the anthrax shot hurt. They actually inject you with a live agent (similar to anthrax). Leaves a wicked bump. And we were given an entire briefing on why we shouldn't scratch the scabby blister that develops from the smallpox shot.

When Willy showed up on crutches, this enormous gray-haired civilian lady who looked like an obese witch grabbed him by the arm and told him to get his commander and first sergeant. She then berated our captain for bringing a soldier on crutches to the deployment process. She pronounced Willy's deployability dead and gave him his, um, walking papers.

At this point Willy sank into a dark hole. This heartless four-hundred-pound gorilla seemed to be in ecstasy at having just squashed a soldier's sole reason for being. She swaggered by (be it from bravado or just the fact that she was a shambling, bitter curmudgeon whale) and said, "One down." I could have strangled her. For the next four hours, Willy sat there trying to cope with the unthinkable: being a brokedick soldier who couldn't be deployed. *I* was nearly on the verge of tears. The idea of going into combat *without* him was incomprehensible to me.

While Willy was ruminating, he overheard a conversation between an officer and a soldier who was also unable to deploy, due to back problems. The officer was explaining to the soldier that he needed a medical review by the head surgeon before he could be officially taken off the mission. Willy interrupted the officer and asked who this surgeon was. Willy then crutched his way to the head surgeon's office, and at this point he was enraged. He said, "There are guys who are *dying* to get out of this mission and they're not being let go, and now you mean to tell me that all I have to do to get out of this deployment is walk in with a set of crutches and an ace bandage on my ankle, and I'm done?!" Moved by Willy's performance, the surgeon ordered the active-duty liaison to immediately take Willy in his personal vehicle to the X-ray center on post and have his foot X-rayed. Once his foot was X-rayed and the slides were returned to the surgeon, Willy started working his magic, before the surgeon even had a chance to make a judgment. He told him how the witch lady had made the call to take him off the mission and how at one point his commander even wanted to take him off the mission. Apparently this really got the head surgeon's goat. "I'm a major! *I* make the determination if a soldier is fit to ship or not! *Not* your captain and not some civilian administrator!" He then looked at the X-rays and pronounced Willy's foot not broken. "Tape your toes together and put on a boot! Your foot is fine!"

The next day, Willy repeatedly used Jedi mind tricks to cut to the front of every line, and he finished before noon a process that for some soldiers took all day and night. That night the crutches were unceremoniously destroyed and strewn across the barracks floor.

October 10, 2003

THE MONASTIC ORDER OF INFANTRYMEN

The last two days have been Death by PowerPoint. Presentation after presentation, and trying as hard as possible to not fall asleep. We still haven't had more than five hours of sleep a night for ten days running. Yesterday was medical familiarization, such as dealing with cold and heat injuries, burns, fractures, etc. The instructor seemed to see it as an excuse to show as many fucked-up photos of injuries as possible—people run over by tanks, stabbings, shootings, frostbite, burns, and a photo of a still-conscious guy who had an explosion take place in his mouth from a blasting cap or something. It left his jaw split in half and dangling, with everything below his eyes a huge mess of hamburger and with his blood-drenched tongue hanging down in the middle of it all to the point where you could see the back of his throat. There was absolutely no reason for the instructor to show half of the photos that she did. Gore porn is all it really was. Fascinating, sickening.

I've been spending a lot of time these days with my friend John, and one of our favorite topics of discussion is how he and I epitomize the single soldier. No wife, no kids, not even a girlfriend. He described us as being part of a subculture that he called the "monastic infantry." Such a perfect description. So we started thinking about who else fell into this category: Willy, Ray, Ernesto, and a few other guys. The funny thing is that all these guys are really decent, normal guys—smart, okay-looking, friendly—but they just can't seem to settle down. I have to admit that the Tyler Durden Buddhist in me takes great pleasure in this. *What I lack is what gives me my strength. I have nothing, so I have nothing to lose.* This of course it not totally true, but not having a wife, kids, or a girlfriend whom I have to call regularly is something I take great solace in. I see these guys at night outside on their cell phones, shuffling around aimlessly, hobbling back and forth from one leg to the other like zombies, mumbling sheepish sweet nothings to the girls they've left behind—and I pity them. I have the luxury of being able to focus on the moment in which I'm living and not dwell on what and whom I'm missing. God, when I think back to my experiences at Fort Bragg and Fort Benning ten years ago, trying to nurture a broken relationship over the phone, I shudder. The telephone is an emotional trauma delivery device. I hate the telephone when I'm in uniform. Putting a phone to your ear is not unlike putting a gun to your head.

I like to make light of topics that most decent people would never touch, but I think it's good to be able to expose the things that cause the real pain and just laugh at them, morbidity and all. For example, one of the guys in my squad, Joel, is on his second wife, with whom he's had four children and who came with two kids pre-installed. I was on the bus one day pontificating about the virtues of the monastic infantryman, and I told Joel that while he's away there are seven people who will have learned how to live without him by the time he gets back. Matt shook his head in disgust and muttered, "That's fucked up, man." Matt is the liberal of my squad and has a very beautiful girlfriend who is also going to learn to live without him. So I suggested that we should start a pool on who's going to get the first Dear John letter. Matt really didn't like that idea, either. He said, "That's *so* bad, man. Guys don't want to hear that shit." Then this guy, Corporal Damion, chimes in and tells me, "Do you really want this many people to hate you this early in the mission?" Then I started to feel guilty. Then I thought about it and decided, fuck that, I don't feel guilty. These guys are being pussies. So I turned back to Matt and said, "Look. Every week in Iraq, three to six U.S. soldiers are killed and forty are wounded. There are fifteen to twenty attacks made against U.S. soldiers *a day* over there right now. The chances of someone we know getting killed are highly likely. The chances of multiple people we know at least getting wounded are pretty much a statistical certainty. If we can't even joke about getting Dear John letters, how are we going to be able to handle the other stuff?" The only thing that seemed to placate these guys was when I determined that by having the least familial liabilities, I was the best suited to be on point.

October 12, 2003

My smallpox shot itches *so* much right now. It's a blistery, scabby mess. The anthrax shot has finally stopped hurting, though.

The temperature at Fort Drum has been unusually warm. The honeymoon before the divorce. There should be snow on the ground before Halloween. I think this year I'll dress up as a soldier.

Today, and for the next two days, I am teaching a class on the M240B machine gun. This gun replaced the M60 (a.k.a. "The Pig") of Vietnam fame. Excellent weapon, the 240, but heavy. Twenty-eight pounds without ammo. Rate of fire at 950 rounds a minute, maximum effective range 1,100 meters, with a maximum range of 3,700 meters. That's right, it can shoot over two miles.

For this mission we will be going as "motorized infantry," which will be something the Army really hasn't done before, at least not since World War II. We are part of something completely new. In other words, the manuals of doctrine for motorized infantry will be written after this deployment, based on our experiences. Despite the inherent dangers of being total guinea pigs, I take a certain comfort in knowing that we will be absolutely bristling with various weapon systems in each Humvee.

October 14, 2003

I can't tell you how many times in my life I've been driving down the street and encountered other drivers so irritating that I just want to ram into them or run them off the road. Anyone who drives feels this way at one time or another, right? My personal fantasy was to mount a computer-controlled machine gun on the roof of my car and program some kind of tracking system where I could lock the gun's aiming system onto the annoying driver's car and lay a few hundred rounds of 7.62mm full metal jacket into it. Oddly enough, this fantasy may be coming true very soon.

As I mentioned before, this motorized infantry thing really hasn't been done before, and the Army is literally making it up as they go. Apparently the tactics will be based loosely on Russian tactics for fighting vehicles used in urban environments. But here's the cool part: I'll command my own Humvee. A Humvee will fit five soldiers snugly, including one guy in the turret. There will be an M240 7.62mm machine gun mounted on a 360-degree rotating seat/turret in the center of the Humvee. Additionally, we will have a second M240 in the back if we need to dismount from the vehicle, at least one guy with an M203 grenade launcher (rifle mounted), a guy with an M249 5.56mm machine gun (or SAW, for "squad automatic weapon"), and perhaps a fifth guy with an M16 assault rifle. The guy with the M240 on top is the true firepower. For us to be effective, this guy has to be a straight-up killer. I'm not sure who my gunner will be, but I pray it's Ray. He's about one step away from being the next world-class mass murderer, but he's a guy who will unflinchingly know when and who to shoot. The way things look, I'll be driving a vehicle in Iraq that any boy who ever watched *GI Joe* could only dream of. Yes, yes, I know, I shouldn't compare combat with cartoons, but seriously, for just one moment let's look at this for what it is: I'll be driving around in a car with a friggin' machine gun mounted on top.

The weather at Fort Drum has been warm and *beautiful*, but that should all be coming to a gloomy end tomorrow. I'll bet we have snow in a week. Also, I almost forgot to complain again about how gross my smallpox shot is. And I only got pricked three times. The guys that were getting it for the second time had to get fifteen pricks. Theirs look gangrenous.

We will be going to the rifle qualification range in a few days. This is where we really find out which soldiers are worth a damn and can perform the single task they were meant to do: shoot things accurately.

October 17, 2003

ELIAS VS. BARNES

Thursday was the big day. Rifle qualification. Forty pop-up targets of human silhouettes, twenty to be shot from a foxhole-supported position, twenty from the prone, unsupported position. Targets range in distance from twenty-five meters to three hundred meters. No scope on the M16, just plain ol' iron sights. Hitting thirty-six gets you the rank of expert. Two guys in my platoon shot thirty-eight, I shot thirty-seven, and the next best was thirty-five. My squad leader, Chris, a police sniper, shot thirty-three, and my other team leader, Kirk, an FDNY firefighter and my new nemesis, shot a plain shitty twenty-six. Yes, I am gloating. And oh yeah, remember Corporal (now Sergeant) Damion, who asked me on the bus if I wanted people to hate me? Well, he couldn't stand me before, and now he can't stop telling me how much of a bastard I am for shooting better than him. Respect comes in all forms, I guess. There's been a lot of tension in my squad due to my style of leading, and this was the perfect way to serve up a steaming-hot helping of "Shut the fuck up."

A lot of the guys in my platoon, particularly Chris and Kirk, have a leadership style that is more rigid than mine. They are both originally from the same company and are used to working together with non-city troops (a.k.a. rule-following upstate white boys). Leading troops from the city forces one to take on an entirely different approach to leadership. John put it best when he said, "You can't push a piece of spaghetti." Willy has said over and over that leadership in the National Guard is more difficult than anywhere else. You can't show up to drill and treat guys that are normally civilians like they're on active duty. If you push them, they resist, and all that comes of it is that nothing gets done and everyone thinks you're an asshole. Additionally, I came from a Special Forces unit, where guys pride themselves on being "silent professionals," looking down on the rest of the Army and their pushy form of leadership. Having worked for the last four years with guys with typical Bronx and Brooklyn attitudes, I have developed a style of leadership that assumes the soldier is an adult and doesn't need to be hounded every two minutes about whether or not his boots are shined to standard. In my normal company I think I'm held in fairly high regard among the soldiers and the leaders. For five months, I was the acting platoon sergeant. Then, one month later, I show up to a new squad and platoon that think I'm too lackadaisical. Funny how so much comes down simply to perception.

October 22, 2003

YOUR MUSIC IS GAY

Things have started to mellow out a bit. Instead of training from 5:00 a.m. to midnight, we've started getting off by 4:00 p.m. most days, at which point we're allowed to change into civilian clothes and do stuff like go to the PX or the mall off post or whatever—so long as we return to the barracks by 11:00 p.m. Despite this, I still find myself going to bed each night at about midnight. The training during the day has been really mellow, too, mostly classes on stuff like land navigation, calls for fire (calling in fire missions from mortars or artillery), first aid, and walking through basics on CQB (close-quarters battles, i.e., urban warfare). Getting up at 5:00 a.m. and exercising outside in ball-freezing weather is a serious drag, though.

We have a little stereo in the barracks, and I recently borrowed a CD from John that is an MTV compilation of alternative '80s hits. I've already been branded as being gay by my platoon for a number of stupid reasons, like looking younger than I actually am, crossing my legs when I sit, being educated, having stylish sneakers, and generally being way more in touch with my anima than your average infantryman. To add fuel to the fire, I was listening to this CD, and Kirk starts haranguing me about listening to gay music. Then in walks Chris and he starts flipping out about how much he likes this CD and how he used to own it. Kirk and I were both shocked. Chris then states emphatically, "My squad needs to know that my favorite singer of *all* time is Morrissey." So Chris flips through the different tracks, commenting on each. While it's on a New Order song, someone yells from the latrine, "Keep it there!" Then in walks Tony, a Brooklyn cop and a real hard-ass. So we're all listening to the various tracks now, talking about where we were when we first got into this music and the memories it evokes, when Joey, a sergeant from another platoon, walks in with a CD case and a big grin on his face and says, "I heard you guys were listening to depressing music, so I came over." Another closet alternative-'80s infantry sergeant! More discussions ensue. Tony asks, "Hey, I've had this song in my head for years, and I can't remember the name of it. It goes like this: 'Heeey now, hey now now . . .'" Then Joey says, "Yeah, that's The Sisters of Mercy. I've got it right here." Now Tony and Joey are flipping through the CDs in the case like it was the new issue of *Tiger Beat*. The whole time all this is happening, I'm ecstatic watching all these trained killers act like giddy schoolgirls as they discuss these bands. At this point, Kirk is in a state of utter disbelief and disgust trying to comprehend how his infantry company could harbor so many apparent fags.

October 23, 2003

THIS IS MY WEAPON, THIS IS MY GERBER . . .

The first and second squads of my platoon share the bottom floor of a two-floor barracks. It's an open bay, and we do most of our squad-level classroom-type training here. It's just one big room with a bunch of wall lockers and bunks, except ours is seriously run down. A few days ago we're all working on disassembling and assembling the M249 machine gun. I had the best time behind Dan. I think I could have beat him, but as his team leader, I believe that the politically intelligent thing to do was to just let him win. I think there is more value in his feeling superior than there is for me in the gratification of beating him. Or I could just be full of shit, and this is my elaborate excuse for not beating him. It's probably a little of both.

Anyway, after the guys got tired of this, we started working on taking the weapon apart and putting it back together while blindfolded. This can be really tricky, by the way. While Jimmy (another cop in real life) was taking his apart, he was having trouble with one of the parts and asked, "Does anyone have a Gerber [multi-tool]?" and he puts out his hand. Without missing a beat, Sean says, "Yeah, here," and whips out his dick and puts it in Jimmy's open hand. Everyone was on the floor, in tears. For about a good ten seconds, Jimmy didn't seem to know how to handle this unprecedented violation, and continued to work on the weapon before finally taking the blindfold off and making an attempt at trying to find some sort of physical retribution for the affront. This incident has become a source of much discussion, and the jury is still out on who is more gay: the guy who touched a dick or the guy who let a guy touch his dick.

One could write volumes about the homophobically homoerotic undercurrents in the infantry.

October 27, 2003

Long before Fort Drum became Fort Drum, it was Camp Drum. The remnants of what was once Camp Drum are a series of aging buildings known as "Old Post." The run-down barracks of Old Post are where National Guardsmen are kept when they train at Fort Drum. Three days ago the barracks we were staying in were condemned. So instead of living in a shitty open-bay barracks, we now live in a shitty four-man-room barracks just down the street.

I think my favorite part of our dilapidated barracks is the latrines. The paint on the floor is at least four layers deep, worn down to the concrete in most spots, particularly in the shower, creating a worn-down-gobstopper rainbow of dreary military colors. The sheer economy of the latrine is the most entertaining part. There are three unpartitioned urinals so closely spaced that if three of us all had to go at the same time we'd all be hip to hip to each other. There is one tiny concrete room in the corner with four shower heads that is supposed to function as a shower for a platoon of sweat-salted grunts. It's rare for all four shower heads to work, and when any of them does, the hot-water pressure oscillates like a bipolar girlfriend, creating a torturous wave of hot-cold-hot-cold. The toilets are actually partitioned, but they seem to always be occupied with guys trying to rid themselves of

MRE-induced constipation or shamelessly masturbating. I think I've been duped. I'm not actually at a modern U.S. military installation but at Sing Sing, circa 1940.

On Saturday we did a little land-navigation training. The standard land-nav training consists of each soldier having to find five eight-digit grid coordinates, in three hours, using a map and compass, but instead we were given one point that a twelve-year-old Boy Scout could have found. Then we did the dead-reckoning course, where you have to find three points given three different directions and distances. Once you reach your point, there is a sign or post of some kind with a code on it. You record the codes and turn them in once you've finished. I was walking back from my third dead-reckoning point when I heard someone yelling, "Help!" from a hill. At first I thought someone was just playing around, but the pleas continued. I walked up the hill (as did another sergeant who was in the area) to find a young soldier who had gotten his foot stuck between two large rocks and had fallen down, twisting his ankle something wicked. He was in a lot of pain and was unable to untwist himself. His leg looked bent in a wholly un-natural way, implying a good compound fracture. The rocks weren't gonna budge, but after a little work we finally got his leg unwedged. Turns out his leg was fine, just tweaked his foot pretty good. I couldn't believe it. Young soldiers are made of rubber, I swear. Later he told me that once he realized he couldn't move and no one was responding to his cries, he fell asleep for a while. Testament to the fact that soldiers will sleep *anywhere*.

November 3, 2003

Training right now is in the "check the box" phase, where the brass want to be sure we cover all the bases necessary to put young men in harm's way. First aid, check; weapons qualification, check; Power-Point presentation on [enter training topic here], check. I wish I could say that the training has been intensive and pertinent, but in reality it's been somewhere between decent and complete-waste-of-time. My squad leader, Chris, is very competent when it comes to CQB, and we've hit that pretty hard, but other than moving tactically through an urban area and learning room-clearing techniques, most of the training has been purely masturbatory.

John, Willy, and I have been thinking a little about who we'd like to induct into the Monastic Order of Infantrymen and have decided that Ray and our friend Ernesto should be the first two. We agreed that for a novitiate to be admitted into the MOI, an act must be performed involving physical pain or discomfort, and public nudity. Assuming that there'd be snow at Fort Drum by now, we were thinking something along the lines of naked snow angels, to be witnessed by at least one of the MOI brothers and at least one innocent bystander. Except there's no snow yet, so we'll have to come up with something else. Ernesto was going to be given a pass on this rite of passage and simply grandfathered in, due to the fact that he's thirty-eight and completely devoid of the familial liabilities that prevent admittance (children, wife, girlfriend), a shining example of the infantry monk. Ray, however, needed no guidance on initiation.

For Halloween, all soldiers the rank of E-4 and below were given a chance to be free from all details for a month as the prize for a costume contest. Considering that we're at one of the coldest posts in America and haven't even been issued cold-weather boots yet, scraping up enough materials to put together any kind of costume turned out to be no small feat, despite the reward (no cleaning latrines, no sweeping, no mopping, etc., for a month). There were the usual entries: first sergeant impersonation; company commander impersonation; guy dressed up in nothing but a black ski mask, black boxer briefs, and combat boots (Bring out the Gimp!); and so forth. And then there was Ray. Covered from stem to stern in camouflage paint (light green on the body, dark green as lipstick and eye shadow) and wearing nothing but a field-expedient string bikini made from bandannas and 550 cord. Public nudity? Close enough. Physical pain or discomfort? Ray: "Damn, it's balls cold out here. And this g-string is kicking my ass!" I'd say it qualifies. The next day, after Ray had spent hours scrubbing cammo off his body, we pulled him and Ernesto aside, taught them the secret handshake, and presented them with their MOI dog tags. Ray: "Wow, I've never been part of an order before. What the hell does 'monastic' mean?"

Ray continues to make us proud. Last night, the battalion commander, recently back from a trip to Iraq, gave us a brilliantly verbose speech complete with the "I won't lie. There will be casualties" line. We all knew what he really wanted to do was quote Gunnery Sergeant Hartman from *Full Metal Jacket* and say, "Most of you will go to Vietnam. Some of you will not come back." Anyway, right around the part of the monologue, toward the end, just before soldiers start asking stupid questions, he starts telling us how we need to be sensitive to the Iraqis and the painful period the people of that country are going through. Ray, like the dedicatedly amoral sniper that he is, yells out, "SIR, GIVE ME AN M24, SOME RAMON NOODLES, AND PLENTY OF AMMO, AND EVERYTHING WILL BE ALL RIGHT!" God, I wish I had that kind of clarity.

November 13, 2003

In the Kill House Under a Dead Moon

Our first day in the field was spent at a CQB live-fire site. There once was a "tire house" that served this purpose, but it was recently replaced with a structure made of giant sectional fiberglass-reinforced concrete blocks—sometimes called a "shoot house," sometimes called a "kill house." Every time one particular instructor said the word "shoot house," I swore he was saying "shithouse." Anyway, the layout consists of some basic building scenarios—smallish rectangular rooms, wooden doors, narrow hallways, etc. In place of a floor there is sand, and at the top of the high walls is a railing where instructors can observe the would-be carnage. There is no ceiling, and the entire building is under an enormous pavilion roof. The way targets are handled is pretty clever. A dummy is hung by a wire that is attached to a balloon inflated inside the dummy's chest. If a proper shot is delivered center-mass of the dummy's chest, the balloon pops and the dummy falls to the ground.

Each squad ran through the same two rooms over and over again, first as a dry fire, then with blanks, then with live rounds. The squad is broken down into two fire teams and led by a squad leader. Alpha team takes the first room, then Bravo team—the team I led—takes the second. Once the first room is clear, my team enters the building and lines up against the wall next to the door of the room we are about to enter. This is called a "stack." In this case, we stacked left of the door. Number-one man in the stack calls that we have a closed door. I am number-three man. I call up the number-four man to the front of the stack to breach the door. In this case it only means he kicks the door in. In other cases he could pry, cut, or blow the door open. Once the door is kicked in, the stack flows into the room, with the number-one man entering the room the way that is easiest for him, usually opposite the way the door swings. In this case, the door swung inward to our left. He entered the room following the right wall, number-two man followed the left, three the right, four the left. In the room there were two dummies in the far opposite corners, one with a cardboard cutout of an AK-47, one without.

Once it came time to perform the drill with live ammunition, I'll have to admit I felt pretty amped. Live-fire drills aren't performed as often as one may think. The Army is fairly obsessed with safety, especially since more fatalities occur due to accidents than anything else, so drills involving live rounds are executed only occasionally. This may not be true for the more elite units, but in general, when soldiers are killing themselves by acts as pedestrian as slipping or falling, I can understand the trepidation a commander may have when it comes to giving a band of bruthaz real destructive power. We donned Ranger body armor—those forty-some-odd-pound ceramic-plated jobs that feel like anvils in the shape of vests—and prepared to run the drill. The entire procedure went down without a hitch, other than Matt's gunning down the "innocent civilian" in our room who wasn't sporting a Magic Markered assault rifle like the other mannequin-at-arms.

The next night, we were to run the same live-fire drill, this time with night-vision goggles. Not a big deal, really, but doing anything with NVGs (night-vision goggles) feels like being underwater or in a videogame, especially since depth perception goes straight to hell. Once you get used to them, it can be manageable, but still somewhat surreal. But then came the wrench in the whole thing. While trying to remove a blank adapter from Matt's rifle with some pliers, Dan pulled a tendon (ligament?) in his left wrist. His wrist hurt him so badly that he was unable to hold up his rifle. Seeing as how Dan was our number-one man and would be doing most of the shooting once we got in the room, his not being able to hold up his weapon put a serious kink in things. For our squad to certify on this task, we had to perform it as a team, including Dan. Chris, our squad leader, decided to make Dan the number-four man, since that position didn't need to shoot anything in this drill, only kick the door in. I would be number one, Matt would be number three and the acting team leader, and Peter, normally the number-four man, would be the number-two man. Since Peter had never had to do any shooting on any of the other iterations of the room, the fact that he was now going to be shooting a target with live rounds a few feet in front of me for the first time, in the dark, gave me some pause. Peter is a really good-hearted kid and a potentially decent soldier, but a bit young and inexperienced, and sometimes this is very apparent. I made him put on his goggles long before we were to enter the kill house, to get him adjusted to wearing them, and then I verbally ran through the drill with him over and over again—in retrospect, I think more for my sake than for his.

All night the moon was full and the sky was clear, providing enough illumination that with the goggles, everything appeared clear as day, although it was all bright green. This of course was too good to last. While we were waiting for our squad's iteration, the moon slowly started to wane. Turns out our two-minute live-fire drill coincided perfectly with a lunar eclipse. By the time it was our turn to run the drill, the now barely visible moon was a dead gray-red. Our NVGs strained under the starlight, making the infrared lasers on our rifles look like light sabers. So there I am, standing in our squad stack outside the kill house, moments away from breaching the door to the first room, and I'm thinking about how the pain in my frozen toes is almost imperceptible now that my heart is racing, and how my weapon is noticeably heavier when it has live ammunition in it instead of blanks. From there my mind wandered farther. It's funny how many simple little beautiful things I've been able to see while doing an ultimately ugly job. Several nights earlier, I saw my first aurora borealis. It was amazing. The waves of light sometimes filled as much as half the sky. I watched it for an hour. Now I was looking at a lunar eclipse. The sky was perfectly clear, and once the moon was gone, the stars were more brilliant than I'd ever seen them, with no light or air pollution from the city to obscure their view from earth. It became almost suffocating for me to try to absorb the overwhelming enormousness of space, to look into the Milky Way and think that I was looking into my own galaxy. I started to feel ridiculous—meaningless, even—standing there wearing an unwieldy amount of gear, the culmination of human civilization's technology, all centered on industrialized death. I'm looking at the wall, thinking about how a few minutes ago I thought it was pretty cool how when a bullet hits it, the concrete and fiberglass are made to crumble just enough to absorb the round and then drop it to the sand floor, inert. I hear, "Closed door on the left!" I'm saying, "Breach man, come to the front to kick in the door." I nod. He kicks. I'm walking into the room, slow and smooth, I scan the first corner, it's empty, I scan over to the second corner, dummy, no gun, I scan over to the third corner, dummy, gun, I press the lever on the PAQ4 on my weapon, a green laser illuminates the room, I paint the dummy's chest with it, I squeeze the trigger twice.

Everything went as it should have. Peter performed perfectly, as did we all. The eclipse came and went, and the platoon slept fitfully in a cramped tent.

Quotes of the Week

After busting his lip open on the rear-sight aperture of his SAW during a react-to-contact drill earlier in the day, Juan then puked due to the dehydration he suffered on our establish-an-observation-post drill later in the day. One of the instructors, bemused by Juan's apparent run of bad luck, tells him, "If it were raining pussy, you'd be the only guy to get hit by a big ol' dick."

In light of the Army's apparent lack of funds when it comes to providing us with adequate gear for our mission, Jimmy announced, "We're not going to be issued DCUs [desert camouflage uniforms] because the Army has decided that it will be cheaper to have us keep the green uniforms and just plant trees in Iraq."

November 18, 2003

Our recent field exercise involved more urban operations, this time with us operating as a platoon and using Humvees—both for the first time. I know that a Humvee on a street is a much more tantalizing target for the enemy than a soldier on foot, but can I just tell you how awesome it was to *drive* to the fight rather than trudge there while wearing over a hundred pounds of gear? With the trucks, things happen at such a faster pace in general. We roll into the (mock) town, dismount, assault the assigned building (my squad's part of the mission), deal with the enemy dead and captured, friendly casualties, and any detainees, then mount up and split.

The nighttime iteration of the exercise was the most interesting. The building we hit had a few surprises. Since Dan and Peter had to stay with the truck as driver and gunner, respectively, my assault team was a little shorthanded, consisting of me, Matt, and Yanko (a seriously cool cat from weapons squad). Our squad quickly bounded building by building until we had the target building in sight. There was a small set of stairs leading to a door—a very convenient entry point. The stack order was Matt on point, then me, then Yanko. The plan was once we entered the building and cleared the first room, Chris would come in with the second team. We started to take fire from a window, which Matt suppressed by returning fire. For the sake of haste, Matt was to open the door, and he and Yanko would enter on my lead. We ran across the open area to the stairs—the entire time returning fire to the window—and stacked on the stairs. Matt opened the door, and I was already starting to barrel in when . . . what in the hell? The other side was boarded up! I kicked the crap out of this thing, and made marginal progress. Between the booms of my boot hitting the board we could hear a woman screaming inside. I think I must have kicked that thing a dozen times. Matt finally yells, "No go! Let's go around!" In retrospect, I should have made this call myself after the second kick. I was just so hell-bent on getting through that board. I won't make that mistake again. The next door wasn't much better. This one was also boarded up, but I was able to get it down after a couple kicks. Once inside, I see the screaming woman sitting in a chair in my sector of the room. The next thing I know, I'm taking fire from a guy who has stepped out of a dark hallway. Matt already had his barrel on the hallway, and he returned fire the second the guy stepped out. By the time Yanko was in the room, a guy in the rafters opened up on us. All three of us returned fire on him. This is where things started to get very third grade. Since none of us, enemy included, had put batteries in the receiver part of our MILES gear (retarded Army laser-tag equipment), there was no good way to determine who'd actually been hit. By the time Kirk's team was in the room, rafterman decides he's not dead and he unloads more rounds into us. We all fire back with what would have been over a hundred rounds. Chris was infuriated. "OH, YOU WANNA PLAY MILES GAMES, HUH?" I think Chris would have stuck his bayonet in him, had he been on the floor. Before things could totally degrade into "You're dead! No, you're dead! No, YOU'RE dead! NO, YOU'RE DEAD, YOU DICK!" the observer-controller guy stepped in and pronounced rafterman killed. We cleared the rest of the floor, then headed for the basement. The stairs were strewn with chairs as apparent obstacles. Still heated about the bulletproof Quasimodo incident, we summarily defenestrated all these chairs via the window at the top of the stairs. The rest of the operation went off without incident, other than Kirk's aggressively manhandling the detainee during the search before realizing she was a woman.

My squad has been developing very well. Generally, I can't stand Rangers and their high-and-tight dress-right-dress mentality, but I have to attribute the success of my squad to our squad leader, Chris, formerly of Second Ranger Battalion and the Tenth Mountain Division. He's a funny and fairly easy guy to work for, but there were times when I found his obsessiveness about training to be annoying, especially when it came to CQB, but now I regret having ever felt this way, because it's really starting to pay off.

A lot of our training has been going through scenarios—or "lanes," as they're called—squad after squad. Almost every time the instructors go through the after-action review (AAR) with us, they say things like "You're the best squad we've seen so far" or "You were the only squad that actually camouflaged yourselves before the ambush." The members of our squad are excellent soldiers, but it's Chris who makes the whole greater than the sum of its parts. He definitely knows the job of an infantryman. And, okay, so the guy is an equipment buff. He personally could keep the tactical gear industry like Blackhawk and Lightfighter in business, and normally this is the kind of guy I love to make fun of, but let me just say how relieved I am that he's leading my squad.

Our squad's proficiency at CQB has garnered us a fair amount of recognition in our platoon, and even our company. This means, in my humble estimation, that when it comes time to kick in doors for real, our squad is the most likely to be the initial assault element. Our battalion commander has decided to create an air assault quick-reaction force (QRF) with one platoon from each company. Word around the campfire is that our platoon is most likely to fill that slot for our company. It's funny to think, "Yay, we did good! We're being given the cool job! . . . Hey, wait a second. QRF does what? Jumps in every time we get in a scrap?! Now, how exactly did seeing extra combat become a reward?"

We're going to the field again in a few days, so it may be a while before I write. Once I get back to complaining, it will most likely be about still not having the right gear, still not getting the correct pay, and (on a personal note) personality conflicts within the platoon. Most of the other team leaders got promoted to the rank of sergeant at the beginning of this deployment and are very new to the rank. I know they'd deny it, but I suspect their need to prove themselves, now that they have the stripes, is a source of some anxiety. Although they are all very competent, there's an infection that seems to have spread, where leading means yelling. I have not been infected yet, nor, god help me, will I ever. The major issues I've had with my own squad have been dealt with for the most part. Kirk and I are on very good terms now, although he still accuses me of being gay at least three times a day, and the serious issues I had with Dan were also put to rest after he and I had a little discussion. (Translation: I took him to a remote area and issued him the most intense ass-chewing of *my* life.) Imagine a pack of wolves in snowy upstate New York where two-thirds of the pack want to be the alpha male. That's my platoon. Right now, as I type, these wolves are all at a strip club (I'm not kidding—an invitation I declined)—and I'm sitting in front of a friggin' computer geeking out. I guess I'm something the pack mentality hates: different. Hell, if I were them, I guess I'd make fun of me, too.

November 24, 2003

We just got back from being in the field for a few days, and the weather was incredible the entire time we were out. Last night I slept under the stars. I figured I'd have to contend with frost or at least dew in the morning, but instead I woke up to an unseasonably warm day. And the training has been pretty decent, too. A little more mission-oriented toward Iraq. In a nutshell, in every exercise we would drive a few miles as a convoy of Humvees, dealing with simulated IEDs (improvised explosive devices), RPG (rocket-propelled grenade) attacks, and other various types of ambushes. At the objectives, we performed a lot of semi-permissive searches of buildings (i.e., knocking on doors instead of kicking them in). Sometimes we would end up shooting, but in most of the cases we war-gamed, no shots were fired, a lot of people and buildings were searched, sometimes yielding a few detainees or weapons. Then we'd drive back to our assembly area and deal with more ambushes along the way, sometimes doing the whole find-fix-and-destroy thing, sometimes just blowing through the ambush, guns blazing. Sitting in a Humvee while the machine gun on top is tearing a seam into hell is an experience—hot brass and links raining down into the passenger compartment like a Skittles commercial for infantrymen.

The day before moving to the field, we were issued all our desert uniforms and gear. It was like a busload of schoolgirls returning from a field trip to the mall—no one could wait to try on all their new outfits. I found myself just as guilty of this as anyone. Posing shamelessly in front of a latrine mirror, I couldn't decide how I liked to wear the boonie cap best—normal style, cowboy style, or Mick Dundee style. I suspect a lot of soldiers were terribly crestfallen when they learned we couldn't wear the desert uniforms until we were one month out from being deployed. We were also finally issued our cold-weather boots to complement the pair most of us already had been forced to purchase on our own to deal with the Fort Drum cold. I can honestly say that half the gear I wear I bought myself. For all the Homeland Security missions we've done, most of us paid for our own gear (pistol belt, suspenders, ammo pouches, canteens, and covers, etc.) to avoid looking like complete dirtbags wearing all the raggedy Vietnam-era gear that we'd been issued. By the time you add in all the knives and crap that soldiers love to buy, the Army is getting a well-outfitted infantryman on the cheap. Hell, Ray even has a friggin' tomahawk. "It's so I can split niggaz skulls open if I have to," he told me, completely deadpan and genuine.

Some major news regarding my squad: Chris is no longer our squad leader. He and Ray are now the company sniper team and will be attached directly to our commander. Chris was reluctant to leave the squad (not that he had a choice) but seems to be very excited about his new job. Ray is on cloud nine and has spent the last few days stripping fiber after fiber out of sections of burlap to make his bushlike ghillie suit. To watch him work is fascinating. Completely absorbed in what he's doing, he'll cut bizarre polygonal shapes from a sleeping mat, then sew and glue them together to form pads for his elbows and knees in the soon-to-be-born ghillie suit to end all ghillie suits. If Uncle Sam could ever get his act together and start paying me my damn housing allowance, I could put together some money and buy a digital camera to keep a record of all this.

I don't have a desire to kill anyone (for killing's sake), nor do I wish death upon anyone. Hell, I'm against the death penalty. But I have to say that I truly hope Ray is afforded the opportunity to do what he seems to be built to do. To paraphrase studies discussed in Dave Grossman's *On Killing*, it's been said that a small percentage of people are born with a natural ability to kill without remorse, and when employed as soldiers, it's these rare individuals who produce the majority of enemy casualties for their unit. The percentage I seem to remember is 60 percent, but I imagine that number reflects training prior to the conditioning that soldiers now receive from shooting pop-up human silhouette targets. Either way, I believe that Ray is one of these people. He's completely unflappable. Imagine John Malkovich in *In the Line of Fire,* but Puerto Rican and with a better sense of humor. If I prayed, I would thank god every night that Ray is on my side.

The fact that Chris is no longer our squad leader is an inexpressibly big deal. Chris is probably one of the most proficient and professional soldiers I've ever met, and having him as a squad leader gave me and the rest of the squad great comfort. Our new squad leader, Whiskey, is an exceptional soldier, and he is the only reason the squad is taking this potentially destabilizing change in stride, but Chris's leadership will be sorely missed.

My team is developing very well. Dan is an infantry wizard. He's currently set to be the driver of the Humvee I'll command. He is very comfortable with this job and very good at it. I also learned recently that he's an incredible shot when it counts. We've spent some time in the last few weeks at the simulation center using their oversize video game setup to practice certain scenarios. Imagine Nintendo's *Duck Hunt* with realistic rifles complete with pneumatic pumps attached to them to simulate the recoil of rounds fired. A reading of the stats after a simulated engagement would go something like this: "Sergeant Hartley, twenty-two shots fired, four hits, three kills. Peter (our SAW gunner), two hundred and four shots fired, two hits, one kill. Matt, fourteen shots fired, two hits, two kills including one friendly. Dan, eight shots fired, seven hits, seven kills, including four catastrophic kills." If rank were based purely on experience, Dan would be the team leader. But since he's not, I'd like to think I'm humble enough to recognize that Dan has an incredible skill set that I can't touch, and wise enough not to be afraid to employ it to the team's advantage. All I have to do now is figure out how to effectively motivate all three of these guys (unlike me, none of them wants to be on this deployment one bit), and I might actually have one hell of a team. Dan says he's happiest when he's blowing up or shooting things; Peter seems happiest when he's on the phone with his fiancée immersed in insipid cuddle babble; I haven't figured out yet what makes Matt happy, which is strange since I think he's the one guy on the team I have the most in common with.

It's after 1:00 a.m. I have to get up at 5:00 a.m. and go on a five-mile company run. I have a laptop now, and I've been geeking on it all day and not cleaning my weapon quite as much as I should. Bad team leader. And I have a few days off for Turkey Day. I've opted to forgo spending it with family, just so I can sleep in my own bed and get up when I'm good and goddamned ready, preferably after noon. I just want to read *The New York Times*, sip a latte at my favorite coffee shop in New Paltz, have an early dinner, drink some Jim Beam with my friends, get stupid, then pass out in my enormous bed, my only real possession in this world aside from my books and Jeff Buckley CDs.

December 10, 2003

I had just finished packing to go back out to the field for a forty-eight-hour operation that would integrate all the various skills we'd been working on—reacting to IEDs and ambushes, traveling in a convoy, cordoning off and searching buildings, performing CQB, setting up roadblocks . . . all sort of motorized infantry stuff with a light infantry twist. After I finished packing my rucksack, Peter looked at it and asked, "Sergeant, why does your ruck have two right-shoulder straps?" All I could do was give a Cheshire cat smile in response to this immensely metaphysical statement-in-a-question my little grunt novitiate had unwittingly proffered me with regard to my dicked-up ruck. "Because that's how it was issued to me," I replied.

So we just got back from six days in the field. Mind-numbingly boring and spirit-crushingly cold. Spent the better part of that six days sitting in cramped but heated (thank god!) rooms waiting for our firing orders to be called. Even the parts where we drove around in the Humvees shooting things was dull, to tell you the honest truth. I sat on the passenger side—oh, I'm sorry, I mean the truck commander position—of the vehicle, and called in targets on the radio as they popped up, yelling at my gunner to engage them. "One-six, this is one-five, be advised, four enemy dismount troops in the open, eleven o'clock, three hundred meters. Engaging at this time. Over." It was the cold that made it so horrible. When the temperature gets in the single digits, even machine guns lose their fun factor.

For the last four days, two platoons (about seventy guys) have lived in a structure that was meant only to feed soldiers firing at the motorized gunnery range. While waiting for firing orders to come up, we sat. Or napped. Or ate. Imagine sitting in the same place for four days straight, getting up only to move a few feet to talk to someone else or to go to the bathroom or to have a cigarette. The incessant chatter and yelling produced an unbearable din. It was so bad. Then, when it came time to sleep, every square inch of flat surface had a body in a sleeping bag covering it. This included the tops of the tables. It was like living on a slave ship. John asked our commander, "Have you seen the chow hall when first and second platoons rack out? It's like *Amistad* over there." The first two nights I slept outside in a cement machine gun-firing position in sub-zero temperatures. I found a wooden pallet that I put a poncho over to make a little shelter for myself from the snow. Soldiering makes you a good bum. It's no wonder so many homeless people are vets; they've all been trained to be professional bums. For six days we lived in conditions that were part central booking, part homeless shelter with a twist of male brothel. One morning, after sleeping on top of the table, Sean wakes up and says, "Dude, I can't get out of my bag yet. I'm not wearing any clothes and I have morning wood."

Having to live in this kind of proximity to each other for this long can sometimes cause guys to find some really petty reasons to fight. For example, the table where the big coffee thermoses sat was covered with coffee stains. Once, when the fresh coffee thermoses were delivered, the genius sergeant who brought them decided to pour water all over the table to clean it off, covering it and the floor with water. This janitorial feat had a lot of guys up in arms. "Yo, we sleep on that floor, you asshole!," someone yelled. Once the brain surgeon had left, the guys were trying to decide how best to dry out the floor. There were two camps: those who thought we should open the doors for a while to let the water evaporate, and those who thought we should just keep the doors closed so the heat could dry it. Personally, I didn't think the doors-open idea would do much except make me cold, and seeing as how all the sleep gear we have is waterproof, I really didn't care if the floor was wet or dry. The dispute was never really settled. Someone would open the doors, then someone else would close them. Then someone would open the doors, then someone else would close them. At one point two soldiers almost came to blows over the most appropriate state the doors should be in. This is what soldiers fight over: the best way to dry a floor.

Pardon Me While I Burst into Flames

It's been a very trying day for me. I can say I truly exploded today, something I have never done with anyone who wasn't my father or my girlfriend. If a human being could detonate, I would have today. Deep within my chemistry is a rage gene that I think I got from my biological father, an evil superpower I have that has been dormant for quite a while now, but I'm realizing it may be reawakening with this deployment.

We got back from the field last night after what collectively everyone agrees was one of the most miserable field exercises of our careers. In an attempt to alleviate a little of the suffering of my squad, I split up a guard schedule so that four guys could patrol for one two-hour shift, then three other guys and I could patrol on the next shift, instead of having everyone on both shifts. It was my plan to maximize our downtime, since being out in the cold was so unpleasant. But when people saw that four of my guys were on patrol and I was taking a nap, it looked really bad. In retrospect, I should have just gone out with both shifts. Hindsight. The gossip channel spread about how I was sleeping while I made my guys go out on patrol. First Kirk tells me this morning how he heard I was fucking his guys over in the field (He was not in the field, because as the platoon's hazardous materials sergeant, he had to oversee the loading of our equipment being shipped to Kuwait.) This turned into a yelling match—the only way he and I communicate in uniform since we are the most mismatched pair of team leaders the United States Army has ever seen. (Our yelling at each other has become something of a spectator sport for the platoon, by the way.) Then I get Whiskey counseling me on the same issue a little later in the morning. By this point I was completely exasperated having to explain the same nonsense twice. In the military, once you've been accused of something, the issue is done. There's no defending yourself; it's already set in stone. The average soldier is very impressionable. This means that the first, strongest, or loudest opinion or perception stated is pretty much always the one that sticks. Case in point: it was observed that my guys were working while I was sleeping, therefore I am a shitbag. And as much as I might bitch about how much I hate this, I have no excuse, because I know as well as anyone that perception is paramount in warrior culture. As much as I loathe the idea of putting the *perception* of correctness before *actual* correctness, I know that perception is really the key. Insert here longwinded metaphysical discourse entitled "What Is Illusion, What Is Reality?" Sticking feathers up your butt may not make you a chicken, but if you can convince everyone that you are a chicken, well, by god, you're a fucking chicken.

After I heard it from Kirk and Whiskey, John runs into me and says, "I hear your entire squad hates you, that you slept while you made them go on patrol." Keep in mind that John is the company commander's RTO (translation: captain's radio man). For him to hear this rubbish pretty much meant that I could assume that Soledad O'Brien was at that very moment convincingly feigning veiled disgust as she read from her teleprompter before a bank of CNN cameras: "Today at Fort Drum, an Army post in upstate New York, it was discovered that infantry team leader Jason Hartley of Bravo Team, Second Squad, brazenly slept while his fellow soldiers sludged through the snow in single-digit temperatures. Sources say that it is a certainty at this time that Sergeant Hartley is a shitbag." At this point I could take no more. I was gonna drop bombs. I stormed back to my room and found to my livid wonderment another gay joke—a picture torn from a magazine and taped to my wall locker of what I was supposed to assume was a gay sailor, bare-chested and tattooed. Then my cup runneth over. I tore the page down. In the margin on the back side was printed the source of this untimely homoerotica: *FHM,* page sixty. I opened the door of the room to Alpha team, the soon-to-be recipients of SPLEEN, JASON TYPE, 1 EA., but they were gone. Ah, lo and behold, there layeth an issue of *FHM.* And page sixty was torn out! So I did the mystery owner of the magazine a favor and took it back to my room and tore out all the rest of the pages to save him time in the future. (Side note: This was the international version of *FHM,* and it actually broke my heart to destroy it like that. There were *so* many hot girls in it.) Then I lay in wait, my rage at a slow boil. When they returned, I entered their room, closed the door, and locked the bolt. I flung the mass of pages to the floor and out of my throat boomed the words, "IF YOU FAGGOTS HAVE A PROBLEM WITH ME, TELL IT TO ME NOW!" It's really embarrassing how when one is pissed off, all political correctness goes out the window and the use of disparaging terms based on sexual orientation are used without thinking. Anyway, once I was done venting and they had explained to me that it wasn't them who'd ratted me out (it was actually my platoon sergeant who'd made an observation that I appeared to be slacking, something I didn't learn till it was too late), all that was accomplished was I had made an ass of myself by being overly furious and destroying a magazine that didn't belong to any of them. It was Kirk's magazine, and his personal joke and my little act of rage was completely lost on them. "Um, Sergeant, whose magazine is that? Did you tear those pages out? I'm confused." I felt like that guy who sprayed manure all over what he thought was the courthouse that had wronged him, only to find out that he had the wrong building.

December 24, 2003

I ♥ RUDI BAKHTIAR

It's Christmas Eve and I'm sitting on a JetBlue flight to Salt Lake City. CNN *Headline News* is on the little TV screen. I've had the biggest crush on Rudi Bakhtiar ever since I became a news junkie after 9/11. I was working at John F. Kennedy Airport for eight months, watching passengers get violated at the security checkpoints, and after work, in the wee hours in my crummy hotel room, I would watch Rudi intently as she told me about the day's stories. She seemed more attractive every night I watched her. Those bewitching Persian eyes, that aristocratic Iranian nose, breasts too small to preclude her from the category of sophisticated beauty. (Before this deployment, I was able to watch the news during the day, and I found I was becoming infatuated with Soledad O'Brien and her mesmerizing smile.) But of course they have to broadcast from Atlanta. How will I ever be able to visit? Why can't they broadcast from New York City? What the hell is in Atlanta anyway? While I was at the airport, I emailed CNN a few times asking them if they could set up a service that would email fans of Rudi each day what she would be wearing the next day. I got no response. So I would stare at the TV waiting for that fleeting moment when the ticker at the bottom of the screen dropped, just before or after a commercial break, revealing her body below her armpits. Willy was my roommate for those eight months, and he found my Rudi obsession amusing and slightly troubling.

January 2, 2004

Tomorrow we leave for Fort Polk, Louisiana. Tonight will be the last night I ever spend at Fort Drum. That's actually completely untrue. I just wanted to say that. After Polk, we come back to Fort Drum. We'll be mobilizing from here to ship out to Kuwait.

The last few days have been incredibly uneventful. The only thing that's really happened is there was a huge battalion "dining-in" on New Years Eve. Basically it was a large kinda-formal dinner for the battalion, with the battalion commander as the guest of honor. One can tell that the dining-in is an event with a lot of tradition behind it. There are a lot of rules, a lot of ceremony, and a lot of toasts. There probably was a time, maybe fifty years ago or so, when this kind of thing was really cool. But with the *Jackass* generation, trying to get soldiers to follow proper dining etiquette, especially after they've been drinking for five hours, is like trying to get a kindergarten class to sit still after they've gotten all jacked-up on red Kool-Aid. And I can't really blame it all on my Nintendo-raised colleagues. We all pretty much let it slide into a drunken brouhaha. It became a two-bit comedy hour. At one point, after the same corporal stood up for the fourth time and yelled at the master of ceremonies, "POINT IN ORDER, MR. VICE!" trying to be as funny as he was the first time he pulled the same stunt, I had had enough and yelled, "SHUT THE FUCK UP!" I found myself sitting there at my squad's table imagining my grandfather, a lieutenant commander in the Navy, at a dining-in at a naval base in Alameda or San Leandro during World War II, adhering to the rules of conduct, remaining silent while the commander spoke, giving hearty toasts and generally getting in the spirit of the event. I'd like to think of myself as being someone who is unafraid to enjoy "grown-up" events like this, but even despite being happily drunk for the duration, I found the whole thing unbearable. I feel horrible for saying this. After all, this was meant to bring a battalion together before they went into combat, but it was undeniable that the dining-in went over like a turd in a punch bowl.

Fort Polk

January 7, 2004

So here I am, sitting on my bunk in a giant warehouse at Fort Polk, Louisiana—a top bunk this time; I let the guy beneath me, one of the medics, keep the bottom bunk he seized before I had a chance to claim one—trying to collect my thoughts on what I want to write about, when a bunch of guys start giggling about something. I look down to the guy on the bottom bunk next to mine. He's dead asleep, his poncho liner half pulled over his head, half falling off the side of the mattress. He's lying on his back wearing long johns (or "poly pro bottoms," as we call them) and no socks. My first thought is, Hmm, with the covers falling off the bed like that, his feet must be getting kind of . . . Hey, wait a second! Oh my god! He has a boner! And it's protruding straight out of the fly of his poly pros! Yuck! Guys would come over, whisperingly giggle like conspiring schoolgirls, then grab as many other guys as possible to witness this foul spectacle, this thing so bizarre and macabre and most abhorrent of all to the heterosexual male: a completely visible and turgid phallus! Then everyone started taking pictures, me included. If a girl shows her tits in a bar, two guys take pictures. A guy falls asleep with an exposed hard-on, twenty guys take pictures. Go figure. Finally someone woke him up by swatting him with a shirt, like he was the village leper, and he rolled over, instinctively resheathing the errant meat saber.

January 14, 2004

WHAT, YOU DIDN'T GET THE WORD?

My company motto is "Let's Roll." Or at least that's what I've been led to believe. We yell it when we're in company formations. I cringe every time I have to say it. But I cringe less than when I hear Delta company yell their motto, "Death by Wire," which is meant to signify their killing the enemy with wire-guided TOW missiles, I think. Or their hanging themselves with piano wire instead of going to Iraq, or maybe their always calling their cheating wives on the telephone (wire) and then eventually eating a bullet. I dunno. Since "Let's Roll" is our motto, we use it colloquially, sadly always sarcastically, but still, we employ it regularly in conversation.

But I have noticed for quite a while now a few other phrases used on an even more religious and fervent basis. Some of them go like, "What, you didn't get the word?" or "What, you didn't hear?" or "You've been here three months and you still don't know that?" or "You're an infantry team leader and you didn't know that?" All this time I thought when guys asked these questions they were being condescending, patronizing assholes trying desperately to fight for the alpha dog position by leveraging themselves ever so slightly with even the most minuscule information advantage like a bunch of petty little bitches, but now I realize they were just being hooah and quoting the new company motto: "What, you don't know?"

February 1, 2004

A couple of nights ago some of the other guys and I went out and got into a little trouble at the last bar we were at. There was a small fight in the parking lot between some soldiers, and we were all out after curfew. I didn't realize I was even at that bar until someone told me the next morning. I barely remember the *third* bar we went to. Anyway, the point is, there was a scuffle. All I really remember was this guy taking off his shirt to fight. Today I was questioned by the company executive officer (XO) regarding the incident. There is now an "investigation" ongoing. What the hell they are investigating is a mystery to me. There's nothing to investigate. A bunch of guys were out after curfew (just like they have been every night for the past four months), got drunk, and got in a fight. Better question: of all the things a company XO could be spending his time doing a month before going into combat, why is he investigating a fucking curfew violation? So now, as part of my punishment, I have to guard ammo on some range for twenty-four hours, starting at 8:00 a.m. tomorrow, with my fellow curfew breakers (except the guy who started the fight; he was out at the mall tonight while the rest of us were on lockdown). But here's where it gets really fucked up: Word is we rule breakers are going to lose some or all of the time off we have before going overseas. We are supposed to have the seventh through the ninth off, and again four days on Valentine's Day weekend. Our deployment ceremony is on the seventh. Plane tickets and hotel rooms have already been paid for by my father and sister so they can come up for the shitbird deployment ceremony. I haven't seen my father since my deployment began four months ago, and this is the last chance I'll have to see him. If I can't spend the night of the seventh with them, there is no point for them to come up for only the ceremony, as it will most certainly be fucking retarded—we'll stand around while every local politician wishes us well. Hey, local politicians, you want to do something for me? Keep your remarks short at the ceremony. We don't know you, and the longer you talk, the longer we have to stand at attention. If I don't get to see my family, I'll live; it's not that big a deal. However, my family may feel differently. They may really *want* to see me before I go into combat. If I get blown the fuck up, what do I care? I'll be dead. But if I get transformed into a fine pink mist because I was on point for an IED patrol as punishment for not clearing my weapon properly before entering a military building, it may draw the ire of my family that they didn't get to see me for that last time because I was being punished for breaking my 11:00 p.m. curfew. I'm a thirty-year-old infantryman who will soon be given the ultimate authority of killing anyone I adjudicate to be a threat, but until then I have the same curfew I did when I was in junior high school. I realize that this kind of argument is really unoriginal and too easy to use, but the thing that really scares me—and I'm being serious here—is that my command makes *this* big a deal about me and a few guys being out after curfew; what's gonna happen when we actually start getting into shit? Am I going to be interrogated every time I pull the trigger? Am I going to be investigated every time I look at someone sideways? My commander is a prosecutor in real life. The guy is a pit bull. He is competent, solid, and ferocious. He loves Hemingway and Melville. His vocabulary exceeds mine. And I love him as my commander. But right now I feel that if he wanted to make a big deal about this, we'd be fucked. This guy prosecutes organized crime in New York City for a living. When I truthfully say that I don't remember shit because I was completely blotto that night, I really mean I don't remember shit. But this isn't necessarily to my advantage. If my commander decided to get involved, he could place me at the scene of the crime wearing a white hood with my boot on the throat of some mentally retarded nun, clubbing a baby seal with one hand and igniting a cross with the other.

February 3, 2004

Dear readers: This blog will be going offline. I have been informed that I have violated operational security and additionally that I am smearing my unit and the Army. I, of course, strenuously disagree.

I am taking the blog offline at the request of my company commander. I do so under protest and I do it as a favor to my platoon sergeant and first sergeant.

I will continue to write, but I will no longer be posting it publicly. The warrior ethos states that I should never give up. So now I have to do things a little more on the down-low.

I love America more than I can describe. I love the Army and the invaluable opportunity it's given me to give back to a country that I love with all my heart. And as much as I love the Army, I love to exalt it by sharing with you exactly how ridiculous it really is. If you can grok what I'm saying, you are among friends. Thanks.

February 11, 2004

RAY AND THE COIN

There's a tradition in the military where if you've done something that merits a pat on the back or if you are in the right place at the right time, someone with rank may give you a special coin, usually engraved with a unit and rank or place. Sometimes entire units are given coins for certain accomplishments, like completing a rotation at the National Training Center in California. In general, receiving a coin is a prestigious thing. How many coins you have and where you got them gives you certain bragging rights. If you are out drinking and someone drops a coin on the bar, you are expected to drop one of your own coins in an attempt to trump it. The guy with the least prestigious coin (or no coin at all) is expected to buy that round. There is no official standard for the hierarchy of coins, but if you have a coin that a two-star general gave you while you were in Bosnia, you can rest assured that the guy with the coin his unit received for attending the Joint Readiness Training Center at Fort Polk is going to be the one buying the drinks. If both you and the other guy have coins from sergeants major, the coin that came from the Eighty-second Airborne Division will trump the one from the Three hundred and whatever Finance Brigade in Toledo, Ohio.

Some guys take the whole coin thing very seriously. I knew a soldier in my old unit in Utah who used to carry around a small coin purse that held his collection, so if anyone ever dropped a coin on him, he'd be prepared to trump it or at least try to impress the other person with the number of coins he had been awarded. There are also guys who do not take the coin thing too seriously. Ray is one of these guys.

On the last day of our rotation at JRTC at Fort Polk, Louisiana, our forward operating base (FOB) was crawling with brass. Generals, colonels, sergeants major, and the like were all visiting to see how the newest batch of soldiers set for Iraq were faring. These guys usually make the rounds to all the command tents and shake hands. Our snipers are part of our headquarters section, so it's no surprise that the adjutant general (AG) of the state of New York (the guy in charge of the New York National Guard) should meet Chris and Ray on that day. Chris and Ray were in their ghillie suits looking like a couple of cold-blooded killers when the AG came around, so not surprisingly he decided to give them coins.

Ray is a no-nonsense kind of guy. He's not a big fan of accolades being given for nothing, so he tends to see coins being given for something as pedestrian as running into a general while wearing a ghillie suit as kinda lame. Ray took the coin, undoubtedly with no expression, but he had been waiting for a moment like this for quite some time. After accepting the coin, he told the general, "Sir, I have something for *you* now," at which point he dropped his rucksack on the ground and started rummaging through it. Knowing that Ray is prone to certain eccentricities, Chris started to sweat.

After a short search of his ruck, Ray plucks from it a coin of his own with the rank of specialist engraved on it that he bought at the PX for four bucks. (Many coins are very elaborate and somewhat pricey to produce, unlike this trinket.) He hands it to the general and says, "From all the high-speed specialists in the Army, I'd like to give you this coin. We think you're doing a really good job, sir. Keep up the good work."

The adjutant general took the coin, thanked Ray, then started to get teary-eyed and emotional. Feeling bad that his jocular ribbing had been mistaken for sincerity, Ray played along and kept a straight face.

A few weeks later we're standing in formation at our deployment ceremony on the basketball court at the gym at freezing-ass Fort Drum. The ceremony is plodding along, as is to be expected—a low-cost master of ceremonies bungling people's names, politicians giving listless speeches, female soldiers passing out in the formation because they forgot not to lock their knees. Then the final speaker, the adjutant general, gives his words. And what story does he tell? The Specialist Who Gave Him a Coin. By this point, everyone had already heard it, so to hear it from the general himself was priceless. We could barely contain ourselves. Thank you, general, for making my deployment ceremony completely worthwhile.

February 19, 2004

I'm sitting at a war-torn '50s-era desk in a small, dirty room of a stuffy, garage-like building that acts as our company's supply building, arms room, and CQ office. I've been in the Army for so long now, I've forgotten what CQ stands for, but I know that it means I have to answer the phone if it rings. The standard answer goes something like this: "Bravo Company, first of the one-oh-seventh infantry, this is Sergeant Hartley speaking, this line is not secure, how may I help you, sir or ma'am?" When I want to savor the absurdity of this verbose announcement, I clearly enunciate it in its entirety. If I'm feeling lucky, I truncate it a bit. But in most cases, what guys do is just smear the phrase into one inarticulate ogreish exhalation, something like what Mormon kids do at the end of every prayer: "INTHENAME OFJESUSCHRISTAMEN."

The bare concrete floor is covered in a nearly even dusting of sand, which is incredibly annoying because no matter where you plant your feet while sitting, you have no traction. This means you have to readjust your feet more often to try to find a comfortable position, but this also means that you have to feel the skin-crawling grind of sand between foot and floor. I swept the area under the desk, but then, because of the still air of the unventilated office, I had to sit suspended in a cloud of dust that only Pigpen would have appreciated. This is what you get for trying to eke incremental gains in comfort out of the Army—different discomforts.

Sitting next to me is Jose, a mortars sergeant I've known for a few years from my original company in the city. He's watching *Carlito's Way* on DVD on a laptop. He turns to me and says excitedly, "Look, look! See? That's me and my baby!" He has the movie paused and points out a man in the near background of a nightclub who looks like a younger version of him wearing a spic-tacular brown polyester suit and wiggling to the club's music with an attractive Latina. I've known for years that Jose was in a scene in *Carlito's Way*, but this is the first time that I've actually seen it. He and his wife appear a few more times throughout the scene, which he proudly points out to me. It's almost as if he bought the DVD just to pore through this part of it. I guess if I were in a film standing right next to Pacino, I'd review it a few times, too.

The funny thing about Jose admiring himself in the movie is it seems to have been a real highlight of his life, something he says he loves showing his kids. But it's the timing of this self-validation that I find interesting. It's almost as if this is the most meaningful record of himself, something that makes permanent a more perfect version of who he is—younger, thinner, and better dressed, and all on celluloid (or in this case DVD).

And he's not the only soldier who seeks a sense of permanence. Every soldier who had a "girlfriend" before this deployment had a "fiancée" once it started. Over the few breaks we've had, more guys have clandestinely gotten married than I can count. The same can be said for guys who made conscious and concerted efforts to impregnate their wives while on leave. There have also been a whole slew of deployment tattoos, most involving religion (a rosary, a crucifix) and loved ones (wives' and children's names). Me, I'm as fixated on releasing myself from attachments as some guys are on establishing them. Well, that's half bullshit. I've worked very hard over the last several years to strip my life down to a state of minimal attachments, but my inner drive to create my own legacy is manifest in this journal, so I can't self-righteously pretend that there are not things to which I cling. I believe that the only genuine stories are the ones that never get told. When someone records history, you get their view infused with their motivations and insecurities and their myopic observations of events. Not only am I no different from any other historian quack, but I'm the worst there is. I'm obsessed with trying to recount events as accurately and honestly as possible, but in practice the only thing I'm really any good at is telling you how I feel.

In a few days we leave for Kuwait. From what I hear, the logistical mosh pit that is Kuwait has hit epic levels not seen since World War II. The fear of going to a place where there are people who actually want to hurt me is something I've never felt before. And I can't seem to overcome the feeling that there is something more I need to bring that I haven't gotten yet. Gearheads like Chris really go bananas at times trying to decide these things, like which optic to purchase for their rifles—the ACOG or the Aimpoint?! I left my room in my apartment basically clean but not organized in any way to make easier the lives of those who would have to clear it out should I be killed. I am a rabid record keeper. I've kept every email, every instant message conversation, every digital photograph. My maternal grandfather helped raise me for the first four years of my life and was my first male role model. He's dead now, and I wish I could have known him better. Maybe someday there will be a grandchild wishing he knew more about me. So I leave every inanity I can find a way to save, for future generations to sift through. So much for no attachments.

I feel like so much has been left undone. There are friends I won't see before I leave; there are bills I still need to pay. I haven't written as much as I've wanted, and there are countless things I've said that I wish I could correct, but this is a process that will never end. When my grandmother died she left a library full of books she never finished reading. This is how I feel now. I don't even know how to end this entry.

But I guess that's the tao of it all. Learning how to leave things undone and still be at peace with it. Nothing ever really gets finished anyway, nothing ever really ends, so why this need to create an end state? Maybe this explains humankind's apparent need to destroy itself.

"There will be no resolution."
Last line from *Smilla's Sense of Snow,* by Peter Høeg.

"This is not an exit."
Last line from *American Psycho,* by Bret Easton Ellis.

February 23, 2004

It's an unusual concoction of emotions I'm feeling tonight on the eve of what will be the longest flight of my life. I keep thinking I should be dreading my departure, but I feel oddly eager to get there. On a basic and immediate level I'm fairly nervous, but I also feel an inexplicable excitement and undeniable optimism about the future. It's hard for me to admit that most of what I feel is positive, for fear that I'll later regret my naiveté. More than ever I find my unremarkable life to be sublimely precious. And it's also hard for me to admit that the rest of what I feel is a sense of incredulity at how colossally absurd it is, what I'm about to do. There are people who are going to try to kill me, and I'm going to try to kill them. (Don't these assholes know that all this killing stuff is dangerous? Someone could get hurt for chrissakes!) But fighting is something so basic to humanity that ruing it is just plain futile. Duality is intrinsic to mortality, so as motivated as we are to preserve life, we still succumb to the lust and necessity to destroy life. To transcend this cycle would mean to transcend our own mortality—not a trivial feat. I don't assume to know so much as even the first step in this process. But I suspect a good start would be a simple sense of compassion and determination.

My heart is full and my weapon is clean.

Camp Udairi, Kuwait

February 26, 2004

We are now at Camp Udairi, Kuwait, by way of Shannon, Ireland, and Sicily. We will be here for about two more weeks before we head up to our area of operations in Iraq. Most of the battalion will be flying up, but my platoon will be part of the convoy that drives up. Yay.

I have a new weapon now—an M4 assault rifle with M203 grenade launcher. Her name is Wazina. She's dark and beautiful.

March 4, 2004

It's sorta hard to talk about what life is like for us right now in Kuwait. We don't really do that much other than walk to chow three times a day, occasionally making a stop at the PX or computer center. We're in the middle of a desert; there's nothing here.

Something I've been puzzling over for some time now: being here in Nowhere, Kuwait, is it more *Indiana Jones* or more *Star Wars*? The *Star Wars* argument is pretty sound, I think. We started out at the snow-covered fields of planet Hoth (Fort Drum, New York), then we made a short trip to the swamps of the Dagobah system (Fort Polk, Louisiana), now we return to the vast deserts of Tattooine

(Iraq/Kuwait). "But *Return of the Jedi* was filmed in Tanzania, which is in Africa, so I'd say this is more *Indiana Jones*," Dan pointed out. Between all the tents and soldiers and sand and the actual setting, the *Indiana Jones* argument is pretty sound, too.

Then we were assigned the Humvees that we'll be driving in our convoy into Iraq, and the argument was settled: this is definitely *Mad Max*. If you could see our vehicles, you'd understand.

Our battalion was given a number of the new "up-armored" Humvees, these bad boys with the powerful engines, air conditioning, bulletproof glass, and more armor plating than you can shake a stick at. My platoon did not get many of these. I think we got two. Then there are the Humvees that have the "bolt-on" armor-plate kits. Once these kits are installed, the armor is pretty damn decent. I think we have one or two of these. The rest of the vehicles we were assigned are plain vanilla unarmored Humvees, which we have now sandbagged the hell out of. We put those Halliburton carpenters to work and have had them make all sorts of stuff for us to help us turn our Humvees into giant rolling mounds of sandbags. For the normal turtleback Humvees, we've sandbagged the floors and the windshield on top of the hood and, best of all, we've had plywood boards cut that now separate the passenger area from the back, so we can stack a wall of sandbags behind us. Some of the seats are now covered with Kevlar blankets. Once you cram all your additional equipment, food, water, weapons, ammunition, and your gear-laden bodies into what little space is left, you have a Gigeresque monstrosity. These fuckers are now uncomfortable as hell, and it'll be a miracle if we make it to our area of operations in Iraq without anyone developing blood clots in his legs from being folded into his seat like a Swiss Army knife. I'm not complaining, really. It's not like I want to get blown up by some shitty roadside bomb. I've placed every sandbag with the outcome of flesh vs. shrapnel well in mind. But I've gotta tell ya, some of these vehicles are just laughable the way they look now. We have a flatbed Humvee that has a mount in the bed for a machine gun. A double-walled plywood box was constructed in the bed to surround the gun and gunner. The hollow space in between the walls was then filled with sandbags. Although neither of us will be the one standing back there, Kirk and I took great care packing in each one of those sandbags. I've seen five-ton cargo trucks that have had similar boxes constructed for their gun turrets, some with welded metal plates. Every vehicle with a gunner turret has also had a sharpened piece of angle iron bolted to the frame of the windshield. The iron stands straight up like a sword to cut through any piano wire that may have been strung across the road in an attempt to decapitate machine gunners. It all looks pretty gypsy. My favorite, I think, is Dan's and Kirk's vehicle. It's a canvas-top Humvee that's had the armor-plate kit applied and a plywood sheet bolted to the roof in place of the canvas. It looks sorta like a half-armored dune buggy—semi-ridiculous. Or, as my platoon leader likes to call it, the Malibu Barbie Humvee.

The First Infantry Division general spoke to us a couple of days ago. The most memorable thing I remember him saying was in reference to our rules of engagement and how we can "crush the rattlesnake that is poised to strike." He said, "What do you do when you see an Arab put an RPG to his shoulder? You draw a bead on his fucking head and you kill him!" He also told us how none of the recent convoys going into Iraq have been attacked. That changed today. One of the First Infantry Division convoys got hit just as it left the Kuwait border. From what I heard, there was one KIA and two WIAs. Score one for the enemy. They hit us the moment we walked out the front door. If I were the enemy, I'd hit the new incoming U.S. soldiers with everything I had right off the bat and inflict as many casualties as possible in an attempt to demoralize the new guys. In a way, I hope this is what they are thinking because I would love to make contact on our convoy. I want to get the trepidation I feel about making first contact out of my system. And I don't think I'm the only one who feels this way. I also want to discard any moral qualms I might have about killing other human beings, and help as many of these fuckers die for Allah as I possibly can on day one. Also, if they bring everything they've got to the fight, it will give us a chance to neutralize more of their assets.

I refuse to call this a war. World War II was a war. This is a fight. And a dirty one at that. The way I see it, our enemy simply wants to kill as many Americans as possible, thereby convincing the CNN-watching public that the price is just too great and we should pull out and let the Shiite clerics or whoever take care of things. In my opinion, this strategy is brilliant. It's cheap, and it has a good chance of working. I pray it doesn't.

I think about the reasons why all this started and how America is commonly perceived as the big evil land of the infidels. When I think of what America must look like to Islamic Fundamentalist Joe, I think of Hollywood. Hollywood makes so much offensively unwatchable garbage and aggressively sells it to the world. Whether we like it or not, *Bad Boys II* is how America gets represented to the rest of the world. This is unfortunate. Then Islamic Fundamentalist Joe looks at the proud and history-rich culture he comes from, and how Martin Lawrence is encroaching on it, and he becomes Terrorist Joe.

America *is* beautiful, from the bustle of her cities to the hiking trails of her national parks, from the snow-mobiling people in Minnesota who talk funny to the grits-eatin' people of Georgia who also talk funny, from the kids on skateboards at strip malls in California to everyone's grandparents enjoying retirement in Florida. But Terrorist Joe sees only Jerry Bruckheimer and his Taco Bell merchandizing tie-ins wiping his shoes on his prayer mat. So I feel for ya, Terrorist Joe.

But some of your buddies attacked me where I live in New York City. They killed people I know. And since a lot of New York City police officers and firefighters are also National Guardsmen, they killed a lot of our brothers-at-arms. So invite all your foreign insurgent friends and anti-coalition forces friends to your place and set the table, because a lot of very pissed-off New Yorkers are coming over for dinner and we're hungry.

March 9, 2004

This will be the last time I write from Kuwait. My platoon leaves shortly for the heart of Iraq, by way of no small convoy.

I've spent so much time existentially pondering all this combat crap, that I've forgotten to complain about the Army. I've always been taught that the most important thing a rifleman can do is shoot straight. This apparently is not very important anymore. We've been sitting on our asses for the majority of the last two weeks, and then finally we went to a range. Since I carry the M203, my weapon wasn't ready until just a few days before we left Fort Drum. So I never got a chance to zero it (adjust the sights) there, the idea being we would zero it in Kuwait. We finally get to the zero range, and they give us just enough ammo to zero the iron sights. Okay, fine, but I don't really use the iron sights to shoot, I use the Aimpoint (reflexive firing optic). But there was not enough ammo or range time to zero both. I refuse to zero only the Aimpoint and not the iron sights, because if the battery dies, I want a reliable backup aiming solution. So I compromised and got a decent zero on the iron sights and a half-assed zero on the Aimpoint. This is totally unsat. We should have spent *days* at the range zeroing the *hell* out of all our weapons systems and doing familiarization fires on all the weapons systems.

Me and the guys of my truck almost didn't get to go on the convoy.

("Road march" is a better term, even though we won't actually be marching.) My commander's Humvee needed a new alternator, so in the meantime, during training, he took my platoon sergeant's Humvee, who in turn took mine. A few hours ago, the commander's vehicle finally got fixed. This gave the guys of my Humvee only a couple of hours to pack our vehicle. Actually, it's not our vehicle. Since our platoon sergeant has been using ours for the past several days, he decided to keep it so he wouldn't have to unpack it and then repack his old vehicle. This is cool (sorta) because this now means that we have his vehicle, which has one of those super-duper high-tech Blue Force Tracker computers in it. This thing is cool as shit. It's a GPS (global positioning system)-linked touch-screen computer that sits in the front passenger side of the truck that allows the truck commander to see a bird's-eye-view map of the battlefield in real time.

Speaking of the Humvee snafu, my platoon was given Kevlar blankets to put on the seats of some of the Humvees. Mine was one of them. This is cool because it literally protects your ass from land mines, IEDs, etc. Well, we had to give them back for some reason. All of the guys in my truck agreed that we would forgo the sandbags-on-the-floor bullshit and just live dangerously and roll without them. The Humvee is uncomfortable enough as it is without a bunch of friggin' sandbags crammed in there for the sake of the time when an explosion happens to take place *directly* beneath me. There are still a shit-load of sandbags in the Humvee, don't get me wrong; we just opted for more leg room.

I am really excited about this drive north. It's gonna take a few days, and I'm sure it will be miserable in several ways, but how often do you get to take a road trip through Iraq?

I have no idea when I'll get to write again. When I do, expect some good stories. After all, that's the whole reason you join the Army is to get some good stories, right?

Iraq

March 12, 2004

Our convoy left Camp Udairi, Kuwait, on March 10, and we arrived at our forward operating base in Iraq on March 12. The drive took the better part of three days, mostly due to the fact that convoys, by nature, are slow. The weather was perfect and the trip uneventful, other than the convoy coming across a dead dog thought to be disguised as an IED on the side of the road a few kilometers before the FOB. It was blown up by the explosive ordnance disposal (EOD) guys with several pounds of C4. There was no IED, and all the explosion did was launch the dog sky high.

We now live in the middle of nowhere in what used to be an ammo bunker. Imagine a Lower Manhattan loft that would be to die for if only it had windows, set in the middle of the Old West. Anything we want we have to build ourselves, out of scavenged material, the *Mad Max* metaphor taken to a whole new level. We get a hot meal about every other day. There is no running water, and therefore no toilets, so we have to burn our own shit. Hearing massive explosions and random gunfire from everywhere is so commonplace we already ignore most of it.

Since the convoy through Iraq was our first combat mission, we were given our combat load of ammo. I got 240 rounds of 5.56mm rifle ammo. I chose to load each 30-round magazine with the first, sixteenth, and last three rounds with tracer, my thinking behind the placement of the tracers being to show me where my first round hits (aiming adjustments can be done very easily once you see where the rounds are striking), to tell me when I'm into the second half of the magazine, and the final three to tell me when the mag is expended. I carry the M4/M203 rifle/grenade launcher combo, so I was also issued a bunch of 40mm grenades: seventeen rounds of HEDP (high-explosive dual-purpose), two green smoke, one red smoke (for marking and/or signaling), and one white star cluster (a fireworks-like round used for signaling). I carry on my person 210 rounds of 5.56, five HEDP, and one green smoke. The rest I carry in an assault pack (fancy name for a small backpack). The Interceptor Kevlar body armor we wear now has big ceramic armor plates in the front and back, making our everyday combat uniform remarkably heavy. Between the armor and the ammo, I feel like a human tank.

Driving through Kuwait just below Iraq, we saw an incredible number of Bedouins. It was like driving through Nevada where there isn't *anything* for hundreds of miles, and then incredibly there will be families just chillin' off to the side of the road, usually with a herd of sheep or camels. As we approached the Iraq border, various messages could be found on concrete blocks beside the road. One read, IRAQ BORDER AHEAD 1000 M. BEWARE OF CHILDREN IN ROADWAY. I can't tell you how exciting it was knowing we were moments away from crossing the berm into "The Raq." Once we made it past the berm and through the one-kilometer buffer of no-man's land, I distributed cigars to everyone in the truck. As soon as we hit the border town, we held our cigars in one hand and our digital cameras in the other. Not the most tactical way to enter the country—puffin' and clickin'—but oh well.

The entire drive through Iraq, stupid American soldier graffiti was everywhere. Like I give a shit that you were in the 367th Pogue Battalion. Idiots. It especially slays me how many white trash soldiers with cans of spray paint have proclaimed love to this or that girl on every overpass along Iraq Highway 1.

The weather was perfect and warm, and aside from being in a combat zone, the trip through Iraq almost felt like a relaxing summer road trip. Except for when we took a wrong turn and drove through the heart of Baghdad at two in the morning, accidentally avoiding a huge daisy chain of IEDs, we later found out. I guess all those prayers for this godless heathen paid off.

I hope god doesn't throw lightning bolts at me for saying this, but for the record, I'm having a ball.

March 17, 2004

For a few days we had to guard a bridge. We got swamped with kids wanting food. "Mister! Mister! Gimme food!" It helped pass the time, playing with the kids. Once we finally gave them MREs, all they'd do was ratfuck the candy out of them and dump the rest.

March 21, 2004

Any vehicles that are parked on the side of the road we inspect to see if they are up to no good or if they just need help. Communicating with the Iraqis is nearly impossible, so we tend to stick to hand signals. To an Iraqi, the thumbs-up usually means "up your ass," but now we have taught them that it means "A-okay." This ambiguity is absolutely sublime. Kids all across Iraq (and soldiers) can now use an obscene hand gesture with impunity.

March 27, 2004

A little bit of all that money that our government is overpaying to Halliburton will be coming to us soon when Kellogg Brown & Root visits us to build us some stuff, including a "dining hall" and a gym. Running water will never happen, but we'd be stoked just to get some port-o-johns. I *never* thought I'd be looking forward to shitting in a fucking port-o-john.

Today I burned shit. Have you ever burned shit? It sizzles. You pour diesel into it, mix it up into a gassy, shitty emulsion, then you burn it and stir it. And the processed food–laden turds that soldiers squeeze out take forever to burn. Strangely, I kinda had fun doing it. When I was done, I had shit-ashes in my teeth. And it smells funny, like funky grilled steak.

I am writing this under the light of a hanging lamp I made from broken table fan parts. We even made a septic tank from ventilation tubing.

April 4, 2004

BRICKS WITHOUT STRAW?!

Iraq right now is not unlike the early American Wild West, and all of my *Indiana Jones*–fueled boyhood fantasies have come true for the most part. We live a pretty primal existence. We have to be creative when it comes to everything. We build what we need by hand, from available materials. Even when it comes to combat readiness, we have to use a lot of ingenuity and elbow grease to make things work. Humvees are being held together with bubble gum and bailing wire half the time, weapons are covered in duct tape to keep pressure switches in place, and recently a slim jim was constructed out of a wire oven rack taken from a home we raided to open a car the owners could not seem to produce keys to. And despite all the high-tech bullshit we carry, personal defense is still the most primal act. Every time we leave our FOB, we lock and load. In the Old West, gunslingers went everywhere strapped, because they never knew when they'd be in their next gunfight. There is nothing different about being in Iraq. It's an oddly exhilarating way to live.

When something does happen, it's exciting. If you are there for the event, there is a certain intensity and elation. If you weren't there, you absorb every word of the recounted stories. I feel like I need to apologize constantly for enjoying myself here. They say that morale among soldiers is incredibly low in Iraq. That sucks for them. I'm having the time of my life.

And I'm not enjoying myself just because of the GI Joe factor. The culture here is fascinating. I feel like I'm in one big Bible story. When I was four years old and living in Spanish Fork, the shittiest hick town in Utah, my recently adoptive father would read me these illustrated Bible stories. Add AK-47s and shabby cars to those stories, and you have Iraq 2004. As a child I didn't understand Charlton "I Loves Me Some Rifles" Heston when he cried out to Pharaoh, "Bricks without straw?! How can we make bricks without straw?!" Bricks need straw? I had never seen bricks containing straw. Well, I have now. And the story about the temple that needed the exposed bricks of its exterior wall mended? That makes sense now, too. Men's fashion hasn't exactly improved over the last three millennia, either. They still wear man-dresses, just like the one Jesus wore as a teen hangin' out at the local Hajji-mart, and later in his life, when people were touching the hem of it. I've seen kids on donkey-drawn carriages in place of bicycles, and men wiping shit off their asses with their bare hands in place of toilet paper. I also was perplexed as a child by a Bible story where someone washed Jesus's feet when he came to visit them. Never having worn sandals anywhere as dusty as Iraq, this seemed like a totally random thing to do. Now I understand that, too.

This place is so harsh and backward and perpetually stuck in the fucking Stone Age in most ways, but you have to love it because of that. There are no shiny new strip malls or housing developments here, no Super Target, no Starbucks, no Jiffy Lube. It's full of people who will die twenty years earlier than Americans and who can't help but understand that life is survival first and owning a PlayStation a distant second. Although there's nothing special about people who live in poverty and squalor, there's something genuine about these people and their life that I can't help but admire. I wish to god I spoke Arabic, because I have a thousand questions I want to ask them.

The first firefight goes to Second Platoon, who went on a night raid in a small town near our FOB. An intel guy and an informant from Baghdad said an attack on a very large FOB in the area was going to be perpetrated by men from this village that night at such and such time. While they were approaching the town, and before they'd even made it to the house to be raided, they took fire. It was an ambush. Ray and John were both on the mission. Some guys returned fire immediately, some whaled away on the enemy with their SAWs, but mostly there were a lot of confused soldiers who took some prodding to kick into gear. Here's a quick scorecard from the stories I heard:

Friendly dead: 0

Friendly wounded: 0

Friendly shoulders dislocated from jumping behind cover: 1

Friendly dislocated shoulders self-relocated: 1

Enemy killed by Ray: 0 (maybe next time)

Overall enemy dead: 0

Enemy wounded: 0

Number of directions in which fire was received: 3

Soldiers' pants pissed: 1

Soldiers with pissed pants who pushed on with the fight: 1

Soldiers who refused to fight and returned to the Humvees: 2

Soldiers who fell asleep on the objective: 1 confirmed (most likely more)

40mm high-explosive grenades John fired: 2

40mm high-explosive grenades it took to convince the enemy to stop fighting: 1

●　　●　　●

Three men of Arab descent and unknown allegiance drove by an ICDC (Iraqi Civil Defense Corps) building in our area and threw an explosive at its front gate, apparently in hopes of baiting them into a vehicular pursuit. The ICDC did what they do best: nothing. They're totally untrained and almost useless. This time it probably paid off. The men in the car had an AK-47 and an RPK (a Russian machine gun). Frustrated that the ICDC did not give chase, the three hooligans drove alongside an up-armored Humvee with its window open and opened fire (probably impulsively) with the AK. The soldier behind the driver was killed and two others were wounded. Immediately a .50-cal and an M240 in the Humvee's convoy showed the three men the flames of hell. Two of the men were shredded by the gunfire, and the third—the driver, as I understand it—ate a self-administered 9mm round. This put all three with rounds taken to the head. Two female bystanders were killed in the crossfire. One took a round to the back of the head, which removed most of her face. Not a good day for heads. I feel horrible about the women. However, I found myself fascinated by what the dead guys were wearing. It was very

Western: jeans, Dickey-like blue pants, white T-shirt, blue plaid button-down shirt, black T-shirt, brown leather belt. All three had well-groomed hair and facial hair. It's not that I expected to see them wearing traditional garb. You know when you're driving and someone on the road does something stupid and you get pissed off and you have to see what they look like, as if you could collect a mental catalog of how assholes look? Well, it's like that. I can't help but want to know what my enemy looks like, how he dresses, how he does his hair.

While on guard duty, I was sitting on a folding stool beside my Humvee, which was parked at a position on the berm that protects our FOB. We heard the unmistakable hollow report of a 40mm grenade being fired. Then, a second later, the even louder sound of the round slapping into the berm not forty meters from us. The sound of it hitting the soft dirt of the berm was loud, but not loud in the way a 40mm grenade exploding sounds. An MK19 on a Humvee, part of a convoy leaving our FOB, had an accidental discharge (now called a "negligent discharge" in military parlance). Had the round been fired about two seconds earlier, it probably would have hit my Humvee, and I'd probably be in a world of hurt right now, another one of those stupid fratricide statistics.

A man on a scooter was trailing a convoy entering our FOB. He was repeatedly commanded to stop—in English, Arabic, and the universal language of an assault rifle being pointed at him. He was unarmed. It is uncertain what he was thinking. However, it is certain that the 5.56mm round that he subsequently took to the chest killed him. His lover, who lived in the nearby town, killed himself the next day when he got word of his death.

•　　•　　•

I've been on two raids now. The first was in response to three IEDs that exploded next to a Humvee as it drove down a road near our FOB. No one in the Humvee was hurt. My platoon, acting as the quick-reaction force, was called to the scene. We cleared about seven buildings in the area of the attack. The buildings were all chicken farms (ranches?) and the homes of the people who ran them. We turned up a lot of weapons, but all were legit. No bad guys or IED-type materials were found, just a bunch of terrified families. I ended up with Jeff, one of our squad leaders, a combat-loving insane former Ranger, and his squad—meaning much fun was had. We trudged through canals and swamps and covered a lot of ground on foot. It was incredibly physically exhausting. (Goddamned heavy-ass body armor. If it didn't protect my vital organs so well, I'd pitch it in a canal.) The squalor these chicken ranchers lived in was sad. But I'll tell you what, clearing a building and entering a room seventy-five meters long and full of thousands of chickens is really bizarre.

The second raid was on a house of an apparent IED maker. The best part of this was how the location was recon'd. Kirk and Jeff were part of a foot patrol that passed by the home of the intended raid. They acted like stupid soldier-tourists and took pictures of themselves in front of everything: the approach to the house, the neighbors' homes, the target house itself, and all its inhabitants, who were more than happy to come outside and pose with them. I guess if the enemy is brazen enough to just drive right up and plant IEDs on the side of the road, we can walk right up to their homes, photograph everything including them, then raid the home a few hours later at first light. The family looked so happy in the pictures, it kinda made me feel bad knowing that I'd be back later, in combat mode. It was good to know that the house was cram-packed full of little rugrats though. We counted four kids in the photos, but after the raid we discovered ten. These Iraqis don't fuck around when it comes to makin' kids. All ten kids slept through the entire ordeal. The raid went off without a hitch, the smoothest operation I've been on, even in training. We were supposed to send a breach team over the wall surrounding the property to open the metal gates from the inside, but once we got to the home, we found the front gate unlocked. It was kinda funny. The breach team and the raid team were lined up against the wall, waiting to go over the ladder. Mike, my platoon sergeant, tried the gate, and it opened. He looked back at us and shrugged and directed the raid team in. When they got to the door, the man of the house was already awake and he let them in. Once inside, they searched the place, and my platoon sergeant found hidden behind the home's AK-47 a plastic bag containing women's lingerie and some booze. There was booze stashed all over the house, actually. The man of the house was none too happy, and I'll bet a big part of it was knowing what a world of shit he was going to be in, not so much for having to explain the IED materials to us but for having to explain to his wife the naughty items we had found. Willy's platoon simultaneously raided another home in the town. They chained the front gate of their target house to a Humvee and pulled it down, along with half the wall. Once again, no shots were fired at either house, no one was hurt, and everything was performed on time. A very successful operation. And for the concerned bleeding hearts out there: all damages are reimbursed.

April 21, 2004

I, Jailor

This morning our battalion conducted several simultaneous predawn raids. The first home my platoon hit went down in a fashion that's becoming the norm for us—moments before the ram is to hit the door for the dynamic entry that turgid grunts salivate over, the door is unlocked and opened from the inside by a man who is probably already on his second cup of Turkish coffee. People here wake up stupid early to get a jump on the long day of chicken herding or dirt farming or whatever.

Some of the intel was of dubious credibility, resulting in nothing but a lot of wide-eyed and confused detainees—as was the case with my platoon's target building—and some intel was rock solid. There were RPGs and belts of machine-gun ammunition found at other target locations today—not a completely fruitless morning of raids.

I missed out on this morning's soiree, pulling a twelve-hour shift of gate and jail guard instead. Our FOB's jail (detention center?) is right at the front gate, a messy configuration where detainees, local civilian contractors, and politicians, along with ICDC clowns, Iraqi police officers, and all the other random visitors we get, are corralled through the same small area. Anyway, everyone was back by 8:00 a.m., at which point they dumped off all the captured men to our reluctant jailor. This "facility" is smaller than my apartment in New Paltz and with twenty-some-odd Ali Baba (the locals' term for evildoers) bound and blindfolded, it can be pretty cramped. One of the first detainees had three thousand dinars (like two bucks), an ID card, and a slip of paper with what looked like some sort of code handwritten on it. When the lieutenant in charge of performing ad hoc in-processing saw this, he thought he might have struck gold by stumbling upon some sort of encrypted message. There were two lines of alphanumeric text; each line was twenty-five characters, with hyphens between every fifth character. Scrawled underneath was what looked like the word "Word." The code format looked incredibly familiar. Then it hit me. I kinda chuckled and told the lieutenant that at best this implicated our detainee in the crime of software piracy. It was a couple of CD keys, for Microsoft Word no doubt.

Once everyone had their restraints cut off, they were farmed out evenly into the four cells, still blindfolded and seated facing the wall. An interpreter instructed each detainee to stay seated, to not talk, and to not remove his blindfold. Each man was also informed that if he followed these rules and acted like a gentleman, he would be treated like a gentleman. Then began the Parade of Piss. "Mister, mister. Toilet, toilet." Once again, Jesus made manifest his displeasure with me for leaving his church. Had I stayed Mormon, gotten married at a ridiculously young age, settled down, made a family, and taken on the inevitable tour of duty of running the nursery at church while the other adults attended various meetings and Sunday school classes, I would already have served my time taking little rascals pee pee. In lieu of this duty I thought I had successfully dodged, I was now taking big rascals pee pee. And these reeked of the body odor only a Middle Eastern diet can create. So when are you being humane by letting detainees urinate (the term this lieutenant kept using was "titrate") as needed, and when are you just plain being taken advantage of by performing an endless round-robin of urinal runs? (There isn't actually any urinal, just a tube stuck in the dirt behind the jail.) Most of the soldiers I had with me had not worked with detainees yet and seemed to also be searching for a sense of what tone to set. I found myself walking a fine line between proper Geneva Convention–esque humane treatment of enemy combatants and being made a fool of by the same guys who had been making fools of us for the past few weeks by hitting our FOB almost nightly with mortars and RPGs, and then slipping away into the night before we could catch them. It pretty much came down to a rule of thumb: if a detainee did the pee pee dance for at least a half hour, he was probably legit and was allowed to go.

Once the initial shock and fear among the herd subsided, the chatter and blindfold fidgeting-with began. I'd say that most of these guys were model detainees, but just like with any Army platoon or company, there are always one or two problem children. First, two guys wouldn't stop whispering to each other. So I put them in separate cells. Then one kept pulling down his blindfold, claiming his allergies were hurting his eyes. We compromised and told him we'd loosen the blindfold if he faced the wall and shut up. He only partially complied. He was warned and rewarned by the lieutenant and the interpreter. But like a child, he kept pushing the limit. Then the lieutenant and the interpreter left. More chatter, more blindfold slippage. He started eye-balling me and some of the other soldiers. (If I had been in East L.A., I'd have been compelled to proclaim, "Why you mad-doggin' me, yo?!") I yelled at him to shut up and pull the blindfold back up. He just smiled and gave me the thumbs-up. I've said that the thumbs-up in Iraq is a way of simultaneously telling someone both "okay" and "fuck you" at once, a trick this little bastard was now turning back on me deftly. I removed him from the cell, took his blindfold off, and put on a new one—a huge one made out of a first-aid cravat—and tied it as tightly as I could. I also flex-cuffed his hands behind his back, also tight enough for him to be uncomfortable. A half hour later, he had pulled the blindfold down with his teeth somehow. Last straw.

Everyone knows that duct tape can fix anything. In the Army, we have five-inch-wide green duct tape that we call hundred-mile-an-hour tape, due to its ability to mend tears in the canvas wings of Wright Brothers–era planes, good up to one hundred miles an hour. I put dickhead on his knees in the middle of his cell, removed the blindfold that he was now wearing as a dashing olive-drab scarf, and wrapped the top half of his head with about ten layers of hundred-mph tape. Then one last piece across the bridge of his nose and around his head again to seal off the small gap that invariably is present at the bottom of one's field of vision when one is blindfolded. I tried to create as much drama as possible with the event. Our S-2 (intel) master sergeant, a mean-spirited quasi sadist, the full-time El Capitan of the jail, was in the process of systematically interrogating the detainees. He kept saying, "Okay, Sergeant, that's enough tape. Okay, that's enough. Okay, that's enough, Sergeant." The distinct sound of duct tape being applied directly off the roll was loud and satisfying as it reverberated off the six cold concrete planes of wall, floor, and ceiling. I tried my best to seem stern and to disguise the fact that my heart was pounding. One layer or fifty layers, I figured it wouldn't make much difference as far as adhesive blindfolds go, I just wanted to give the impression of an excessive and final response to the guy's juvenile game of tit for tat. I felt like my pious disciplinarian father; I felt like I was on the wrong side of recurring anxiety dreams I've always had of being imprisoned; I felt stupid and petty and cowardly.

Discipline that has some constructive end or transparent layer of camaraderie, like the relationship a soldier has with a drill sergeant, I have no problem with. But having to assert my assumed authority in front of my prisoners and my peers to make an example of this miscreant had no positive result as far as I was concerned. There's a darkly intoxicating aspect to this kind of thing, though. I'm overarmed with my rifle and grenade launcher and the veritable ammunition dump that is the vest over my body armor. Because of this, my power over these men is near absolute. I can see how the bully feels, how one could grow fond of this darkly amusing massive imbalance of power. In the end, I just wanted to maintain order, I wanted to assert a measure of authority, but most importantly still, I did not want to perpetrate something on others that I am deeply phobic of myself—to be imprisoned and tormented.

I let this guy sit and think about what he had done wrong. Isn't that how our parents used to put it? He finally broke his macho stoic silence after about forty-five minutes. "Mister. Mister. I'm sorry. I'm sorry." I was furious at this asshole. Not only was he apparently contrite now, but his English was getting better, too. But mostly I was furious that he had "made" me do this. I yelled some nonsense at him about how it was too late to be sorry, that he would continue to be sorry before I did anything for him. Not my words, just rhetorical crap I was regurgitating from a lifetime of being caught in a punishment-lecture-punishment-lecture cycle for serial rule-breaking.

Working with me at the time was a medic, this forty-somethingish Hispanic specialist with an improbable number of vowels in his name and a thick salt-and-pepper mustache that seemed to exude an avuncular warmth. He had a pleasant and attentive demeanor and looked like he could be a dentist or a good-natured washing machine salesman at Sears. All day he had been eminently respectful to me. Everything was a snappy "Yes, Sergeant. No, Sergeant"—something that always makes me uncomfortable when coming from someone so clearly my senior. He looked at me now like he had been suffering along with this guy the whole time, maybe empathetic because he's a medic or because he knew it would probably be his job to help separate tape from eyebrows in a few minutes. I assured him that I'd let the guy stew for only five more minutes, tops, but after I hemmed and hawed for about five more seconds, I finally just said, "Fuck it, let's just give this jerk his reprieve." With him on his knees again, we unwrapped his head, and then I absurdly lectured him in an unavoidably paternal (patronizing?) way in a language I knew he couldn't understand but a tone that I knew he would. He looked up at me, his eyes red and watering (had he been crying, or were his eyes actually irritated?) and he reverently uttered, "Thank you." After we locked the cell door (padlock on a grillelike door—not quite totally archetypical for a jail), all inside either sat or slept quietly, unmoving.

Hours later, it was the problem child's turn to be interrogated. He was escorted by several soldiers to an out-of-sight location by the master sergeant. I sat outside by the front gate, eating an MRE. My knife, a beloved Spyderco Delica with a green handle and a black blade, slayer of MRE packages, lay in front of me as I shoveled beef and mushroom into my mouth like the engineer fed coal into the furnace of his engine in the old Popeye cartoon. As they were walking by, the master sergeant stopped for a moment to talk to someone, and my favorite detainee now stood in front of me. He eyed my knife, then eyed me. I looked back at him, and he didn't look away, or I should say he *wouldn't* look away. Honestly, I couldn't tell if he was trying to read my eyes like I was trying to read his or if he was just trying to memorize my face, or maybe he just plain hated me and was indulging his fascination with the object of his hate, a thirst you can never really slake.

I paid little attention to how he looked, not nearly as much attention as he seemed to pay to how I looked. If I saw him on the street right now, I probably wouldn't recognize him. Shame on me, I guess. The first step is to remove the person-ness from your enemy. Once you remove his humanity in your mind—distance him from you, the human—it's easier to kill him if it comes down to that. He wore a green camouflage jacket over his man-dress, making him stand out from the rest of the white and gray man-dress wearers. In the back of the jacket, at the bottom, was a buttoned flap. Ever since the advent of the man-dress, when it came time to go into combat, you'd reach between your legs, grab the back hem, and pull it up into your belt in front, creating a big man-diaper. My seminary teacher in junior high said this was called "girding your loins." My guess is the flap on the back of his jacket was made for this same purpose, to be pulled between the legs and buttoned in the front, to turn the flowing man-dress of would-be fighters into MC Hammer pants. His hair was neat and short-cropped. I only know this, really, because I had to pull all that tape off his head. He was probably in his early twenties. I'd say if it came down to hand-to-hand, this guy, being most likely in the same weight class as me, would give me a run for my money. But most non-farmer Iraqis are in absurdly bad shape, so I'd probably prevail. If not, I'd at least bite his nose off or something really dirty like that. So there he was, staring me down again, who knows what machinations going on in his head.

April 23, 2004

I ♥ Dead Civilians

The man in the passenger seat lay slumped against the dashboard, a massive wound to his head. Kirk pulled the body upright and cut the man's pockets open looking for ID. When he was done and let the body fall back against the dashboard, he said that what was left of the man's brain fell out of the opening in the back of his head and onto the ground. He could handle the guy with the brain and both the dead women, but it was the three-year-old-girl, he said, that got to him.

Roughly an hour earlier, a convoy of fuel tankers and Humvees came to a halt a little north of our forward operating base when what looked like an improvised explosive device was spotted on the side of the road. Since the suspected IED was spotted mid-convoy, the vehicles were split, part to the north and part to the south, leaving the area around the IED open to prevent any of the trucks from being destroyed. Our explosive ordinance disposal team was being called in, and our quick-reaction force was going to escort them. I was in the QRF staging area that day, but I wasn't on the mission. We were listening to the radio in a Humvee as one of the officers in the convoy was communicating with our headquarters about the IED when the convoy started to take small arms fire. They took contact from multiple directions. Then the mortar rounds started to fall. The people who attack convoys and FOBs seem to have no end to their supply of mortar rounds, a common means of attack and the primary charge of the IEDs they leave for us like Easter eggs. Thankfully they don't know how to aim them any better than they do their rifles.

When our QRF made it to the scene, shots were still being fired, so they laid down suppressive fire as best they could. Even though this attack took place in daylight, there was much difficulty pinpointing the location of the enemy assailants. There was a building and a parked vehicle in the distance, and the guy on the ground who was calling everything up on the radio was unsure if fire was being taken from these locations. Restraint was exercised and fire was directed toward less collateral damage–inducing areas.

But to the north, another QRF also responded to this ambush, an active-duty unit newly in country. This was their first mission. Since this other QRF was on a separate communications net, the response attacks were not coordinated. This isn't particularly important, other than it's anyone's guess what the communication between them and their battalion leadership was like. They also spotted a vehicle, this one on the move apparently, but less restraint and less positive target identification were exercised.

The vehicle was a white pickup, a small Toyota, one like most Iraqis stack their families into the back of, just as this family was. Everyone has these trucks in Iraq; it's like the national vehicle. It's also the preferred vehicle of the ICDC and insurgents alike. I can imagine that the man driving it, most likely the father of those on board, just wanted to get his family out of the area of the fighting as quickly as possible. I can also imagine that the other QRF got word that a fast-moving vehicle was our attackers' likely means of attack and escape, a completely plausible and reasonable possibility.

From what could be gathered afterward, the Humvee gunships engaged the pickup with a SAW, an M240B, and an M2 .50-cal—or, in other words, a shitload of machine gun fire. The truck contained six people. Two men, two women, and two young girls. As is the custom in Iraq, the men were in the cab as the females huddled together in the bed of the truck. Among the dead were one of the men, both women, and a three-year-old girl, apparently smothered to death by the two women's bullet-riddled bodies as the women tried to shield the girl from the fusillade of gunfire—the tragic irony being that this ultimate protective act was the very thing that killed the girl. The man driving was still alive when the casualty evacuation team (comprised mostly of members from my squad) got there, but he was probably on his way out. Matt said the man had numerous wounds to his legs and a gunshot wound to the scrotum, an entry wound for a bullet that had no visible exit and was most likely lodged in his pelvis or abdomen. As Matt held a pressure dressing to the man's bleeding thigh, he felt the shattered pieces of femur grind against each other. The only one who seemed certain to survive was an eight-year-old girl who had gunshot wounds in both of her upper arms. The man and the girl were medevac'd via Blackhawk, along with another girl from a separate location nearby, who had taken a round through her cheek and leg. Whiskey and Kirk had the grisly duty of stacking the dead bodies in the back of a truck to be moved to the aid station at the FOB.

As I try to fathom what it must feel like to be a poverty-stricken eight-year-old girl and to experience the epic pain of having your family suddenly and violently killed in front of you, I have to pause and ask myself, Now what am I doing here again? I know this kind of thing happens in combat, and I kind of expected to see it, but, Jesus, the record is pretty bad so far. Since I've been in Iraq, in situations that my platoon has responded to, there have been three dead bad guys, two wounded civilians (one critically), and seven dead civilians, including four women, one three-year-old girl, and one mentally unstable homosexual man on a moped. Hell, if you count the suicide of the latter's lover—an excellent two-for-one dead civilian deal—and the de-family'd guy who got his balls blown off who, even if he lived, would have wished to Allah that he was dead, that makes the tally 3 to 8, a near 1:3 ratio of dead evildoers to innocent and ridiculously poor Iraqis who couldn't have cared less who led their country just so long as they were able to feed themselves. Now that I think about it, there have actually been more civilian casualties in our area, but these are the only ones I remember right now. Thank god none of this carnage has been carried out by anyone in my platoon or even my company, for that matter. My battalion has sustained only one casualty of its own so far, and there has been at least one engagement by another company that netted a few dozen dead bad guys, so the numbers are at least decent in that regard, but, still, I'm having a hard time being okay with all the dead civilians. But it happens so often. It's like we should have bumper stickers that read, I ♥ DEAD CIVILIANS.

But let's get back to the family in the truck who were killed. Like I said, I wasn't with the QRF that day and didn't see any of this first-hand, and all the information I got was gleaned from the guys in my squad who were. Even though Matt said it was better that I hadn't seen any of it, I wish I had been there—to bear witness, I suppose. So tell me, why would I wish for this?

I've been stewing over this dead family thing for a couple of weeks now. I've been painstakingly mulling over in my mind the things these insurgents do and the things we, the U.S. Army, do and the unintuitive peculiarity of how the *drive* to be violent seems to precede the *purpose* to be violent, and how rampant it is to meaninglessly develop one's identity through injury, but frankly I don't think I've figured it all out well enough yet to even kludge together a coherent line of thought. Introspectively, I'm blindly trying to sew together the absurd lateral progression one unwittingly goes through when pulling legs off grasshoppers as a child and how it is a precursor to compulsive sexual infidelity as a young adult, among a million other uncoalesced thoughts. I'm unprepared at this time to write the *Gödel, Escher, Bach* of my own self-loathing.

But what does any of this have to do with the dead family, you ask? Well, nothing directly. It's just another one of those things I'm having difficulty reconciling in my mind, I guess.

April 25, 2004

WOMEN IN THE INFANTRY

A topic of discussion that I always seem to find myself embroiled in sooner or later once people learn that I am in the Army is that of women in the infantry. My feelings on the subject are very conflicted. Actually, that's a lie. I know exactly how I feel, it's just that I wish I could say that I felt differently.

I agree with the policy that women cannot be in the infantry.

The topic of women in the infantry is a very tricky one and is the one thing in my personal philosophy that I am sexist about. I see that there are two reasons why women are not allowed in the infantry (or most other combat arms jobs). The average grunt is fairly in touch with his primal self and therefore wants generally only two things: to fuck and to fight, in that order. And the main reason they fight is to be tough and therefore attract more women with whom they can fulfill their desire to fuck. As soon as there are any women within spittin' distance, prime directive number one kicks in, and all things, especially job discipline, go straight to hell. Anyone who thinks this is stupid is right, but is also an idiot if he thinks this will ever change. Grunts are grunts. The thinking man finds meaning through some sort of higher pursuit. The grunt finds meaning through fucking. And if he can do some fighting between coital sessions, that's cool too.

The second reason women are not (and should not) be in the infantry is as equally based in the primal side of human existence as the first. Women can't do a grunt's job worth a shit. I wish I were wrong about this because it goes against all my notions of gender egalitarianism, but it's the truth. I have trained with women on many occasions, and I can only say that their presence completely alters the training environment. Not only are the guys distracted for reason number one, but also the intensity level of training is shot all to hell. Your average female will not push herself in training the way a man will. I've seen guys in training literally push themselves until they die. I saw a guy finish a PT test two-mile run then collapse and die from a burst aorta. I saw a guy march in the sun until he collapsed from heatstroke severe enough to give him brain damage. I've seen guys march despite broken bones, dislocated joints, and torn ligaments. Dying in training is dumb, but it is a testament to the degree to which a soldier is willing to push himself. In all my experience training with women, I've noticed that their commonsense gene (which guys seem to lack, thankfully for the military) kicks in and they say, "Fuck this, I'm not gonna kill myself doing this." I'm sure there are women out there who probably are hard enough to train themselves to death, but in a society where men are raised with the incredible force of macho peer pressure, men who will push themselves like this are much easier to find than women who will.

And I haven't even yet gotten to the fact that your average man is much physically stronger than your average female. Even if female humans were as strong as men and willing to push themselves to the same extent, there will always be Reason One. There are, like, four women at my little base. The other night, the QRF had to move out, and we couldn't find three of our guys. We ended up leaving them, including a .50-cal gunner. Turns out they were asleep in a room with one of the girls who lives near the QRF staging area. (*Note:* The QRF staging area has since been relocated.)

There may be a time when these factors don't matter as much and women will be in the infantry. In the meantime women can always join the MPs—what they call the "chick infantry." In combat, MPs end up doing most of the same stuff as the infantry, at least in Iraq.

Other issues with women in the infantry:

- menstruation and vaginal health—Living conditions can be very harsh, and having to deal with, say, a yeast infection while going without a shower for several months can be very difficult, I imagine.
- rape—(especially if captured)
- pregnancy—There is no time for prenatal care in the field.
- breasts—If they are large enough to get in the way of wearing gear and body armor, low-crawling, and the other physicalities of soldiering, you are totally ineffective as a grunt.

I wish I had more things positive to say about women in the infantry, but there are so many things that make it not a very good idea. Women deserve equal opportunity, but equality in certain combat jobs may not make the best tactical sense.

April 28, 2004

In preparation for the scores of anticipated refugees who would flee Fallujah, our battalion recon'd an old bunker complex not far from Fallujah as a place to temporarily accommodate them. The bunkers and buildings at this complex were *really* spread out, more so even than the old ammo bunkers where we live. Gas masks and gas mask filter canisters were found littered everywhere. Rumor has it that the people who live in the area won't graze their animals on the complex because when they have in the past, entire herds have gotten mysteriously ill. The buildings we cleared were very strange—incredibly high ceilings with tiled walls—and they reeked the way I would imagine old slaughterhouses reek. Outside, there were what looked like enormous pump tanks that had been ripped out of the buildings. Kirk said, "Thank god I already have kids, cuz you guys are fucked! When we get back and you guys have kids, they're gonna be *all* fucked up. Ha ha!"

While we were there, a First Infantry Division guy shot himself in the foot. This was the first time I'd seen a wounded soldier firsthand. It was a little disturbing to see one of my own on the ground, bleeding. Then I got over it. We waited about thirty seconds before we started making fun of the guy. Matt treated him. He had shot himself perfectly between his fourth and fifth toes, a very lucky shot. A medevac chopper was already en route, and there was no use in canceling it, so toe-blaster got a free ride. Like any soldier, I am constantly checking to be sure my weapon is on safe. And on top of that, you should never have your finger on the trigger unless you are ready to let loose hell on bad guys. How this guy, a full-time soldier unlike us National Guard shitbags, managed to do this is embarrassing. He was a private. I felt so bad standing there, looking at him, trying to decide whether or not I should take a picture. I didn't feel bad because he had been shot or because I was contemplating doing something in bad taste like take a photograph; I felt bad because this guy's pain was going to last a lifetime, being a soldier who shot himself in the foot. He wasn't even doing anything at the time. He wasn't getting on or off a vehicle; he wasn't running to an objective or clearing a building. He was just standing there and, *BLAM*, all pretense of professionalism right out the window.

Oh yeah, and another thing: This is the same complex where that Hamill guy had been held prisoner. He escaped a few days later. How cool would it have been if we had found him? It kills me that we could have; we just hadn't gone to the building he was in.

May 2, 2004

We did a raid today. As we cleared the house, we corralled all the women and children and put them into one large room. The guy whose house it was had four wives, two of whom were pretty old and two of whom were pretty young and really attractive. The old wives were weeping, the young wives were pissed, and the kids were excited to see soldiers. It was a little comical to burst into a room to see the young boys grinning from ear to ear and with their hands in the air, like we were playing cops and robbers. I had written on my arm the phrase "Et med ded," which is supposed to mean "Lie down." It didn't work. Everyone in Iraq just squats.

Raids are so strange. The first few I did, as I would perform the search of a room, I'd try to put things back in place when I was done. Then I realized how much of a waste of time this was. I was just looking for a way to ease my guilt for having invaded someone's home. After missing a hidden weapon once that someone else found because I was being too "nice," I decided to check my politeness at the door and search for the weapons that these guys were trying to kill us with, like I was fucking supposed to. I still feel bad; I just make a bigger mess now. If this lady is sad now knowing that we're taking away her husband and sons, she's gonna be livid when she sees that her home looks like it got hit by a tornado. They hide the weapons pretty well, so we really have to tear things apart to find them. This house had a lot.

May 7, 2004

Since truck driver Thomas Hamill was held captive in the bunker complex on the outskirts of our area of operations (that we now refer to as the chemical plant), I suspect our battalion commander wanted to see what else was there. Recent intel intimated that chemical weapons had just been discovered there by a local. My conspiracy theory was that we had been sitting on some chemical weapons for months, and an opportune political moment awaited for some New York boys to "find" them. Most of my platoon donned their protective masks and spent the day clearing bunker after bunker, finding nothing.

Since the area where they were working is a ways from our base, a retransmission site had to be set up about midway so that communications could be maintained with our tactical operations center. My duty for the mission was to guard the retrans site, located at the top of a large underground bunker along with about a squad's worth of men. Given that we were sitting on a bunker that was not secured in any way and was left open for anyone who might happen upon it to hole up in it, we decided it was best to clear it. All I can say is, Holy shit. This thing was enormous. It was probably the most exciting and spooky thing I've ever had to clear. It was completely dark, and we had to navigate through the structure entirely by flashlight. Long corridors, hundreds of rooms, massive iron doors like the kind on bank vaults. If I had to venture a guess, I'd say it had been a research center of some kind. There were rooms that were most likely used to house network servers long removed by the invading force. Conduit trenches ran from room to room under removable concrete tiles, most likely used for network cables. There were a lot of small rooms that looked like they could have been offices, a lot of medium-size rooms that looked like they used to contain a lot of equipment, and a few larger rooms full of petroleum-like sludge and water (perhaps lubricant?) in the compartmental areas in the floor. This was possibly the location of some since-removed industrial equipment and machines. The main entrance into the office complex, deep within the heart of the bunker—an architectural security plan probably borrowed from the Egyptian pyramids—was where the massive metal doors were. There was an intermediate vestibule area with a small round portal one could look into or fire into should the person entering be deemed an enemy, an idea borrowed from medieval castle architecture. This structure was the kind of thing that David Macaulay would do a book on. Or better yet, it was like something created by video-game designer John Romero. I felt like I was playing *Doom*. I am not joking when I say that all the hours I spent pissing my life away playing *Quake* were actually not wasted at all. The techniques used for any first-person shooter to safely and systematically go from room to room translate over to real life in situations like this. The next time your mom lectures you about the time you waste playing *Half-Life*, telling you that there is no benefit whatsoever in it, tell her that if things keep going the way they have been, you'll most likely serve time in the Army sooner or later, and being familiar with basic room-clearing concepts could save your life. But then she could just as easily explain how algebra skills are necessary to accurately call in indirect fire missions and that you should finish your homework.

We spotted some figures on the horizon. Didn't look like enemy. Wait, it's a bunch of kids. One of them is carrying something. They're coming toward us, I think. Let's see what they want.

I don't know where these barefooted kids could have come from. There weren't any houses for at least a couple of miles. Unbelievably, they had carried a complete tea set to greet their temporary neighbors. A pot of tea, two saucers, two small shot glass–size glasses, two small stirring spoons, and a pot of sugar, all served on a large metal platter. The tea was hot and fresh. They also brought several loaves of unleavened bread. We all squatted down, broke bread, and had a perfect Middle Eastern moment. This is one of the coolest things I've seen; it was sublime. Of course the whole ploy was to see what they could weasel from the soldiers, but we were happy to oblige. We dumped onto them as many MREs, bottles of water, and bags of candy that they could carry. They were tempted to leave the tea set. Then one of the girls carried it back on her head.

May 12, 2004

Today's mission was to escort payroll money from our base to the town bank so people like the ICDC guys and the police could get paid. Iraqis have no concept of waiting in line, so the whole process was a melee. After we were done paying them, we fired a bunch of them. All this madness took the better half of the day.

While the payroll fiasco was going on inside, we stood outside to secure the building. Kids mobbed us annoyingly. They try to sell us high-quality knives and sunglasses that have fallen off Halliburton trucks or been stolen from other soldiers. I bought two DVDs with the name "Ballone" handwritten on them in black pen. Then they bugged us to give them stuff. Their English is getting better, too. "Mister, Mister, gimme gimme." I got fed up with it and was telling one kid, "All you kids know how to say is 'Gimme this, gimme that,'" to which he replied, "Gimme shit. You my bitch." I was nonplussed. Another kid pointed at my chest, saying "What's this?" Thinking he was asking me about my ammunition, I looked down and he flipped my nose. So I tried out some of the grappling moves on him we had learned at Fort Drum. This didn't phase him, so I just kicked a few kids in the shins and threw rocks at another. Any ideas I ever had of coming back to Iraq to help with education were killed on the spot. What these kids need is a good spanking and to go to bed with no dinner. Wait, they already get that every day. What the hell am I doing messing with kids? I thought that the infantry was all about running around in the woods and trying to kill enemy soldiers, not about being made the bitch of a band of unbathed sandal-wearing eight-year-olds. When I was discussing this with one of the guys in my platoon later that night, he said, "That was your first time in town? Ha ha! I don't mess around with the kids anymore. When we go into town, we take sling shots and paint balls. Fuck those kids. This one kid I hit was wearing a man-dress and was pissed; he thought I'd ruined it. He was yelling, 'Fuck you! You my bitch! Suck my cock!' but once we showed him it was paint that easily washed off, he was all 'You my friend!' Fucking kids."

May 13, 2004

When we first got to Iraq, it was easy to find things to write about because everything was new. Now that we've gotten into a pretty good work rhythm and have captured most of the bad guys in our area, things have gotten a little routine. I look at all we do during a week and it's more exciting than any five years of my life before Iraq, but I still can't help but admit that I think we're getting used to it.

A friend of Willy's sent him the complete series *Freaks and Geeks* on DVD. I had to liberate those DVDs from Willy; he wouldn't have understood suburban teen angst. I watched all eighteen episodes back to back, taking a short break in the middle to sleep for three hours and to go on a raid. It breaks my heart that something as optimistic and genuine as a show like that could be so completely dismissed by the majority of TV-watching America. Who is creating anything worthwhile anymore? We need to encourage this kind of thing, not discourage it by worshipping vapid garbage like *Friends*. The raid went fine, by the way.

AN IGNORAMUS'S TIKRIT PALACE TOUR OF ART

Duality is implicit to mortality.

This is something I spend a lot of time thinking about. One of those basic but mysterious principles of life that we spend a lifetime trying to unravel, understand, then knit back into something meaningful. I love talking about duality and the math behind systems of opposition and pseudo-intellectual things of this ilk, but with most any group of people you bring this sort of thing up with you get everything from polite smiles—the same ones you'd give a child who says he wants to be an astronaut, a fireman, *and* a doctor when he grows up—to simple dismissive eye-rolling. Trying to subtly segue into a dialogue about anything even remotely philosophical with an infantry platoon is an exercise in futility.

Anyway, something I always surprise myself with is how I am able to simultaneously feel both bummed out and excited every time we get called to go on a mission. Most times I'll be geekin' out on my laptop, engrossed in what I'm doing, and while I work I'll be planning, in the back of my head, how I'm going to allot my time to the various tasks I want to accomplish—weapon cleaning, laundry, reading, responding to email, writing, editing photographs, showering. Then someone will come in and say, "Get dressed! We have a mission. Team leaders and above, op order in fifteen mikes." Then there will be that initial feeling of terrible disappointment, knowing that how I will be spending my time is now dictated by the caprice of a mission— that reaction of laziness denied. I'll think to myself, "Dammit, I don't want to have to do anything right now. I was totally chillaxing. Now I have to put on all my shit and go raid some stupid house that won't even have anything in it, get all sweaty, and then go to bed late as hell.

Ugh." But not one second later, the childlike soldier excitement will kick in. "Fuck yeah! I think it's my team's turn again to do the initial entry. Wait, maybe I can be on the breach team this time. Hell yes! I'm gonna smash the fuck outta that door! It's going to be awesome! What if we make contact? Oh god, this could be so cool!"

Another dichotomous pair of desires regarding this whole combat experience thing are living conditions. When soldiers tell stories, the ones they are most proud of are those that involve things sucking. *Black Hawk Down* would not have been nearly as interesting if everything had gone as planned. You never hear soldiers say, "Man, basic training was so easy. I had the easiest training cycle ever." "No way man, *my* training cycle was *way* easier. Shit, it was so easy, we got off every day at four. And the drill sergeants didn't even yell at us. They politely *asked* us if we'd please do push-ups and shit." Hell, we want our soldiering experience to suck as much as possible. We'll never openly say this or admit it to ourselves. You can't *want* things to suck. That would be stupid. It's like you want it to suck, but you don't want to go so far as to ask for it to suck or to purposely make it suck. But the more it sucks, the better the stories. The whole idea is for it to suck so you can try to make it suck less. That's the whole game.

Originally we were told that our company was going to act as the division quick-reaction force and that we would be stationed in Tikrit, where the division headquarters would be. This changed, as things do in the military. We now live on an ammo bunker complex in a swamp near a smallish town. Accommodations are pretty spartan. But this is good in a way, because the experience seems a little more in keeping with the theme of what we are doing, which is combat. Not far from us is a very large base complete with a movie theater, chow hall, and lots of girls. One's natural inclination is always to want the better setup, like to move to the base up the street, but we sort of like having our own little base. It's quiet here, and we don't get attacked that often. There are things that make living where we do cool, but overall we have it much harder than probably most of the servicemen and women in Operation Iraqi Freedom.

Our platoon has recently made a few trips to Tikrit on various escort missions. I was on two of them. The first trip I went on was brief. We had a chance to grab some chow at the very respectable chow hall at the First Division's headquarters, located at the palace complex, then it was back to our mosquito-infested bunkers in the swamp. The second trip afforded us the opportunity to spend the afternoon there. After chow, we headed over to the morale, welfare, and recreation (MWR) center, located in Uday Hussein's old palace. This base is impressive. It pained us to think that this is where we were supposed to be stationed but then weren't. You can't help but envy the lucky bastards who get to do a tour at this place. It's gorgeous. The view of the Tigris is incredible. There is so much cool stuff. I mean, it used to be a fucking palace complex, so there are swimming pools and ridiculously decadent living quarters and all that. When I wake up at my base, I stand on a dirty concrete floor where bombs used to be stacked. When the soldiers in Tikrit wake up, their bare feet kiss cool, smooth marble. You can't help but want desperately to be stationed here. Conventional wisdom says that when you go into combat, you must live in a way that is substandard to the way you were previously used to living. Not true here. If I were stationed in Tikrit at this palace, I'd never leave Iraq.

I think I would make a crappy dictator. I wouldn't get anything done. I would totally squander my time fucking off all day at my ridiculous palace. Think of the parties you could throw! God, I have to stop thinking about this. The more I do, the more I lose all sense of Zen-like contentment about living in a swamp. I wanted to strangle all the undeserving pogues who lived here. And the girls. So many girls. The number of women in combat in Iraq has got to be unprecedented. Some graffiti on the wall in one of the shitters read, ALL ARMY GIRLS: HOW DOES IT FEEL KNOWING THAT WHEN YOU GO BACK HOME YOU'LL BE UGLY AGAIN? The cruelty of this remark made me feel better for all the rooms with marble floors upon which I'll never tread barefoot, belonging to female soldiers I'll never know.

Like everything in the world of the buck-sergeant infantryman, you are poorly informed about anything beyond platoon-level operations. I wish I could tell you all the history and significance of Tikrit, and all that took place during the assault there, but I can't even tell you definitively which palace belonged to which Hussein. I know very little about architecture and even less about Middle Eastern architecture. I don't know the proper names for these structures or any of the style elements. I hated my art history professor in college more than I can express, and I'm one of these people who fail classes because they hate the teacher. Had she not been such a raging bitch, I would have paid more attention and been able to speak more intelligently regarding this sort of thing. But seriously, this lady fucking sucked. On one test you were supposed to match up certain terms. I was supposed to match the word "parallel" with another word. "Crosshatching" and "posts" were both options. Both things involved parallelism, so I thought I'd just pick one and hope for the best. I chose "posts" since posts were always standing straight up and were parallel with other posts, such as in stone doorways, e.g. posts and lintel. Crosshatching involved parallel lines, but only in little textured groups, so I figured she might get stupid and make an issue about that. I chose wrong. Apparently she thought the lines of crosshatching qualified better as parallel. When I met with her a few days later to contest her marking my test wrong, I figured it would be a trivial feat to present how posts were always parallel and therefore I deserved the points. But she refused. So I asked, "When are posts ever *not* parallel?" I study calculus, dammit, and even a fucking third-grader knows what it means. As long as two lines that go infinitely in both directions don't ever intersect, they are parallel. And you know what her response was? "Look at Stonehenge. Those are posts and they're in a circle; they're not parallel." I was dumbfounded. Circle, not parallel?! Either she was pulling my leg or she was trying to pull some novice-level apples-and-oranges Jedi mind trick or she was just actually that retarded. She kept a straight face. She was serious. Trying to not be condescending, I argued, "Fine, they are in a circle, but even so, the lines they represent still never intersect. . . ." She wasn't paying attention. I gave up. I slept in through most of the final then showed up absurdly late. I failed the hell out of that class. I was such an idiot. I could have settled for a B-plus and never thought about that old maid ever again, but instead I failed the class as if to spite her. I have a bad habit of having to learn everything the hard way.

So here I am, wanting to be able to intelligently describe for you some of the things I saw in Tikrit, but I can't really because I refused to absorb anything from my Art History class at Utah State University eleven years ago. But hey, remember: If things don't work out in your life, you can always just turn to drugs or join the Army.

On our way to Tikrit, northbound on Iraq Highway 1, we drove under a magical arch that had been constructed over the highway that will stargate you to ancient Sumeria where you can witness the beginning of human civilization, a regional accomplishment the people of Iraq are very proud of. So proud, in fact, that they haven't really done anything since then other than rest on their laurels. People of Iraq, it's time to get a new schtick. We're all very impressed by Hamurabbi and algebra and everything, but it's time to do the next insanely great thing. A cure for cancer or usable cold fusion would be cool, but I'd settle for a *fatwa* denouncing jihadis' beheading my countrymen and detonating car bombs. Or maybe the secret to those tires that are supposed to never wear out. And by the way, I don't think the arch was working right. When we drove through it, I didn't see any cradle of civilization, just a bunch of absurdly poor people juxtaposed with ridiculous despotic wealth.

At the side of the road as you enter Tikrit, there's a crumbling concrete monument with a painting of an oil decanter and a sign welcoming you to town. I'm curious what the oil-decanter thing symbolizes. Maybe wealth, or bounty? It brings to mind the Bible story about the miraculous oil vessel that never ran out of oil. Maybe that's what we're doing in Iraq—looking for something that will keep giving oil.

The palace complex in Tikrit, relative to all other architecture I've seen in Iraq, is beautiful. The palace where the MWR is located was full of intricate woodwork, elaborate inlaid marble floors, enormous chandeliers, and an abundance of relief sculptures. But to be perfectly honest, your average cheesy Vegas casino has more class.

One of the rooms in the MWR palace had been converted into a rec room and was full of computers, PlayStations, and TVs. While I was there, I decided I'd send an email to my mom:

Hi Mom.

In Uday's palace. Have a nice view of the Tigris. Still looking for the bathroom with the solid gold toilet and silk toilet paper. Was going to pee in the pool, but was closed today. Made a joke to the girl behind the snack bar that I wanted to pee or poo in the palace, even if it meant doing it on the floor, but she told me this wasn't Uday's palace, that this palace belonged to the soldiers now. Why does no one get my sense of humor, Mom? Love you.

The relief sculptures that covered the exterior of the palace told the history and tradition of the area. The thought that kept going through my mind as I looked at them was about the person who did all this carving: did he do it out of love for the Husseins, or because he had an unfortunate talent and did it to spare his family from being slain and/or raped by Uday? One particular piece was military in flavor, depicting soldiers holding AK-47s, and it made me think about how many times this part of the world has been overthrown. If you figure how the Sumerian civilization was here, through to the Ottomans, and all the warring peoples in between, this is a place that has pretty much never known peace. Would this palace survive over the centuries? It's made from sandstone and sits by a riverbed. Not likely is my guess. I was in a place that was once the domain of the dictator du jour, and now *I* was the arm of the new sheriff in town. Of course my cause is righteous, so I guess I'm supposed to see the overthrow of Iraq—for what, the twenty-fourth time in less than a century?—as a good thing. The relief sculpture depicted soldiers we just trounced. I felt sad when I thought of these guys trying to find pride in being soldiers, the way I'm of proud of being a soldier, but who, really, were being betrayed by a despotic ruler who cared more about his cheesy palaces and fantasy art-filled bachelor-pad apartments in Baghdad than his own people. And now here I was, part of the most recent conquering army, an army whose commander-in-chief isn't exactly William Wallace. Oh well.

The motto "Professionalism, Vigilance, Pride, Lethality" had been painted across the threshold you drive through as you leave the walls of the palace complex. I liked the message, but I'm not a big fan of painting messages directly onto what would otherwise have been a nice building. Oh well. That's all I can think to say for almost everything I see in Iraq. Oh well.

Thus ends our tour. Thank you. Come again. Watch your step.

June 19, 2004

A Very Special Message

A few days ago we held a ceremony at our forward operating base to award a Purple Heart to a soldier in one of our companies who had been wounded. A few soldiers from each platoon were sent to the ceremony to stand in formation while the award was being presented. Somehow I was chosen to represent my platoon along with a few other guys, a duty I frankly could have done without. Not that I don't want to show my respect to the guy who was getting the award, it's just that it kind of sucks to stand at attention in ungodly Iraqi heat in full battle rattle listening to our battalion commander speak.

I was driving my company commander to the ceremony—we were late—and out of the blue he asks me, "So how's the writing coming?" He asked me this once before, when I ran into him in our shower trailer a month or so ago. Back in February, he demanded that I "dismantle" my blog when he discovered it on the internet. It was a bit of a fiasco, so I took down my website but continued to send my writings to friends via email.

I have a penchant for openness and honesty, so I immediately responded with, "It's going well." I paused for a moment, then added, "Actually sir, I haven't written in a while because there hasn't been that much to write about lately." "That'll change soon," he said matter-of-factly. We have a lot of missions planned over the next few weeks to—how shall I put it?—to "celebrate" the turnover of power on the thirtieth. It's been mostly quiet around here, other than the damn lucky shot of a rocket that killed two soldiers and wounded dozens of others at a nearby base.

By the way, the ceremony was good. This is soldier-speak for it was short. The guy got his award for getting wounded, a distinction for an award that has always seemed a little odd to me. When I was a kid, my dad once gave me a prize for having the most number of bones in the piece of fish my mother served us for dinner that night. The bullet is still lodged in this soldier's shoulder. Apparently it entered the Humvee through an open window on the passenger side, shot the night-vision goggles off the helmet of a soldier in the backseat, ricocheted off the vehicle's radio, then struck him in the shoulder. The battalion commander didn't mention any of this aside from the night-vision goggles part, something he seemed to find hilarious and macho. I got the rest of this information from Ray, on the drive back to our bunkers. At the end of the ceremony, everyone sang the Army song and the First Infantry Division song. Oh my god, what an abortion that was. "Blah blah blah and the Army keeps blah blah along!" "Blah blah blah blah the Big Red One! Blah blah blah blah!" It was embarrassing. Not one person in my company knew one word of either song. The chaplain, however, sang with gusto.

We're attached to the First Infantry Division and, hell, we're even wearing their patch on our right shoulders now to signify that we've been to combat with the Big Red One, or the "bro," as we like to call them, a unit patch I've never worn a day in my life. The First Infantry Division is cool and they have an incredible history—but what active-duty unit doesn't have an incredible history?—and I'm proud to wear the patch, but some guys think it would be more correct to wear our own unit patch as our combat patch, the patch of the Twenty-seventh Infantry Brigade. But here's the thing: with all the restructuring and shit that the National Guard is going through, there is no Twenty-seventh Brigade anymore, or at least not for us. Why wear the patch of a unit that doesn't really exist anymore? All the guys who got left back home from our unit have now been absorbed into the Forty-second Infantry Division (another unit with an incredible history). A lot of guys are not excited about this because the unit patch for the Forty-second is a rainbow. The very same patch the guy in the Village

People had on his uniform, incidentally, only he wore his improperly. A rainbow was used for the patch since the entire unit was originally an all-Irish militia once upon a time, and later the patch became half a rainbow to signify how half the soldiers got wiped out in a single battle. The Forty-second has fought in every major conflict since the American Revolution. Their history is awesome. But this is all lost on today's soldiers. Guys will literally leave the Army because of a patch. "I'm not gonna wear that fag patch!" was a common response to the news that we'd be folding into the Forty-second. There was a time when our New York National Guard unit wore the patch of the Tenth Mountain Division—a cool patch with crossed swords and the word "Mountain" across the top. The irony is that the Tenth Mountain is located at Fort Drum, New York, nowhere near a single fucking mountain. Anyway, retention rates were astronomical, and unit strengths were well over 100 percent back then, something that could be attributed to the simple fact that guys got to wear a cool patch.

Unquestionably the coolest unit patch in the Army is the Special Forces patch: it's in the shape of an arrowhead, to symbolize the Native Americans and their guerilla fighting style. There are lightning bolts to symbolize swiftness and power, and a sword to symbolize whatever swords symbolize—who really cares what swords symbolize; swords are cool!. Now *that's* a patch! For most of my career, I was in the Nineteenth Special Forces Group, in Utah. I loved wearing that patch.

When I moved to New York, I had to start wearing the Twenty-seventh Brigade patch. It isn't a very cool patch. The brigade isn't that old and it was named after Major General O'Ryan. When they were designing the patch, I think one of the patch-planner guys said, "Okay, they want us to make a patch for the brigade and it has to be in honor of O'Ryan. Hmm . . . Hey, we're from New York and we're all Yankee fans, let's just wear their symbol!" I'm sure this got presented to the patch-approver guys, who said, "Um, that's the stupidest fucking idea anyone has ever come to us with. We're not going to let you wear a baseball team patch. Try again, you assholes." So the patch-planner guys went back to the bar for another think-'n'-drink session. After a few months of brainstorming they came up with a patch that was the Yankees symbol with some stars. An extra line was put in the *NY* of the Yankees symbol to make it *NYD*, meant to mean "New York Division." For those of you who listened to punk in the eighties, it looks reminiscent of the Dead Kennedys symbol. And some stars were added to symbolize the constellation Orion. Never mind the fact that O'Ryan, an Irish-American soldier, and Orion, a Greek mythological hunter, don't have shit in common other than the fact that their names are homophones. Just as I was warming up to it, I learned about the whole O'Ryan-Orion nonconnection thing, which totally ruined it all for me. And now I am wearing the Orion patch in combat. Whatever. It's a dicked-up patch, but it's *my* patch, so I'm proud of it.

When my battalion moved into our forward operating base here in Iraq, our battalion commander decided to change the name of the base from "Lion," the name that it had for a year, to "Orion." So it got changed. But here's the thing: no one was sure how to spell "Orion." Throughout the tactical operations center, every possible spelling could be found, including on official documents. So this sorta forced the issue to clear up what exactly the spelling was. It was recently decided (after a few months of waffling) that the official spelling would be "O'Ryan." Um, but isn't our brigade named "Orion," like the stars on our patch? And isn't our battalion call sign "Hunter" in honor of Orion the hunter, a moniker our battalion commander adores to no end? And if anyone dies from our base, it will undoubtedly be renamed again, and knowing our luck, the new name will be something like "Rodion Romanivich Raskalnikov."

•   •   •

I suppose I should mention the *Time* magazine article. (I wish I could be mentioning a *New York Times* magazine article instead.) Since you are terribly sophisticated and would never normally read *Time* unless someone happened to leave a copy in the restroom, let me be the first to tell you that they mentioned me. It was an article on blogs (dated June 21, 2004), and *Just Another Soldier* was the only one mentioned as a military blog. It was mentioned that I had wandered through one of Saddam's empty palaces. Um, I didn't do that, I wandered through Uday's non-empty palace. Close enough for mass media, I suppose. But hey, who I am to bite the hand that feeds me, right? I seriously don't know why they mentioned me. But hey, who cares! We have fun in my blog! If you want news about Iraq, congratulations, you've come to the wrong fucking place! If you are distrustful of the media and want to know exactly what's going on in Iraq, you'll have to pray for divine enlightenment, because only god knows what the hell is going on over here! But I can't really help you with that either, because I don't believe in god (or at least not in the traditional sense), and I think the phrase "There are no atheists in foxholes" is semantic proof that "god" is essentially a construct borne of necessity, in fact I regularly ridicule Christian doctrine. This is only natural because I am a recovering Mormon.

However, if you want to know how it feels to be a soldier in Iraq, to hear something honest and raw—that I can help you with. There is so much to discuss! Urban warfare tactics! Killing civilians! MASTURBATION!

But hey, I'm a madman, a clown prince, a heretic. I am most likely out of my mind. I mean, seriously, what kind of an asshole joins the infantry?

My platoon went into town with our company commander recently to perform a number of short tasks. I suppose I lack the ability to take anything seriously because everything we do just seems so . . . well, funny. It's not to say that what we do isn't important. We do many good and sometimes necessary and important things. It's just that sometimes, when you stop and think about it, like I do every time I write, you notice how humorous everything is. I started my day by going through the remains of an air-defense artillery site we had bombed, sifting through piles of unexploded ordnance, picking up explosive fuses to prevent someone from coming along and . . . *picking them up*. They're explosive, you know!

Most of the ordnance exploded when the site was destroyed, but the fuses that screw into the nose of the shells contain a small amount of explosives and can be dangerous, particularly to all the kids who play in the area. "This goes against everything we learned about UXOs [unexploded ordnance]," Matt remarked. What he meant was our training taught us to not mess with unexploded ordnance, *ever*.

Everywhere we go, we get mobbed by kids. They are impossible to get rid of. What makes it really complicated is that they commonly have really cool shit to sell. Like today, one of them sold Matt a Benchmade automatic, a knife that sells for $180 in the PX, but here he bought it for thirty bucks. They mob, annoy, and insult us to no end; they steal knives, pens, and sunglasses right off our vests; they steal cameras and GPS devices out of Humvees; and they basically make it impossible for us to do our jobs. Later in the day, I would whack one of these kids in the shin hard with an Asp baton in an attempt to get him to go away, but it didn't work. His response was basically, "Dude, that really hurt. Why'd you do that? I'm not gonna leave you alone." I got in a staring contest with another kid—and lost. Just like the detainees we commonly deal with, they know how to posture, they have the macho front routine down pat, they even know how to take a beating, but they will flip into abject apology mode in an instant if it suits their purposes. If they're not shamelessly begging us for food and water, they're spitting at us. I'm no sociologist, but this behavior seems endemic of Arab culture.

Our next two stops were to a couple of the poorest families in the area. We dropped off some food for them. None of the men were there when we came by, so very little organization was imposed on how to disseminate the goods. The children disputed bitterly and sometimes violently.

The next stop was an abandoned set of buildings in which four families were living. In the seventies, these buildings were a club-house for the town's semi-pro soccer team. But after some of the people in the area attempted to assassinate Saddam, he decimated the town. The soccer field was destroyed, and the clubhouse was converted into an air-defense artillery site. These families were using the buildings to house a group of water buffalo and about a dozen cute little snot-nosed ankle-biters.

Our company commander is an assistant district attorney in Manhattan. He is the kind of guy who uses terms like "broad" and "fella." In my humble opinion, he is the only sane man in our command structure. We trust him. And he's no dummy. He made sure to take his helmet and sunglasses off before offering an open packet of Pringles to an Iraqi girl because, you see, the civil affairs guys were snapping pictures of everything he did.

A common task for us is to record the daily prayers broadcast over the loudspeakers at the local mosques, to see if they contain anti-coalition messages. It was a Thursday, so of course someone was getting married. Today the celebratory gunfire was very close and a bit excessive. "Hold your fire, men! It's celebratory fire!" our commander barked. Every time someone says, "celebratory," all I hear is "celibatory." Then the ICDC came on the scene, right into my sector of fire! Moments later, a shiny new car drove by all covered in colored ribbons, trailed by a bus full of singing revelers.

After we were done hanging around the mosque, we secured the town police station while our commander attended a meeting there. The same kids always know where to find us. They are insufferable. They now know elaborate curses in both English and Spanish, most involving them pimping out your sister and mother while you are sucking a dick because you are a piece of shit. Today a kid showed us his push-up prowess. "Schnow" (rhymes with "now") means "Do push-ups" in Arabic. We gave him a dollar for doing enough to pass an Army physical fitness test.

June 23, 2004

BLOOD AND SOAP

My gloves smell of blood and soap. I washed them yesterday after everything that happened, but instead of just the sweet musky smell of blood—that smell that is both subtly repugnant and strangely appealing, appealing because your viscera knows its own, but repellent because it seems too personal, like the smell of someone else's sweat or breath—they also have the cheap smell of scented antibacterial soap, a smutty fakery like the aborted attempt of scented tampons to obfuscate the stench of menstrual gore.

Today a good part of my company was involved in a mission to nab a fairly high-profile local politician in a somewhat spectacular manner during a city council meeting in the town where we work. But homeboy never showed up. I was on the secondary snatch team, the guys who would have physically intercepted the target individual should he have chosen a less-expected egress route from the target location. But once we realized that there would be no fandango, we just sorta milled around the dance floor like a bunch of high school chess club kids. So I had a lot of time today to indulge in an obsessive-compulsive and repeated sniffing of my gloves, seeing as how there was no other stimuli to focus on in the madness-inducing heat.

As things become busier as the transfer of authority in Iraq approaches, missions that are normally performed by other companies get passed around to cover the ebb and flow of requisite manpower. Yesterday, about fifteen of us were picking up some slack for another company by checking up on a couple of "named areas of interest." Essentially this means going to an area where bad guys have been roosting, and nosing around looking for anything less than kosher.

The area was somewhat new to us—something always exciting, being somewhere for the first time. The terrain was dry, hard dirt cut deeply and randomly in places by water. In the abrupt ravines and gullies, tall dense grass grew in stark juxtaposition to the dry ground. After our initial clearing of the area, we poked around in all the abandoned buildings and abandoned fighting positions. After an ample amount of dicking around, my lieutenant asked me, "Sergeant, do you have any HE?" (This means, "Do you have any high-explosive rounds for your M203 grenade launcher?") What? Phft. I was like, "Hellz ya I do, sir. Shit!"

"See that steel and stuff over there?"

"Roger, sir."

"I think it's attacking us."

"Roger that, sir!"

By this time everyone who had a 203 was already instinctively loading rounds. When it comes time to lay down HE, the Force kicks in and you have one in the tube before the Obi Wan in your head can even clear his throat.

I fired first. *Doonk!* The target was about 150 meters away. I overshot horribly—I don't have a sight for my 203, so I was using the Force to aim, which happened to fail me miserably on this occasion. *BOOM!* The 'splosion was cool as shit. None of the other 203 gunners did much better, but all said, it was good training to fire a few live grenades, not to mention a lot of fun. *Note to self:* Bug the supply sergeant for some fucking quadrant sights for the 203.

You might be thinking that this is going to be a story about soldiers indiscriminately firing a few grenades for no good reason and accidentally hitting some innocent civilians. Well, this is not one of those stories. We were careful and fired into an area that we had just cleared thoroughly of puppies, three-year-old girls, and baby seals. I've already written about soldiers killing civilians, and I never wish to do it again.

We mounted up and moved out. It would be a bit of a drive to the next place, so we were expecting a smooth ride through a basically unpopulated area. But before we got far, we saw an Iraqi guy running with a limp toward the road, waving his arms frantically. We were in the middle of nowhere. It looked as though he had come from an area that was nothing but a lot of big gullies. This guy was obviously hurt, and without knowing a single detail, it was clear that somewhere there would be other people hurt. I was the last vehicle in a four-vehicle convoy. We followed the guy as he hobbled back in the direction from where he came. The terrain here was hilly and mostly non-navigable, a real tactical challenge. There were innumerable places for the enemy to engage us from. We were apprehensive as we rolled down into the gully where he led us. We were basically entering a textbook ambush location. Everyone dismounted from the vehicles except for drivers and turret gunners. The natural focus was to get to whoever was hurt, so a lot of the guys started running down the incline. We walked by a blood-soaked rag. It looked like a young boy's underwear. We couldn't see anyone yet, but my heart started to race. I started to worry about how bad the injuries would be. I was also worried about our position.

Anytime something draws everyone's attention, I assume it's an intentional distraction, and I start looking in some other direction. I worked at John F. Kennedy Airport for a while with the National Guard. I was one of those dicks who just stood there with an M16. Eight hours a day, for eight months, I watched everything that went on at Terminal Four's security checkpoint. (This happens to be the terminal for the Middle East flights. After September 11, all eyes were on the airborne Arabs and therefore my terminal. But oddly, the Arabs were the well-behaved ones. It was the customers flying on El Al who were the pains in the ass. I could write an entire book titled *The Hasidim: The Rudest Fucking People to Ever Walk the Earth*.) You want to know how to get something through a checkpoint? Have a girl with big tits put a bag through a scanner that has a set of kitchen knives in it—a gift for grandma. She needs to be wearing something tight and revealing. She needs to be a garrulous coquette. All eyes will be on her cleavage—every Port Authority cop, every soldier, and most of the passengers. With this distraction as your smoke screen, you could pass off a hand grenade as a PalmPilot.

I climbed to the top of the gully and out of the potential kill zone. This is not the part where I tell you something totally unexpected happened. Life can be extraordinarily unoriginal. This is the part where I tell you that we were right. There were two Iraqi men on the ground where the gully turned to the right and opened to a wider area. We ran up, quickly assessed them, and found that they both had gunshot wounds to the upper thigh.

One of the two, a young man probably in his twenties, died before we could begin treatment. "Sergeant, this one's out." A large pool of blood had soaked into the ground under his pelvis. It was bright red. Just like we'd been trained, a few guys pushed out a security perimeter while we worked. The question that would perplex me for the rest of the time that we were there was, Where was the gun or guns that shot these guys and who shot them?

Whiskey and I stood over the other man, a potbellied gentleman who I would guess was in his fifties. Someone grabbed the combat lifesaver bags out of the Humvees. We cut the leg off his pants. There was an entry wound on the front of his left thigh. It was a good-size hole, big enough to fit my thumb. The wound was dark red and bloody, but not bleeding profusely. We cut more of his pant leg off to try to find the exit wound. On his inner thigh, close to his groin, there was a hole about twice the size as the first wound. The hole was jagged and it welled with dark blood. I opened a field dressing and got ready to apply it by grabbing the man's leg. The wound looked soft and fresh and wet, like a bloody macabre vagina. As I lifted his leg, the hole opened slightly, and I thought of sashimi. I was worried that I was hurting the guy. I applied the field dressing to the wound, repeating the same action I had dozens of times in training. Whiskey did the same for the other wound.

There was minimal bleeding at this point, but we had to put a little effort into keeping the guy awake. I put my hand on his chest, looked him in the eye, and told him that he was going to be okay. I felt like an idiot, assuring him in English, but I figured he'd get the point. Why the hell else would a man put his hand over the heart of another man? As we finished up the dressings, a couple of other guys started an IV for him. Giving IVs is not something I know how to do (something I mean to rectify now), so I let them have at it.

I went back over to the guy who was out. He was just lying there, ignored. Maybe he could be resuscitated, maybe he wasn't all the way dead yet. I wanted to do something, but I couldn't even decide if I should elevate his feet or his head. I kept thinking that no matter what I elevated, it was just going to make him bleed out faster. I contemplated giving him CPR, but without treating the wound first, I had no inclination to kiss a dead guy and break his sternum with compressions that would only make him bleed out more. But, Jesus, what was the point? He was already dead, I guess; his pants were soaked in blood, as was the ground around him.

His eyes were half open. Being a product of American pop culture, I knew that the thing you were supposed to do now was shut his eyelids, one of those archetypical things that everyone wishes they could do just once in their life but knows they never will, like leaving a small stack of worn cash on a whore's nightstand. I put my hand over his face and tried to shut his eyelids. They didn't really move, or they just moved back to the half-shut and dead-looking position. I tried harder. Still not working. Now I was just feeling stupid, it's not like making him look more like he was asleep instead of dead was going to be giving him any comfort, and frankly I didn't care how he looked, I just wanted to give him some dignity in death. We grabbed a poncho out of one of the Humvees. I arranged his arms and legs, and we put the poncho over him, tucking it under him. Is it weird that the first time I've "tucked someone in," it's a dead guy?

The guys were having a little trouble with the old guy's IV. His veins were basically nonexistent, and I could see, judging from the new blood on his arm, that there had already been a few failed attempts. Had the situation not been so serious, I would have given them shit about this. But I knew they had it in hand—they just needed to give it another try—so I walked over to the first guy, the one who had flagged us down.

This guy had been shot in the calf. His wound had been dressed and we had him drinking water. The temperature in the sun was at least 135 degrees Fahrenheit. I asked him if he was doing all right. Again, stupid that it's in English, but I felt that this was one of those times that people understand what you mean regardless of language.

He Arabic'd that he was fine, but he was pleading with me to do something for his friend. I stupidly told him that we were. I didn't know what to say. His eyes welled with tears, and he wiped them away with the same hand that held the bottle of water.

We called in a medevac, but we were denied. I am not the lieutenant, so I don't know what the conversation was like, but I imagine the message was basically that we don't provide valuable air assets to local nationals who get hurt. On a human rights level, I find it reprehensible that we had that dumb First Infantry Division motherfucker who shot himself between the toes airlifted out, but a critically injured Iraqi didn't warrant a bird. However, on a tactical level, I understand that we can't be tying up vital resources on every Iraqi who decides to get hurt—something that happens too often for us to be giving up Blackhawks.

We put the old guy on a poleless litter and onto the hood of a Humvee. We put the calf guy in one too. Again he asked me (I'm assuming from his gesticulating) to please help his dead friend. I repeatedly assured him that we would put him on the other Humvee. Which was true. But he wasn't going to want to watch that. The Humvees rolled back up the gully.

No one seemed to really want to deal with the dead guy. This sorta bothered me, but I'm not gonna harp on guys for it. No one wanted to get blood on himself. This is what happens when you have a platoon of soldiers who are all either cops or were raised in the city— they're all convinced that getting blood on you is the fastest way to catch all manner of untreatable disease. This may be true in New York City, but in Iraq the AIDS rate is like zero-point-zero. I said, "Okay guys, let's get this guy on the hood." No one seemed too eager. I didn't need help yet, so I went to the dead guy and rolled him over so the poncho was under him rather than over him. When I rolled him, it felt like a body, it moved like a body, had the heft of a body, but it was strange to think that this body was no longer a person. It had been a person just a few short minutes ago, but now it was a mass of meat that I was going to throw on the hood of my Humvee like a deer. I tried to think of it as only a body, but I couldn't help but think that he was a man, and I wanted to respect him as a man. So I chose to not be offended by him or his body or any of its functions. After a little coaxing, I managed to get three guys to grab the ends of the poncho. I tried giving very explicit instructions on how I wanted to get the guy on the hood, but the guys weren't too stoked on the idea of getting physical with a dead man. Touching a poncho is one thing, but touching a bloody dead body is another. We finally got him on the hood but almost lost him. I was not going to drop this guy on the ground. I yelled at them to stop being squeamish and to just fucking push. I decided that his not falling was more important than his comfort, so once I got him on the front of the hood, I just rolled him up it until he was right in front of the windshield. It wasn't very graceful, the whole procedure, to say the least. But he didn't fall. I stayed on the hood with him, along with Justin, our radio guy, for the ride up to the road.

I was looking at the dead guy's face and noticed two deep cuts in his brow. They were not bloody. I wondered how he got those wounds and if maybe they'd played a role in his death. Then I realized that since they weren't bleeding it must have happened post-mortem—shit—and that I had probably done it getting him onto the hood. I felt bad that I had inflicted a wound on him that would normally have caused him to be scarred for life, but right now it didn't really matter because his lifespan was a number less than zero. I guess at worst I slightly fucked up the open-casket thing for his mom. I don't know how to express that I'm genuinely sorry without sounding like an asshole.

We had to wait longer than I care to mention, but our CASEVAC escort finally made it to our location with the field ambulance to evacuate the wounded. Out of the sight of the others, we transferred the dead guy to a body bag. We then loaded the body onto the back of an ICDC truck, a compact white Toyota with a machine gun shoddily mounted over the cab, a stand-in hearse that just seemed cheap and undignified, but oh well. At least we had a body bag. This is not an item you really want to make a priority to remember when you load up the vehicles. But lugging a body around in a poncho that's on the verge of bursting apart, lifeless limbs dangling out the sides, is not a cool way to roll.

The wounded were escorted to our base to be treated, and the dead guy was dropped off at the ICDC station. We opened the body bag to search for ID. The bag was full of blood now and the guy's white shirt was almost completely saturated in red. Whiskey did the searching, a guy I love for not being one to ever back down from the most repulsive of tasks. There was no ID, so we took a few pictures of the dead guy's face in hopes of being able to ID him later. The two places where I cut his head were now a blackish red. Damn.

The first thing we wondered once we got the chance to was, Why had these men been shot? Who would have done something like this? Had these men refused to cooperate with the local Al Sadr guys or something? Then we thought maybe it was an Arab thing, a score that needed to be settled, a family or clan issue—none of our business! Then we wondered if maybe the men were child molesters and the father and brothers of their victims had done this. This gave us temporary solace. After all, we did see what looked like a young boy's bloodied underwear; the symbolism was all there. But the answer, we would later find out, was pretty much our first guess, the most obvious and, the least original.

When we got back to our bunker, my hands and arms still smelled of this guy's blood. And his sweat. I took a thorough shower. I felt guilty washing his smell off me.

• • •

This afternoon, once we returned from the unsuccessful mission to snatch the local politician, we got some follow-up information on the three men. They were local contractors who were painters for the major base up the street from us. While leaving the base, they were carjacked by people who were none too pleased with their working for the coalition. They were then driven to a remote gully far from any base, an excellent location to kill someone. It's near a major road, and therefore an escape route, but completely out of sight. The last thing one of these men did was take that long walk down the gulley. Then each of them was shot and left for dead. They could have been shot in the head and killed on the spot, but they weren't. They were all shot in the legs, forcing them have to fight to live. And to suffer. And if they survived, to remember.

I've been thinking about this a lot and I've realized that I was so overly concerned about the dead guy, the guy I couldn't save, the one I *didn't* save, that I hadn't realized until now that I had saved someone's life, or rather that I had helped save someone's life, that *we* had saved someone's life. I've never saved someone's life before.

June 27, 2004

How to Blow Up Trucks, Dogs, and Mosques

A couple of days ago me and about fifteen guys from my platoon were doing our NAI ("named area of interest") run along with the EOD ("blow shit up") guys. There was an alleged cache of mortar rounds or something near the NAIs that the EOD guys wanted to blow up. So we drove to the first one, dismounted, checked things out, mounted up, and moved out. We came to the area where the cache was supposed to be, but we didn't find shit. Then we went to the second NAI.

The NAIs are somewhat large areas of real estate, so each time we go, we try to inspect a different part of them. This time, while tooling around, we found an abandoned tractor trailer. Abandoned vehicles are never a good thing in Iraq, so we usually destroy them when we have the means. Since we never found the cache of mortar rounds we were looking for, EOD was happy knowing they now had something to destroy.

First we had Johnny-O, one of our .50-cal gunners, unload a few bursts into the tractor trailer. For you non-killers out there, mounted machine guns have a device on them called a T&E, which controls the weapon's traversal and elevation. Basically it's just a thing that keeps the gun from climbing up as you fire it while allowing it to swing freely from side to side. When Johnny-O shot the truck, he didn't have the T&E engaged. It's fine that he chose to free-gun it—it was good experience—but it made it so he could put only a short burst into it before it started to climb. We try to be careful about this sorta thing because, after all, there are people living all over the place, and collateral damage from errant bullets isn't cool. Free-gunning is cool when you need the freedom of movement—say, for a close-range engagement on a highway—but if you want to actually put lead into something accurately with nice long bursts, use the damn T&E.

After shooting the truck, EOD got ready to blow it up. They had several bricks of some Russian explosives they wanted to expend, so they put the whole shit in the cab of the truck on a timed fuse. We then drove several hundred meters away and waited patiently.

"Thirty seconds!" the EOD guy yelled.

So we're all watching the truck, waiting for the fireworks display, when, Hey, wait a second, is that a dog? Oh, shit! What are you doing? Get the fuck away from there, you stupid mutt!

A dog had wandered toward the truck right as it was about to explode. I've never seen so many dogs get fucked up in my life as I have over here. This one had the luckiest day of his life, though. However, I don't think he'll be answering to any more whistles. The truck blew right next to him, then he tucked tail and ran. Aside from the fact that innocent animals (almost) dying is not cool, it was pretty damn funny.

Then, on the way back, while we're driving through a little neighborhood, I notice all these bricks and rubble strewn across the road. I thought to myself, Hmm, what's all this shit? I look out the front of the Humvee (I was in the backseat, so my sector of fire was out the window) and thought, Is something missing? Holy shit! That one mosque is gone!

This small village had a mosque that was now no more. We stopped and got out to investigate. It was handy that we had EOD with us because they were able to poke around the rubble and determine that the explosion had come from the inside (as opposed to an air strike or an exterior detonation). The locals who came out told us that someone was seen planting the bomb that destroyed the place. It must have been a good amount of explosives, because the place was leveled. As you may well know, I'm no fan of religion, but it still made me really sad to see this. The mosque was Shiite. What's strange, too, is that this area is considered to be less than friendly to us, so for it to have been a retaliatory strike against the local people for being sympathetic to the coalition didn't make any sense. The mosque and the village are within the boundaries of a different unit's area of operations, so we reported it up and headed home. We may never know what the story was. What can I say? The Iraqis are as busy being assholes to each other as they are to us.

July 9, 2004

ALL HAIL WILLY! THAT BASTARD! PART ONE

My girlfriend Heather and I were expelled from high school less than a week before graduation. This is because the First Amendment does not protect suburban Utah high school students. Our parents were heartbroken and wouldn't speak to us, and we became pariahs in our own town. But these were the least of my worries. Heather had already been accepted to Utah State University, in Logan, and they would never be the wiser that the girl whom they would eventually graduate with honors in psychology and sociology had never technically finished high school. But this created a serious problem for me, because I couldn't leave for infantry school until I had a diploma. And I wasn't just expelled from my high school, I was expelled from the whole goddamned school district, something that I think was unprecedented. I tried to get my diploma through the alternative high school—the one where the criminal, sociopathic, drug-addicted, and pregnant students went—but they wouldn't take me in. I made an appeal to the superintendent of the Murray school district. He was the first government administrator I ever met who could talk and talk and talk and never actually say anything. "Something must be done. We are going to have to decide what should be done. Something will have to be done," he droned on ad nauseam. There was a special meeting of the school board to determine my fate. That's when they decided to boot me from the district and, according to the superintendent, to actively pursue barring me from transferring to any district in the state of Utah. He broke the news to me when I called his office from my work, a telemarketing job, an unfortunate trade I acquired that would help me pay my way through college, hone my verbal communication skills, and eventually cause me to develop a love for New Yorkers. That day at work, after all his blathersome circumlocution and beating-around-the-bush, the superintendent finally gave me the verdict. "After much deliberation, blah blah blah, the school board and I, blah blah blah, regret to inform you, blah blah blah . . ." I then told him, as professionally as I could, to go fuck himself. "Sir, Heather and I would like to cordially invite you and the school board to go have sex with yourselves."

To give you a proper background, I feel compelled to tell you my entire goddamned life story and all that David Copperfield kind of crap, but nothing is quite so boring as having to endure an autobiography. It's like looking at the personal photographs that cubicle dwellers put up next to their computers or deployed soldiers put up around their bunks. You don't know the people in the photographs and you don't know the stories in them. It's totally abstract. And if you're like me, you couldn't care less. For example, I have two photos on the bookshelf next to my bunk. One is of me lying on a bed in an apartment in New Paltz with two girls, Wazina and Rachel. The girls are spooning and looking at me. I'm looking at them. We had just finished our first performance of the *Vagina Monologues* for the weekend. I had performed the only male monologue that is allowed when universities do the show—original material on the subject of *What the World Would Be Like Without Violence.* (I started my monologue with a joke about how Michael Bolton would never have to worry about getting his ass kicked in bars, but no one laughed.) The other photo is of another pair of girls, Erin and Kristin, my roommates in New Paltz. I stole the photo out of one of their albums from our apartment when I realized before I deployed that I didn't have any pictures of them. These photos, or rather the memories captured by each photo, mean volumes to me. To you, they mean absolutely nothing. (Unless, of course, you are Wazina, Rachel, Erin, or Kristin.)

It's like trying to explain a dream where the emotions are intense and poignant, and you want so badly to try and get these feelings across to whomever is your unfortunate audience, but trying to explain how you fell in love with a girl you met on a spaceship run by lizard dogs really kinda kills the delivery.

Despite the inherent risks of trying to explain feelings and personal histories, here's the flashcard summary of my life: I'm born in Provo, Utah, to George and Linda. My mom would later describe George to me as a "chiseled Greek god." The marriage ends after I'm a few months old. My mom and I move to San Leandro, California, to live with my grandparents. My grandfather, a retired Navy officer, becomes my father figure. At the age of four, my penchant for large words and all things fecal has already developed. Jim, an earnest and conservative man, starts courting my mom, despite her having a child who has a predilection for running around the yard stark naked with a yellow ribbon wedged between his little baby buttocks yelling, "DIARRHEA!!! DIARRHEA!!! DIARRHEA!!!"

Jim and Linda wed and move into a small house with shag carpeting next to a cow pasture in the hick town of Spanish Fork, Utah. I am taught to refer to Jim as my father. Small, backward working-class town plus community of religion-induced sexual repression and perversion equals five-year-old me being sexually molested by twelve-year-old boy across the street—"Let's pretend we're tied up . . ." One Sunday morning, following a day of playing in the sprinkler and getting my first sunburn, I get spanked by my new father for watching *Mr. Rogers' Neighborhood*—you can't keep the Sabbath day holy by indulging in entertainment, ya know! I would be spanked more times that I can count over the years. Oddly, I'm also taught that one should never fight, but to "turn the other cheek," a fucking idiotic philosophy that would haunt me during my childhood and later shape my adolescence as I shed it. I start having terrifying recurring nightmares about a dragon and a mustachioed man who dwell in the foundation of an unfinished house and force me to choose a different method of death each night—"So what's it gonna be, kid? Cut apart by the dragon's claws or crushed to death under his feet?" My dad tells me to chant the phrase "Kook-a-munga rickety-rack, mean old dragon, never come back!" to make them go away. It doesn't work. I finally learn to simply refuse to comply with the sinister man's *Sophie's Choice* bullshit by just letting him know that he and his dragon can go fuck themselves. I never have the nightmare again.

It finally dawns on my parents that Spanish Fork is fucked up, and we move into a new rambler style house in Murray, Utah, fifteen minutes from downtown Salt Lake City, where I make many friends and have a happy childhood, despite being sheltered and repressed. Things start getting a little sketchy between me and my father once my critical reasoning skills start to kick in, at around age twelve. I learn to play the piano. I become an Eagle Scout. By the time I am fourteen, I am well on my way to becoming a very difficult and rebellious teenager. I learn that I love to write, but my parents find what I write troubling. I will have incredibly good English teachers in Utah for ninth, tenth, and eleventh grade, who, simply put, will have a bigger positive influence on who I am today than anyone aside from my mom. At fifteen, I meet a transfer student with perfect skin and a Germanic face named Lori who teaches me how to skateboard and introduces me to the whole self-destructive, bad-poetry-writing, Winona Ryder–in–*Edward Scissorshands* smoking-clove-cigarettes thing. I go to my first concert with her—Oingo Boingo at the Salt Palace during the Boingo Alive tour—against the express instructions of my parents (girls: bad; rock-n-roll: bad; combinations of the two: total and utter damnation). I sleep at a friend's house the night after the show.

After years of dealing with their "troubled" teenage son, my parents decide they've had enough. The following day, I am picked up from school by my mom, who is dressed like she is on her way to church. We meet my dad at a place called Benchmark, a mental institution north of Salt Lake. To the crowd I run with, being institutionalized is considered a badge of honor. ("They stuck me in an institution / Said it was the only solution / To give me the needed professional help / To protect me from the enemy, myself.") But "mods"—what goths were called in Utah before the word "goth" was coined— tend to go to the Western Institute of Neuropsychiatry, or WIN, at the University of Utah, while stoners and rockers go to Benchmark. I am torn. The dilemma is immaterial, because the insurance company refuses to pay for the cost of institutionalizing a noncrazy basically drug-free kid who simply doesn't get along with his dad.

I start seeing a therapist, who diagnoses me as having an atypical anxiety disorder—bullshit psychobabble for "pissed off at his dad." The therapist is Mormon. My whole issue is the religion shit. As a compromise, I move in with my aunt Cheryl and uncle Lauren for the second half of my tenth grade year in Alamo, California, a wealthy bedroom community on the east side of the San Francisco Bay. My aunt and uncle and cousins are another huge Mormon family, except they are eccentric, wild, and fun, like something out of a John Irving novel. At San Ramon Valley High School, I see students treated like adults. The school newspaper is remarkably good. In it, I read an editorial about the death of Jim Henson called "It's Not Easy Being Green" that I will remember for years. The kids here are being prepared for adulthood, and it makes me feel empowered. I fail both quarters of English, however. The teacher fails all my unconventionally written essays. I write short stories instead of normal essays to fulfill the requirements. The teacher is short, pugnacious, and ugly as hell, with greasy, pockmarked skin, thinning wiry hair, and a green tongue. (She would use her tongue to scratch her chin! Blech!) We get along fairly well, and I like her.

I return to Utah. Public education in Utah is excellent, but students are not treated like adults. My citizenship grades in school are horrible. I am chronically tardy or absent. Each unsatisfactory citizenship grade has x number of community service hours attached to it. I have hundreds of hours to do. I move out of my parents' house and begin living in an apartment with a friend. The best part about living on your own while in high school? Qualifying for free lunch tickets—technically, I am utterly poverty stricken. I guess there can be free lunch after all!

I am a decent student—my grades are good. I get a 29 on the ACT. I have Advanced Placement credits in English and Chemistry. I am part of the literary magazine staff. But I am overwhelmed by these infernal community service hours. I do janitorial work at the school to fulfill them. I also work at the local firehouse, washing the same sparkling clean fire truck, day after day. I forge numerous hours for myself. I still cannot work or forge fast enough.

Then I see the movie *Pump Up the Volume*, a wonderfully eighties flick about pirate radio, starring Christian Slater. I am inspired. The previous year, a senior at school printed an underground newspaper. He harped on how bad our school newspaper was and he wrote some innocuously funny things. He got in a bit of trouble, however, for writing that Mr. Such-and-such, one of the teachers, should have a tie with I'M A MEAN OLD BASTARD, AREN'T I? printed on it. A light goes on in my head. I will publish an underground newspaper! I have two months before the end of the school year, so I have to get to work.

I should tell you that I renewed my faith in the Mormon church (religion recidivism!) after returning from California and after going to Basic Training with the Army following my junior year. At the beginning of the school year, I was made the president of my seminary class. In Utah, you are allowed to take a period of seminary each day.

At the beginning of every class I made some sort of military analogy in order to teach a religious principle. (Mohammed Jason Al Sadr!) But by the middle of the school year, I find a new religion; her name is Heather. Heather, Heather, Heather.

We are inseparable, we are each other's evil twin cum guardian angel, we are partners in crime, like a pair of dragons soaring through the medieval night sky in search of villages to lay to waste. Though I have dark brown hair and brown eyes, and she has blonde hair and blue eyes, eyes I drown in every time I look into them, we look a lot alike (big forehead, toothy grin, general air of mischief) and are commonly mistaken for brother and sister. An uncommon familiarity that shows, I suppose, because we feel and act as though we have been friends for millennia, spanning countless lives. She is incredible. She makes me feel like I can do anything. And I can, so long as I can do it with her. But when you have a sense of self-worth based *through* someone else and not first through yourself, your insecurities will inevitably get the better of you. I learn this the hard way. Eventually I ruin everything I have with Heather, and our relationship spirals into an abominable co-dependency.

But I suppose character is built based on what you have lost more than on what you have. I love who I am today, but I hate what I had to lose in order to know myself. But back to underground newspapers and how I found time to write one during the hour each day when I was supposed to be spiritually leading my seminary class.

At first, my intentions are mature and adult. I know that anyone can criticize something they don't like, so I want to offer feasible solutions along with my criticism. I want to present a rational argument against the current citizenship grading policy. There are also a few other issues I want to provide intelligent alternatives to. Then I smarten up. Students are treated like children at my school and their opinions are not given any credence. This becomes apparent to me when a committee of students and teachers are formed to discuss an issue. (I forget what the topic was exactly, but I remember that after all the hullabaloo, the decision reached was the same as it would have been if there had been no committee.) It is a farce, a front. Something they can say was done to come to a mutual decision that took into account the desires of the administration, the faculty, and the student body. I now know that this is simply how the world is run—most everything is bullshit, like makeup on a corpse, like China calling itself a republic, like invading a country that is a "threat" to our national security then telling them they can form their "own" democratic government. But at the time, my idealistic eighteen-year-old mind cannot reconcile this affront to reason and democracy. My voice, the voice of the student, in this case the voices of a few student representatives on the committee, are summarily ignored.

I hate to be ignored. So I scrap all my ideas and start over. That's when the *Murray High Muckraker* is born. We become literary terrorists. We take on a scorched-earth policy. ("We'll use their guts to grease the treads of our tanks!") I berate the fascist citizenship policy. I write a tastelessly vulgar horoscope and an article on how the word "fuck" can be used for all parts of speech. (Did you know that "fucking" is one of the only infixes in the English language? Prefixes and suffixes are ubiquitous in English, as they are in most languages, but not many words can be used like this: "Absofuckinglutely.") Heather goes off on how physical education for girls is useless sexist hogwash. She makes an unspeakably sacrilegious Mormon trivia crossword puzzle. We write all manner of offensive material. But the real coup de grace is my indiscriminately venting my spleen on every single administrator, even those of whom I am fond, all in the name of libel fairness. It is nothing less than an act of terrorism. We use multiple pseudonyms to make it appear as though there is a small army of revolutionaries hell-bent on burning the school to the ground. The staff photos are fun: my armpit, my ass, my crotch; Heather in her under-wear; our friend Mandy's feet.

It is all a secret. We tell no one. I figure the way to do something and not get caught is simply to not tell anyone, not even friends. Heather and I bring Mandy in at the eleventh hour, when it comes time to make copies. We can't afford to print hundreds of copies of an eight-page paper at Kinko's (not to mention the security risk), so late one night we steal the keys to Mandy's dad's place of employ-ment. It almost doesn't happen because the photocopy machines need a code to be entered into them to work. I search every workspace in the office until I find where someone has written the code down—a trick I learned from Matthew Broderick in the movie *War Games*. (Thanks again, American pop culture!) If I remember right, we made five hundred copies, double-sided. Collating and stapling them all is a chore. Once we finally leave, as the sun is about to come up, we lock up and walk out, passing an employee coming in to work. Had we left ten seconds later, we would have been in a world of hurt.

I am very proud of myself. I plan everything very meticulously. I map out where all the lockers in the school are and how many there are in each section. I break it down by class—seniors, my target audi-ence, will get the majority, one for every other locker, while juniors will get one for every third locker. The actual distribution is another coup I am proud of. Given that I now have intimate knowledge of the janitors' schedules at the school (thanks, community service hours!), I know that there is a thirty-minute window each Saturday when the school is completely devoid of any adult supervision. So I recruit a gaggle of losers who party at my apartment and who don't go to my school, give them each a bundle of newspapers folded lengthwise, and instruct each one on which row of lockers is their responsibility. The newspapers are slipped through the horizontal vents of the lock-ers. It takes us less then fifteen minutes to inseminate the school with our demon seed. There is no turning back.

I came to school early on Monday. As students started to show up, the buzz began. "Oh my heck! Do you have one of these in your locker? Read this part!" By the time everyone was there, minutes before the bell for the first class was to ring, the school was in a state of complete pandemonium. Like an amorous pyromaniac admiring his work, I walked up and down the halls and took it all in. A few teachers were running around the halls, trying to collect as many of the illicit newspapers as possible. There was shock and disgust, there was laughter, there was speculation on the identities of the authors.

I made it through only the first fifteen or twenty minutes of first period before I was pulled out by the vice principal, who was the attendance enforcer and the butt of most the jokes in the newspaper. His name was Mr. Long, a man ironically named, I surmised publicly. He was former Army and a total stress case. He made it very clear to me, once we were alone, at our most excellent moment together, that he wanted desperately to kick the living shit outta me and that Mrs. Long could attest to the fact that his name was not an oxymoron. I later found out that he would mow his lawn every single day to relieve his tension. Apparently it didn't work, because he died of a heart attack a few years later. He was not old. I wish I could have a beer with him now.

So how did they catch us? I covered every base. Except one. Or maybe two. No matter the lengths I went to in order to hide our identities, I couldn't disguise my writing style. The English department most likely sang in unison like a Greek chorus, "JASON DID IT!" Once they determined that it was me, and therefore Heather as well, they took us both separately and told us that the other one had already admitted to the deed. Heather took the bait and just said, "Yeah, I did do it, and I'm glad I did! Fuck you!" I held out for about an hour, but now that Heather really had admitted it, and the fact that the lady who ran the computer lab could corroborate that she had seen me print out one of the pages (drat! foiled!), I knew I was screwed. (I had had to go to her to retrieve a page I had printed, and she looked offended by its content. I remember explaining to her that I was writing an essay for an "adult" magazine. I was eighteen! I was an adult! It's possible I could have been a contributor to an adult publication, right? It was a pathetic explanation.) So I folded and admitted to it.

The fallout from *The Muckraker* was pretty extensive. One of my English teachers criticized me for not putting my name to my work, calling it a cowardly thing to do. In a sense, she was correct, but like I said before, I wanted to be heard, the way a suicide bomber wants to be heard, and this approach worked far better than any other. Besides, it was much funnier and a lot more exciting to go the route of typewriter terrorist. The seminary teachers advised their students not to read it. You know you've hit the big time when local religious leaders devote time to speaking out against your work. I egotistically imagined that it was a spiritual triage situation for them. A lot of people thought it was funny, a lot of people thought it was in colossally bad taste. I think they were both basically right. My mom, in a state of anguish, wrote a letter to George, my biological father in New York, whom I had only recently met for the first time, essentially blaming him and his genes for my transgression. She sent him a copy of the paper, as if to show him the product of all the bad parts of his genetic contribution to his wayward son.

The one thing that I didn't plan on was the reaction the students' parents would have. That's where things got complicated. I really didn't plan on any of the chaos leaving the school. In addition to the newspaper mess, I had recently been arrested on two counts of criminal mischief for exploding two mailboxes with dry-ice bombs. My dad, Jim, had opened a letter he found in our mailbox that I had written to George, where I bragged about the deeds, so he ratted me out to the cops. One mailbox was a random act of violence and the other belonged to Heather's ex-boyfriend, my ex–best friend. When the detective came to my house and read me my rights, I couldn't help but giggle. One more thing I could scratch off my list of archetypically lurid things to do before I died: being Mirandized.

I don't mean to get sidetracked with more stories about my behaving badly, so let me just establish that because of this dry-ice bomb thing I had already become fairly well acquainted with the attorney for Murray city.

When my court date came, the city attorney and I were waiting outside the courtroom and he told me he had heard about *The Muckraker*. This sorta shocked me, that it had gotten as far as him. He tried to argue how my characterizing the attendance policy as the love child of Hitler and Stalin was inaccurate in terms of political theory. I had used the pseudonym Holden Caulfield for some of the articles, and the attorney argued how he thought *Franny and Zooey* was better than *Catcher in the Rye* and would have been more appropriate to reference. He wanted to articulate how he thought my message was flawed. But what I couldn't get across to him was that there wasn't really a rational message, just the simple fact that it blowed up real good.

But then he told me that there were four separate parties who were putting "political pressure" on the city to prosecute me for various things like libel and lewdness or whatever. He told me he didn't think it was much of a case, that if someone wanted to sue me they would do it themselves and not ask the city to do it, and he said outright that he didn't want to pursue any of it. But he told me I could discuss this with the judge. I was perplexed and a bit overwhelmed. Sue me? Discuss it with the judge? Jesus, I never thought it would go this far.

Judge Burton happened to be the father of one of my classmates and was part of the local Stake High Council. In Mormon-speak, this meant that he was part of the church leadership in my area. He knew my dad and thought well of him. My case number was called, and I stood before the man. We discussed the dry-ice bombs, and I pretty much spilled my guts about them. I never had a chance to get my story straight with Heather or the others involved before the detective questioned us, so I let the truth set me free. So to speak. Then the judge brought up the *Muckraker* incident. I wasn't sure that this was appropriate, but who was I to say anything? He basically repeated what the city attorney had already told me. At some point I think I explained that I needed to resolve my current legal problems and get a high school diploma so I could leave for infantry school. Then the judge asked me about my dad, I guess to be friendly. I told him we didn't get along. I had to be honest. I mean, I was under oath, right? He asked me why not. I said, "We have a difference of religion. He thinks he's god, and I disagree." I didn't come up with that joke, but the judge thought it was hilarious. My dad's religious zeal was well known. That was when the judge told me something I'll never forget. He said, "I like you, Jason. So we'll make you a deal. The city will agree to dismiss the charges against you and not pursue any further charges with regard to the newspaper incident, if you agree to leave town." Leave town? WTF? Are you kidding me? That's all? I wasn't sure how any of this was appropriate or even legal, but I loved the Old West feel to it. Leave town. Classic. The judge spat on his palm, and I spat on mine, and we shook. Then I saddled up, lit a cigarette, gave him and the city attorney an acknowledging tip of my hat, and I rode off into the Utah desert sunset.

I took a geography class through an adult education center, which got me residency in another school district. The superintendent of that district said he would back me up if I wanted to go the whole ACLU route and fight to get my diploma through my own district, but by this time I just wanted to take the path of least resistance, Heather even more so, because this wasn't really her fight to begin with. This could have been a sensational battle, but my priority was the Army and Heather's priority was college. I paid the fine, got a letter from the Granite school district stating that I would "graduate" through Hunter High School with the class of '93, and a few months later I was on my way to Fort Benning, Georgia.

The End.

The whole reason I've shared this story with you now is because I recently recounted it (in a more abbreviated format) to Cesar, the newest member of my team, along with the story about how our commander made me take this blog off the internet. I figured he'd be able to identify with it and I wanted him to know that I could empathize with his current situation intimately.

Before I explain Cesar's little imbroglio and how he came to join my team, I think it's time that I got you up to speed with regard to my squad. When we originally deployed, our squad of nine men was led by Chris, a New York cop and an outgoing former Army Ranger. I've said this before, but Chris is like a blonde with big tits; he's like the hottest girl in school and pretty much acts as our idol. I know this sounds like a grotesque amount of ass-kissing, but it's the best way to explain it. He's just a really good soldier with a lot of experience and training under his belt. When he was our squad leader, we were the best squad in the company. In reality our squad was completely average, he just made us look really good. He's long since left the squad to lead the company's sniper section. He's in a position now where he arguably is more of an asset to the company than he ever could have been with a regular squad, but truth be told, our squad never survived his departure.

Our new squad leader is Stan, or "Whiskey" as we call him, for having an incredibly long last name starting with a W. Whiskey is a really easy-going guy, and is a very decent squad leader, but he's not part of the inner conclave of the platoon leadership (the Army version of the popular kids in school), so he's commonly out of the loop on information and planning. This sucks because this means the team leaders, Kirk and I—we lead three men each—are usually left out of the loop as well. Whiskey's capacity for sleep is unrivaled, and he spends most his free waking time watching the same DVDs over and over again. He's literally turned this deployment into an extended vacation for himself. It's remarkable. But don't get me wrong, he's not complacent. He plays by the rules and is a hard worker, and his amiable attitude makes for a much less stressful work environment. It's just that our platoon (which is four squads) is run by an unspoken social structure that he is not a part of.

Since Chris's exodus, our squad has become a revolving door for soldiers. Take Alpha team: Joel, one of our original members, left when he became the company medic. Cola, the guy who replaced Joel, later joined the sniper section with Chris. Cola was then replaced by Johnny-O, a big Irish lug of a guy who, unfortunately, is now the butt of most of the squad's jokes, some of which he deserves, some of which he doesn't. The other two members of Alpha team are Anthony and Juan, two soldiers from my original company whom I've known for years. They are led by Kirk, an excitable firefighter from the Bronx, who uses the term "big titties" at least five times a day. Kirk has attention deficit disorder so bad that it's virtually impossible to have a conversation with him about anything for more than six seconds, unless it's about sex, preferably including the phrase "big titties." Here's a fictitious but plausible conversation:

"Hey, J, who's that package you got from?"

"Just from a friend of mine, this girl I know in New Paltz."

"Oh yeah? Were you fuckin' her? Does she have big titties?"

"What? Dude, she's married and I'm friends with her husb—"

"Oh yeah? I love big titties. I was chatting with this girl online last night. Damn, she had"—he then pauses for a split second to reflect—"BIG TITTIES! They were like"—he bites his lower lip and cups his hands out in front of his chest in mock mammae—"bam! *Out* there, and shit! I was like, *yeah!*"

Kirk is like the unapologetically two-dimensional co-starring character from your typical romantic comedy who acts as a foil to the protagonist. As human beings go, he's a study done during god's drunken ham-fisted chiaroscuro period. On one side, he's incredibly caustic: He's rude as hell to all Iraqis and won't hesitate to put a barrel in the face of anyone with a name he can't pronounce. He loves to yell for yelling's sake and becomes legendarily ecstatic with assumed rage anytime he finds any garbage or clutter in our living area. And he generally treats lower-ranked troops with totally unwarranted disdain and contempt. His preoccupations with sex, big titties, and homophobia are near pathological. But the other side of this prurient and churlish brute is a very genuine nature, and he can be unassumingly affectionate, friendly, and inclusive. With Kirk, you always know what you're getting. He's completely free of guile and utterly upfront with everyone. His loyalty and forthrightness are like that of a dog you've had since you were five, who seems never to get tired of viciously barking at everything one moment, then the next, chasing his own tail and humping all your friends' legs.

Originally, Bravo team, the team I lead, had as its SAW gunner a young kid named Peter. He had a bad reputation with his original company for being a bit of a shitbag. He seemed to me to be somewhat unfairly picked on, and I believed I could easily rehabilitate him. He was egotistical and self-assured and ultimately turned out to be a defeatist shitbag. Somehow he managed to catch narcolepsy during training and get tagged as nondeployable. Before you tell me how narcolepsy is not contagious, understand that he was borderline enough to enlist but was able to use his condition as an out when it suited him. I tried really hard with this kid, and he made an ass of me. I tried to be understanding, but all it did was give me a reputation for being soft. Throughout training he was having trouble with his unfaithful teenage fiancée and wanted nothing more than to not deploy. But the song he sang was all about how badly he wanted to go into combat with his team and never let us down. Everyone told me I was wasting my time trying to help him, and I hate that they proved me right. Note to future soldiers: get your priorities straight before you join the Army. Your job is to fight, usually far away from your nubile girlfriend, and if that doesn't work for you, don't fucking enlist. Oh, and don't count on her being faithful either. You won't be, so why do you expect her to be?

Peter was replaced by Orlando, another guy I've known for years. Orlando is one of these guys who always seems to be in a good mood. I love this guy. He likes to watch *I Love Lucy* DVDs and has a collection of animated Disney and Disneyesque DVDs that would make your kids jealous. He's also a guy you can always count on to bring porn to the field. He's not the most articulate guy, but his heart is in the right place, something that goes a long way with me. The thing that most of the other guys in the platoon don't know about Orlando is how he used to be a real badass back in his days growing up on the Lower East Side. Orlando has been in the Army for over twenty years now and was recently promoted to sergeant. Normally, you need to be in a sergeant slot to get the promotion, but his promotion was one of the kind where you just get promoted because you've been in the military for so long, or something like that. I have no idea how this is possible, but regardless, my SAW gunner is the same rank as me.

One of my riflemen is Matt. He looks a lot like me, tall and thin, brown hair and eyes, and he is a paramedic in Poughkeepsie in real life. Matt is intelligent and level-headed, and his medical skills are an invaluable (and comforting) asset. But he's former Air Force and has a real penchant for doing his own thing while flaunting his disdain for military regulations, particularly about the wear of the uniform (such as having the pockets removed from the front of his blouse and sewn onto the arms like some fucking Delta Force operative). I'd say that Matt is an exceptional soldier other than the fact that he doesn't know his place. He has single-handedly made a good part of this deployment utterly miserable for me with his condescending self-importance and self-righteousness. I've tried reasoning with him and I've tried smoking him. But he still manages to act like he's a five-star general by always having his hands in everything: he attends op orders; he automatically makes himself the platoon spokesman anytime we meet other units while out on missions; the way he wears his uniform and gear makes him look like he's in the Special Forces to the degree that he's even managed to con the first sergeant into giving him his 9mm Beretta. And he gets away with it because he's part of the good ol' boy club, where people like our platoon sergeant are referred to as "Mike." In this regard, he's a team leader's nightmare. But despite how much his attitude infuriates me and how much he undermines my authority, and the chain of command in general, I really can't see the point in spending much energy to make him stop trying to be an effective soldier. If I really wanted to, I could squash this behavior altogether (at least that's what I tell myself), but I'd rather have my energy and his energy spent on more productive activities than infighting, so I permit most of it, despite how much he sometimes makes me want to pull all my hair out.

Up until a few weeks ago, Dan was a rifleman on my team, but he has since been promoted to sergeant and is now a team leader in another squad. Peter and I used to mockingly but affectionately refer to Dan as the "infantry wizard," because of how much knowledge he has about being an infantryman. But he was accustomed to acting as a team leader and resented that he had to be led by someone less experienced than him. This made my job very difficult because he is one of the grumpiest people I've ever known. He would make it his job to show me up or correct me publicly whenever possible. In the Army, they call this "sharpshooting." He and I had a talk about this early on, at Fort Drum, and he slowly got better about it. Now that he's finally an NCO, his demeanor is remarkably more amiable. He strikes me as bipolar. When he's in a good mood, he's one of my favorite people to be around. He's a bit of a geek about things, like I am, and he loves to tinker and figure stuff out, and we've had a lot of really good conversations. He's incredibly observant and resourceful and has a natural talent for soldiering. But when he's grumpy, he's a fucking troll. The fact that he's short, with a really broad build, adds to his trollness. His gait is even CroMagnon-like. Were it a few hundred years ago, he would most likely be carrying a battle-ax and have a long braided beard.

And this brings us to Cesar. Cesar has always reminded me of the character in the Looney Tunes cartoons who insists he's a chicken hawk. ("I'm not a chicken! I'm a chicken hawk!") He's a diminutive Dominican firecracker who walks with his elbows back and his chest puffed out like a red-breasted robin trying to attract a mate. When he first came to our unit in the city, he was barely seventeen and had an arrogance and bravado that only the truly Napoleonic can achieve. He made his distaste for Caucasians readily known and directed a lot of his contempt toward me. (This was back when Willy and I were the only white soldiers in our company.) He was the rank of E-1 at the time, and I was an E-4. The first time I ever had to pull rank and put a soldier in his place was with Cesar. But that was a long time ago, and he's since grown immeasurably, due largely in part to having Willy as his team leader.

Up until the point where Cesar joined my team, he'd been in

Third Platoon as Willy's SAW gunner and protégé. Cesar's development has been rapid and noticeable. All the hard work and tough love of turning him into a soldier from the unruly little fucker he was less than a year ago is something that I think Willy can be really proud of. I'm stoked as hell to finally have a soldier who is both worth a damn and can follow instructions. I don't really deserve him, I'm just riding Willy's coattails in having developed a good troop.

Willy and Cesar's platoon sergeant was our former platoon sergeant back in our home unit in the city. He's a black city cop with an Italian first name and an Irish last name whose best talent is his ability to employ his argumentative and combative nature to get what he wants through coercion. Think Denzel Washington's character in *Training Day*, but played by someone who looks like Wesley Snipes. His resemblance to Snipes is so uncanny, in fact, that we've taken to calling him "Daywalker" behind his back. His bullheadedness is unrivaled. Between Willy's stubbornness, my smart mouth, and our utter inseparability, Willy and I were public enemies number one with Daywalker back in the city. Before we deployed, a drill never went by during which we weren't being disciplined by this guy for some petty offense, usually in the form of him publicly pulling us aside or into his office for a private ass-chewing.

Daywalker's grudge against Willy didn't diminish a bit just because I wasn't with him anymore. And once chicken hawk Cesar got added to the mix, things really started to simmer in their platoon. Willy has already gotten four negative counseling statements from Daywalker since the deployment began, not to mention countless verbal confrontations. And the acrimony toward Daywalker is not only from Willy and Cesar. Almost everyone in their platoon now has an ax to grind with him. But one day, Cesar had had enough and decided to put his manuscript where his mouth was.

That day, on the Third Platoon dry-erase scheduling board, Daywalker found taped a letter addressed to him from "a soldier." In it was a list of his deficiencies that read like a cargo manifest. After two handwritten pages of his being slapped in the face with the journalistic equivalent of John Holmes's cock, the real stinger was the last line—a reminder that we all knew his original job in the Army and that at his core he'd always be a pogue, probably the most subtle but egregious of insults against a grunt: "To us, you'll always be Supply."

This of course warranted a witch hunt in Third Platoon. Daywalker interviewed each soldier individually. Cesar eventually admitted to it without too much arm-twisting. My guess is he really wanted Daywalker to know he'd done it, in that Jack-Nicholson-in-*A-Few-Good-Men* kind of way. ("Did you order the code red!" "YOU'RE GODDAMN RIGHT I DID!")

Justice was swift. Cesar got a one-way ticket out of Third Platoon and an Article 15, which included a one-time loss-of-pay and demotion from specialist to private first-class. The irony about the timing of the Article 15 is that Cesar, while on a raid only a few days earlier, had distinguished himself while under fire and arguably saved Willy's life.

ALL HAIL WILLY! THAT BASTARD! FINALE

Willy's mother is dying. She has cancer, and it has moved to her lungs. What especially sucks about his mother dying is that his grandmother, whom he had shared an apartment with in the Bronx for years, also passed away during this deployment. His grandmother, the tiniest cute little old lady, who couldn't have weighed more than eighty-five pounds, seemed to always be sitting in her recliner—engulfed by her recliner would better describe it—watching TV, flipping channels, looking like a delicate sculpture more than a person. Until she spoke. From that tiny throat came a voice so enormous it was like a kick in the shins for your having dared think she might be feeble. "WILLY! WHERE HAVE YOU BEEN? DO YOU WORK TONIGHT?" (She was always very interested in where Willy was going and when he planned on being home and whether or not he was going to take it easy on the alcohol.) The first time I heard her speak, I think my fight-or-flight response kicked in, and if I had known karate I would have popped into a fighting stance. I was like, Holy shit! Where the fuck did that voice come from! Jesus! I think I just crapped my pants a little bit!

The evening she died, she had complained of a cough, and Willy's parents were going to take her to see a doctor in the morning. She sat down at the dining room table in a chair she never normally sat in, then apparently just gave up the ghost. She was eighty-nine. I've always been fascinated by the way she passed. To me it seemed dignified. It's like she knew she was about to die, so she said to herself, Well, I guess I'd better sit down for this.

When I first moved to New York City, I was a bit apprehensive about my new National Guard unit. I knew it would most likely be populated with city kids who had grown up on the streets, who were tough in ways that a mewling suburbanite like me could never convincingly have replicated. And although I had been to infantry school, I hadn't done any real infantry work in years and was a little nervous that I wouldn't remember the battle drills properly.

The groups that soldiers hang out in tend to be divided down racial lines, so when I arrived it was basically assumed that I'd hang out with Willy since he was the only other white guy. The platoon was mostly Puerto Ricans and Dominicans, with a handful of bruthas and the occasional random ethnicity like Moroccan, Guyanese, or Venezuelan. One of the first things Willy told me when I met him was, "Yo, I didn't show up last drill. I didn't call the first sergeant or anything. Oh well.

Fuck it." He told me this while we were smoking in front of the armory on Lexington Avenue, hiding out from whatever was going on at the moment. I remember thinking, Okay, this guy is a shitbag, I need to find someone else to hang out with before this guy gets me in trouble. I was in a slight panic thinking that I'd just shown up at a new unit and was already shamming out of work and associating with this lazy bastard.

But once Willy was in the field, he was an entirely different animal. The guy was hardworking, tough, and a clear thinker. For one of my first drills, our platoon went up against some West Point cadets. We were in the rocky wooded training area at Camp Smith, New York, in a standard defensive perimeter, and the cadets were an assaulting element, or OPFOR, as they're called in training, for "opposing force." I remember Willy had set up some early-warning devices outside our perimeter consisting of tin cans and a trip-wired chem light, something that is perfectly natural to want to employ, but I would never have thought to do it. I was so concerned with following plain-vanilla doctrine as closely as possible, while Willy was thinking in terms of practicality. Before this drill he was just some portly rookie cop from the Bronx with an Irish last name that I could never seem to remember how to pronounce. But after seeing how he worked in the field, I became immediately attached to him. I remember thinking that as long as I stuck by this guy, I'd always be safe. I was doing my best to hide the fact that I didn't know what the fuck I was doing on so many different levels—as an infantryman, as a New Yorker, and (to be perfectly honest) as a man. I had moved to New York City several months after my relationship with Heather came to its indescribably horrific end, and the only way I'd been able to cope with it all had been to strip everything away from my life except the most basic elements of myself and start over. There's no better place than New York City to reinvent yourself, and the solidness that was Willy could not have been better timed at that point in my life.

I think it was George Carlin who said he never really understood prayer. He said when people pray, they basically are just telling god all the things they want. He said it would make more sense if you told what you wanted to someone like Joe Pesci, because Joe Pesci seemed like someone who could get things done. I don't pray and I don't know Joe Pesci, but I'll tell you what, Willy knows how to get things done.

When the Red Cross message came through about his mom dying, Willy was granted emergency leave to return to the United States. Normally the trip from Iraq to the United States is this three-day ordeal, but Willy managed to do it in twenty-one hours, despite numerous obstacles. Here's the compressed version of the story:

Willy pulls a guard shift from midnight to 3:00 a.m. Goes to bed but can't sleep, so watches *Die Hard*. Falls asleep around 5:30 a.m. Is woken up at 6:15 a.m., told that the Red Cross message has come through. Catches a ride to the Balad Air Base at 9:30 a.m. Sits in traffic as an enormous convoy slowly makes its way through the gate. (Think traffic jams suck? Try being stuck in traffic worrying about being blown up or shot.) Finally makes it to the airport, but the base gets hit with mortar fire, impacting right in front of him near the airstrip. His flight indefinitely delayed, he makes friends with some pilots and plays a game of whiffle ball with them while they wait for air traffic to be restored. Mentions his predicament, which is overheard by a lieutenant colonel. Next thing he knows, he's on an empty C-17 by 2:00 p.m. with some pilots bound for training in Germany. (He was supposed to get a flight in the morning to Kuwait.) Lands in Germany at 6:30 p.m. The logistics rep tells him he can catch a flight to JFK in the morning. Screw that. Notices some soldiers on their way to Atlanta for R&R. Unsurprisingly, he talks his way onto the flight, but is told he'll have to pay his own way to New York. Right, whatever. Is told to check in at 3:00 a.m. Drinks three German beers, returns to his room to shower and get ready, but is more drunk than expected and instead passes out on the bed. His infantryman's internal alarm clock goes off and he wakes up on the floor at 3:45 a.m. (he does this for some reason when he's drunk—sleeps on the floor). Freaks out, runs to the terminal but finds to his relief that boarding doesn't begin until 6:00 a.m. Notices he's hungover. Gets on the flight and sleeps through most of it. Once in Atlanta, uses his Jedi gift for bullshitting to convince the Delta ticket guy that he was supposed to be on a flight to New York. The Delta guy diligently finds a "fund code" to pay for the flight. Visits the USO in the airport. He's still wearing body armor, so attracts a lot of attention. Patiently answers questions from well-wishers despite a splitting headache. Has a conversation with a Special Forces guy who says twelve-month complacency-inducing deployments are too long. At the ticket counter, is upgraded to first class (bear in mind that he never paid for this flight). Has a stiff Jack and Coke and passes out in the plush leather seat. Lands in New York and from the airport goes straight to the hospital, where his mother nearly goes crazy when she sees him.

Just before the transfer of power took place in Iraq, we had a very big operation planned in the small town where we worked. One of the most powerful men there was a cleric who lived in a mosque in the center of town. He had ties with Al Qaeda and pulled a lot of political weight in town. I don't know all the details about who he was and what he had his hands in, but I know he was considered a "high-value target" and had to go. This was the guy we had hoped to nab from one of the town meetings, who never showed, so it was decided that we would raid the mosque in which he lived.

This operation was by far the biggest thing we'd been involved in on this deployment. There were a few homes in town that were going to be raided at precisely the same moment that we'd perform the raid on the mosque. Willy's platoon would do one of the homes, and it was my platoon's job to do the mosque, but eventually the raid itself was given to Special Forces. This was a bit of a disappointment, but I suspect the politics of the situation were a consideration. The raid was actually performed by the Iraqi National Guard, a team trained by Special Forces, with only a few A-team guys actually taking part. My platoon was given the task of providing a cordon for the mosque, which basically means preventing anyone from leaving or getting near the mosque during the raid.

I don't normally get very nervous before operations, but this one was a recipe for disaster. There was a lot of suspicion that enemy activity would increase as the transfer of power neared, and I couldn't imagine the townsfolk taking too kindly to us barging into their mosque in the center of their town. In this case, the raids would take place about an hour before dawn. That way the streets would not be crowded, and if things got funky, we wouldn't have to wait long for daylight. When we heard that the raid on the mosque was going to be done by the ING, we all collectively groaned. Most all the ING soldiers we'd seen were such utter shitbags (the platoons we trained were actually half-decent), the idea of a complicated raid being performed by them was completely preposterous. In the mission briefing, when we were told that an ING team was doing the raid, we were advised that their faces would be wrapped. This is a key bit of information because normally we are told to shoot people carrying rifles who have their faces wrapped. Then the rumor got started that the guys doing the raid would actually be Army Rangers dressed to look like ING. That way, the spin on the story could be that the raid was done by Iraqis, not American infidels ignoring the transfer of power and hell-bent on soiling sacred places of worship.

Once all the vehicles and units were staged early in the morning prior to the mission, I took a walk to the truck the raid team was on to see if they really were Americans dressed up to look like Iraqis. But, alas, they were all Iraqis. I wasn't sure if that was a good thing or not.

Then I took a walk over to Willy's vehicle. He was with Cesar and a few other guys I knew from our original unit in New York. I have to admit that it makes me jealous when I find him bullshitting with the guys in his platoon and I have to step in like some fucking outsider because I'm in a different platoon. Normally he and I were inseparable, but our commander made it a point to put us in different platoons when they made up the platoon rosters before our deployment. At first I thought that maybe this was a good thing, to let us "grow" separately with different soldiers under our leadership, but I've since changed my mind about that, and I'm just plain resentful that I finally got to go into combat with Willy and had to be in a different platoon from him. Anyway, I forget what we talked about, but when I left to go back to my vehicle he told me, "See ya later, little buddy." For years it would drive me up a wall whenever he called me "little buddy," like I was some sort of subordinate to him. But when I finally told him I hated it, he told me it was supposed to be a *Gilligan's Island* reference. After thinking about this, I realized that it was pretty goddamned funny. After all, his resemblance to the Skipper and mine to Gilligan were somewhat uncanny. I don't mind it so much anymore.

Once all the vehicles left our base, it looked pretty impressive. Normally when we go out on missions, we usually take between four and eight vehicles. For this operation, we had an absurd amount of firepower with several dozen vehicles. We rolled out with Abramses, Bradleys, more Humvee gunships than I could count, five-ton trucks full of additional dismounted guys, along with Apaches and Kiowas as overwatch. Most of the brawn that tagged along was for in the event that things went sideways, à la *Black Hawk Down*.

Once we came to the town, each team of vehicles broke off in different directions. My platoon was going to approach the town from a small dirt road off the highway, but we got a little lost trying to find the turn, something that really sucks when you have several vehicles all following the same lead. I was thinking that if we couldn't do something as simple as find the right turnoff on the way to the raid, we were in for a world of hurt once things actually got more complex.

Synchronization among all the teams was an important aspect of this undertaking, and we were a few minutes ahead of schedule, so we quietly parked all the vehicles on the dirt road just outside of town. We could see the mosque's minaret, only a few hundred meters away. I was pretty amped, and having to wait gave me time to think about all the things that could go wrong. I thought about a mob of people with torches and pitchforks blocking the road. I thought about IEDs exploding beside us on the way in. I thought about all the homes clustered around the mosque crammed full of women and children and the men who all had AK-47s under their beds. So I did an idiot check on my rifle to make sure there was a round in the chamber. Checked my Aimpoint to make sure I could see the red dot through my night vision (which appeared green). Checked my night vision to make sure it was mounted securely on my helmet. Put my hand where I had the 40mm illumination flares in my vest, then where I had the high-explosive 40mm grenades—although the two look completely different, you wouldn't want to mix them up and load HE when you wanted illumination. I visualized exactly how I'd load a round into the tube. I visualized changing magazines. I visualized a man on a roof pointing a rifle at me. I visualized putting the green dot on his chest and squeezing the trigger.

Two minutes out. The vehicles started up and we made our approach into town. There were more trucks on the roads in town than I expected. There were a few men here and there doing god knows what at this time of day. The area around the mosque was clear—no legion of activists performing a human shield sit-in, no candlelight vigils, no platoon of Sadr's men. My Humvee stopped next to the front gate of the mosque and I dismounted along with Kirk and Whiskey. The three of us crept down the tight alley adjacent to the outer wall of the mosque, our sector for the duration of the raid. I peeked into a window of a home and saw six people sleeping side by side on the floor. The alley opened up to the left. I scanned around the corner. Multiple doors, multiple windows, an area around the wall to the left that I couldn't see behind, two spaces between buildings I couldn't see down either, a half-stripped car. The buildings in front of us had two levels, and each level had a roof. The alley continued between an apartment complex and another house. To our right was the back door out of the mosque courtyard. We were to kill or capture anyone who might try to engage us from any of these buildings, anyone approaching through the alley, or anyone fleeing out the back door. For three guys in a small alley, this was a total shit sandwich. With my thumb on my weapon's safety, I scanned door, window, door, window, roof, door, roof, window, alley, roof, door.

Then *CRASH!* A Humvee rammed the front gate of the mosque then pulled back, and the ING team poured into the courtyard. A few shotgun blasts (to breach the inner door), some yelling, then footsteps on the roof of the mosque. I couldn't really watch any of this. All I could do was listen, which can be a lot scarier. A Special Forces guy came out the back door, looked around, nodded to us, then went back in. It looked like the ING guys had gotten their man without incident. So far so good.

Then, not far away, there were a few bursts of automatic fire, and some tracers streamed into the night sky. At first I thought it might be one of the vehicles in the cordon, but it was a little farther away than that. There were a few more shots, then silence. I looked back at Whiskey and said, "Who the fuck was that?" Then I remembered that Third Platoon's objective was in that direction. That bastard! If Willy made contact before me I'm gonna be so pissed. It had to be Willy.

Shit. Since our deployment began, Willy and I have been competing to see who would make enemy contact first. I was part of the convoy that drove up from Kuwait, so I thought I'd win for sure with that movement, but it ended up being a completely uneventful trip.

A minute or two later and we were back in our Humvee and on our way out of town. I was impressed that the raid had gone as quickly and smoothly as it had, and surprised that the target individual had even been there. I had bet Kirk five bucks that he wouldn't be, and when we were back in our seats, he yelled at me, "Ha ha! Pay up, motherfucker!"

There was no word over the radio of any casualties, so none of us knew what the fired shots had been about. Once I finally had a chance to talk to Willy and some of the other guys in his platoon, I got the whole story.

Willy's platoon has a thing for performing breaches on outer gates by chaining the gates to a Humvee and pulling them down. So on this raid, Willy's squad is stacked on the outer wall by the gate, and they've hooked the gate to the Humvee. But this time when they let 'er rip, instead of the gate coming down, the whole goddamned wall came down.

Onto Willy and Cesar. Willy said that he could see the wall coming down on top of him like it was in slow motion, but there wasn't anything he could do. There was no way to move out of its way fast enough. Willy is one big motherfucker, and there isn't much in the way of physical force that can phase him, and his tolerance for pain is completely ridiculous, but he told me, "That brick wall coming down on me rocked my world. That shit really hurt." Cesar is not a big guy but is smart enough that when he stacks, he's right on Willy's ass. Willy says this sometimes really bothers him, to have this little guy basically crawling up his butt when they're on raids, but I can understand the desire to want to be as close as you can to Willy when you know things are going to get hairy.

"Man down, man down!" Willy and Cesar's squad leader was freaking out. Although the wall had rung his bell, Willy managed to summon his retard-strength and force his way out of the rubble with Cesar. When he realized that the "man down" shit was about him, he got pissed and just kept yelling, "I'm good! I'm good!" The body armor we wear can really suck sometimes, but Willy said what really saved his ass were the ceramic plates in the armor and his knee pads. And what saved Cesar's ass was going down next to Willy. Once they got it together, the raid continued, even though Willy said he doesn't remember the next several minutes. Willy's squad leader tried to get him to sit out the rest of the mission, but Willy just kept saying, "I'm good, I'm good!"

Willy kicks in the front door and stumbles in with his team, reeling like a drunk. Once inside, they find a large door that the other team is unable to kick open. "Get the ram!" someone yells. Still pissed about the wall and not about to let some stupid door ruin his flow, Willy runs into it full force with his shoulder, and it bursts open. Willy has been perfecting the one-man breach-entry technique.

After the building was cleared, Willy and Cesar came back out to the front of the house. From the rooftop of an adjacent building, a man fired a burst at them with an AK. Cesar immediately returned fire with his SAW (arguably saving Willy's ass), the rounds zipping off the low wall around the roof and barely missing the guy as he ducked, and Willy took cover behind an outhouse. Since the rounds were directed toward Willy and he didn't want to expose himself too much, he put his rifle over the top of the shitter, Vietnam style, and shot back blindly. Then one of the Humvee-mounted M240s opened up, raking the roof with a stream of 7.62mm. This deterred the guy enough from firing again. Another soldier from Willy's platoon was on the roof of the cleared building. He had clear line of sight to the guy with the AK and looked right at him. Instead of shooting him, he yelled, "Freeeeeeze! Don't mooooove!" The guy then ran across to another roof, dumped the gun, and disappeared into the dark.

A few days later, Third Platoon raided the same house again. The demolished brick wall had been replaced with a spanking brand-new super-strong cinder-block wall. This time when the gate was pulled by the chain, the entire wall came down in one solid piece, missing flattening a soldier by a few inches.

July 10, 2004

UXO, EOD, WTF

There is an incredible amount of unexploded ordnance in Iraq, and the method in which it is discovered varies. A lot of the time locals will report it. Sometimes they'll point it out while we're out on patrols, and sometimes we find cache sites when locals rat each other out. Sometimes we'll find it on our own, either from patrols on the ground or from aviation units that spot it. And of course there are times that UXOs are found the hard way. Not long ago, there were some local contractors on our base cutting steel with a blowtorch. What they were cutting was on the ground, and just below the surface were some armor-piercing rounds. The torch hit a round and it exploded, injuring a few of the men. One guy caught some shrapnel in his neck and was bleeding. Rather than waiting for us to give him a ride to the hospital, he grabbed a cab and caught a ride into Baghdad. (Sometimes Iraqis do some pretty punk rock stuff. Baghdad is a bit of a commute from our base.) Regardless of how the UXO is found, collecting it is usually a matter of the EOD guys driving out to the site, picking it up, and putting it in their truck. Recently, an empty field was discovered to be full of buried UXOs, apparently left there by Republican Guard when they hightailed it out of their camp during the invasion. We escorted EOD to the field. They then dug all the UXOs up with a backhoe. (This is usually when I put a Humvee between myself and the EOD guys. EOD is the only unit that seems to wear the Kevlar groin protection religiously.)

Once EOD has collected enough UXOs, they load them all into a dump truck and we escort them out to a remote area to destroy the ordnance. While they prepare everything, we create a security perimeter around their work area with our Humvees.

On this particular day, the temperature was well into the stupid hot range, and simply sitting in our Humvees while EOD prepared to detonate their stash was incredibly painful. So I took a walk over to the massive pit where they were working to ask them if they could possibly work any fucking slower. When I saw the quantity of explosives they had amassed in the pit, I changed my mind. I told them that I intended to bust their balls for working so slowly, then I told them that on second thought they could take all the time they wanted. A lot of the stuff they were handling looked unstable as hell, and I didn't want to be anywhere near it. On the walk back to my Humvee, I noticed something smoking. Like an idiot I walked toward it and realized that it was an artillery round with its ass end on fire. I didn't know what the hell to make of this, other than the fact that it was probably dangerous. I later found out it was most likely a white phosphorus incendiary round. It scared the shit outta me. I ran (sorta for my life) back to my Humvee and backed it way the hell away from the flaming ordnance. That's how hot it was: shit-spontaneously-combusting hot.

July 16, 2004

APACHE DOWN

Today we got a call to help recover a vehicle that had run over a land mine. This is the first land mine I've seen detonated in the traditional running-over-it method. Sometimes tank mines are used in IEDs, but they are usually rigged for command detonation. In this case, the mine was a type that didn't really contain or create much shrapnel, so these guys lost a tire on their Humvee and that's basically it. No one was hurt.

On the way back to our base with the disabled Humvee, we got a call that there was an Apache down. We were all like, "What? Apache down? Are you kidding me? Is that supposed to be some kind of joke?" But apparently it was real. It was frustrating as hell because we were the nearest unit to the Apache, and not knowing what the situation was exactly, we assumed the worst and wanted to get there as soon as possible. But we had a tow truck with us carrying this stupid blown-up Humvee, and couldn't move very quickly. We finally managed to pass the tow truck off onto another unit that responded, and we moved out to the site of the crash.

Once we'd made it to the crash site, we found both the Apache pilots, and they were fine. One immediately started telling us about how someone on the ground had fired a rocket at them, and when they did the evasive-action thing, they ran into some high-tension power lines. They definitely clipped some power lines, two different sets to be exact, but no one seemed to buy their "guy with a rocket" story. I felt pretty bad for these guys, especially when the brigade commander flew in wanting to know what the hell had happened to one of his birds.

The power lines tore the bird up a bit, doing damage that the recovery guys said would cost about twenty million dollars to fix. Ouch. After night fell, the Apache was carried back to its base by a Chinook.

August 5, 2004

"NOBODY FUCKING MOVE!"

You know that scene in so many bad movies where the car is teetering on the edge of a cliff and everyone inside freezes and tries to find a way safely out without tipping the balance of the car and causing it to go over the edge? I can now (kinda) add that to my list of unbelievable things I never thought I'd ever experience. Out on patrol last night, we're driving beside a large canal on a small dirt road when suddenly—*BANG!* —we hit a large outlet from the canal that juts out into the middle of the road. This is just one of the things that can happen when you drive with the lights off, night-vision goggles or not. Almost half the Humvee was hanging over the edge, but we weren't quite to the "teetering" point. Regardless, once we came to a complete stop, and since I was sitting in the seat at the opposite end of the balance point, I actually had to stop and think about whether or not I should get out. It was a major canal and if the Humvee flipped, everyone inside would almost certainly drown. Hell, even without being trapped in a ten-thousand-pound armored vehicle, the body armor we wear alone would cause you to sink faster than Jimmy Hoffa in cement shoes. Thank god we weren't going very fast. All I want is to die in a cool way, preferably when I'm really damn old. Drowning in some shitty canal in this dumb country is not cool.

I Still ♥ Dead Civilians (Well, These Aren't Quite Dead)

One of my battalion's responsibilities is to patrol a large segment of an oil pipeline. The pipeline runs through an area where there's a whole lot of nothing. Just flat dirt from horizon to horizon. Why anyone would live out there is beyond me, but there are a few shitty little houses here and there.

Last night my platoon ran a patrol along a segment of the pipeline. The mission was simple. Drive out to the pipeline at night, park the Humvees, a few guys dismount from the vehicles and walk a few miles, then the Humvees pick them up and we drive back. Our platoon leader explained all this and what we would do if we were to encounter the evildoers who like to attack the pipeline. Then he said, "Look, guys, we all know the chances of us actually catching anyone out there is, like, zero. The only chance of us getting shot at out there is if there's some farmer who thinks we're cattle thieves, and we'll probably just end up wasting his whole family. But that's okay. Whatever."

So there I am, out in the middle of nowhere, there's no moon and it's dark as hell. We're walking along on the uneven furrows of hard-packed dirt in a wedge formation, trying not to trip while we watch the ground through our night-vision goggles. I have Cesar on one side of me and Orlando on the other, both of them with SAWs. There are a lot of dogs that roam around these areas, and there were about half a dozen going berserk barking. It's pointless trying to achieve any kind of stealth through noise discipline when you have a pack of dogs announcing your position to the world. I could tell that Cesar was nervous about how close one of the dogs was getting to him, and Matt even pulled out his pistol. Then in the distance I heard someone whistle loudly. The dogs stopped barking and scurried away. That was nice, I thought, These dogs must belong to this guy who has gotten them to shut up and come back to the house.

Then I heard a familiar metallic sound. *Kuh-chunk.* I looked over toward the sole structure in this absurdly empty land of dirt and I could barely make out someone in a white man-dress holding a rifle pointed up diagonally. I knew what was coming next. *Boom!* The muzzle flash and the bang were not quite simultaneous. He was probably 150 meters to the left of us. I went down to one knee and started deliberating whether or not I wanted to shoot back. I knew most likely this guy just wanted to scare off whoever was lurking around his home, but I thought, Then again, this is the same story we're always told when farmers shoot at us. This thought process went on for about one second, then *Brrraaaaaaappp!* Cesar let off a long burst with his SAW. Then a few other rifles immediately started to chime in. I saw the guy with the gun run around to the back of the house. I thought to myself, Okay, I guess we're shooting. The hell if I'm gonna miss out on this. I rotated Wazina's selector lever from safe to semi, looked through the Aimpoint, put the green dot on the roof of the house, and squeezed the trigger. *Click.* What the . . . ?

When you load and reload the same round at the top of a magazine over and over again, a slight dimple starts to form on the primer from the firing pin hitting it slightly each time it's loaded. I guess when the dimple gets deep enough and the firing pin hits it for real, it may not be enough pressure to ignite the primer. Whatever the reason, my first round fired in "combat" was a dud. This was very disappointing, and frankly quite frightening. I assure you this will never happen again. I charged another round, aimed at the roof, and fired. I have to admit that it really felt good to finally shoot.

Cesar was really going off with his SAW. I yelled to him, "Don't shoot at them!" At the moment I didn't know how to best explain to him that I wanted him to shoot, just so long that it wasn't actually *at* anyone. I didn't believe the guy with the gun was much of a threat, and I didn't want to kill him per se, but I saw no reason not to suppress him. I continued to fire rounds into and over the roof of the house. I noticed that most everyone else's tracers were also going over the roof. I don't know if this is because they were thinking the same thing I was or they just didn't know how to shoot at night very well. When it's dark and you don't aim properly, your rounds always tend to go high, it's a known fact. Anyway, this shooting the roof thing felt really stupid, so I scanned for a better target. The windows? No. The car? No, no one's trying to use it and no one's even standing anywhere near it. The tractor? No. Goddammit, there's nothing worth shooting! I put a few more rounds into the roof, then the lieutenant called a cease-fire.

The lieutenant yelled to me, "Fire an HE!"

I thought to myself, HE? Are you kidding me? Isn't that a little overkill? So I yelled back, "HE?"

"No! No! Illum! Illum!" he yelled back emphatically.

Oh, illum. Okay, that makes more sense. Shit, I thought he said HE. I called back, "Illum comin' up!" loaded an illumination round into the 203, and—*Doonk!*—fired it into the air. *POP.* As the flare ignited and hung in the air, all the nothing in front of us became more visible.

The lieutenant again calls to me, "Start bounding your team!" From here we performed a textbook example of clearing an objective. The two teams bounded one after the other toward the house. My team moved to a flanking position as overwatch, and the other team cleared the house. By then the vehicles had moved up to our position. I then moved my team, and we cleared the remainder of the property while trying not to get gored by the bull in the backyard.

There were four men, one AK-47, and a ton of women and children. Apparently Allah didn't will any of the bullets to hit the family that night (thank god), except for a few fragments of one that struck one of the young men in the chin. He bled on his man-dress a bit, but he was fine. We seized the rifle, but we didn't detain anyone.

The scene was the same as it always is when we raid homes: The men were fairly collected, the oldest woman wept, wailed, and beat herself, and the young boy was ecstatic at the sight of soldiers. I took pictures of all the men. Then the youngest boy tugged on my sleeve. He didn't want to be left out; he wanted to have his picture taken, too. As I pointed the camera at him, he did just like the men had and he tried to put on as serious a face as possible. After the picture was taken, he went back to hyperactively running around like he was at Disneyland.

We then gave them a box of MREs, a box of bottled water, and tried as hard as possible to emote, "Sorry we almost wasted your family. Please take this gift of food and water as a consolation."

August 18, 2004

The Cutest Girl in Qatar

In retrospect I'm not sure if I would have been better off going to Man Lake. It's not like you have a choice when you're sent on a four-day pass whether you'll go to Camp Chili's, in Qatar, or to the resort in northern Iraq known as Man Lake (but sometimes also called Dick Island). During the orientation that preceded the few days I'd spend at Camp Chili's (actually named something completely forgettable), I was given a map of the base with very little actual information on it. You aren't allowed to make notes on the map, nor are you allowed to write down building numbers for fear that if an annotated map fell into enemy hands, the enemy might be able to mount a coordinated attack once he knew which building number went with which rectangle.

Impressively, the base in Qatar is built entirely around a Chili's restaurant. This is where soldiers on pass end up eating almost every meal. But just as the lingerie section of AAFES shopping catalogs sent to soldiers in the Middle East are devoid of any actual photographs of non–burqa-wearing women and are replaced by more empty gray rectangles, the Chili's is devoid of any pork products. Every day a new group of hungry soldiers shows up on their first day of pass. They've been fed canned corn daily for months, like caged veal. They get off the shuttle bus singing, "I want my babybackbabybackbabyback ribs," only to sit down at a table and open a morbidly abridged menu and proclaim, "No ribs? Are you shittin' me? And what the fuck is beef bacon?!"

Adjacent to Chili's is a good-size pool, surrounded by an eight-foot-high brick wall. This walled-off area is part of a small campus of buildings, all of which are surrounded by a high chain link fence with armed guards acting as sentinels at the sole entrance to this complex that sits at the heart of the post. The guard duties at the entrance are performed by an alternating roster of unbelievably sloppy-looking overaged contractors with hillbilly accents and missing teeth and overzealous underage fresh-faced pogue Army privates who think that obstinately standing in my way as I approach the gate is good soldiering. There's only one entrance into the inner sanctum of the walled Chili's/pool area, and even that entrance is obscured by another wall, making a T-shaped infiltration route. Once within the wall, the pool acts as a water obstacle, preventing a direct approach to Chili's from the entrance and forcing any would-be attackers to file around the pool and through all the deck chair obstacles, another tactical genius stroke. Central Command is located at Camp Chili's (seriously), and I suspect that the super-secret entrance to their massive underground command center and Bat Mobile garage is through the kitchen's walk-in freezer. I did not note any of this on my map, however.

The thing about going to Qatar on pass is you can count on seeing females who will also be on pass. Forget what you may think about pass being a time to relax, because it simply isn't. It's just as stressful as not being on pass, because all that matters is getting laid. At Man Lake, the other "resort," you may be able to have your own room in the hotel, which is a godsend in that you'll finally be able to masturbate in privacy, but instead of the male-to-female ratio being twenty to one, as it is at Camp Chili's, it's something more like a hundred to one. At Camp Chili's you're allowed three beers a night, but at Man Lake alcohol is prohibited. At Camp Chili's you can go off post for certain activities, but at Man Lake you wouldn't want to go off post even if you could because you're still in Iraq. Keep in mind that while at Man Lake you still have to have your chemical suit with you in the event of a chemical weapons attack. I've always found it difficult to relax while wearing my protective mask.

When you leave to go on pass, you're stuck with whoever else from your base happens to be going at the same time. If you're lucky, you'll get put with cool guys, but you could always get stuck with total assholes, too. I lucked out by getting put with guys who were really easy to get along with. The senior man in our group was a fair-skinned, red-haired E-6 mortars sergeant named Earl, from another one of the infantry companies. There was this enormous Puerto Rican kid named Karl, who was a Bradley gunner, and also with us was one of the fuel specialists, a slightly off-center eccentric named Lawrence.

Before flying to Qatar, we had to spend a day at the Balad Air Base, where soldiers can in-process, withdraw cash, and take care of whatever tasks they need to before flying to their pass destination. This base is probably the biggest one in Iraq and considered a luxury resort by Iraq base standards. But the real crown jewel of the base is the Olympic-size swimming pool—easily five times the size of the pool in Qatar. When the Army first took over the base, the pool was a shambles, and from what the contractor who oversaw the reconstruction project told me, there was actually a broken jet in the empty pool when they found it. The four of us agreed that our main goal of the day was to spend as much time as possible at the pool after our errands were done.

First we went to Finance to get some money. Apparently the process of visiting the Finance Department can get really ugly, so there are a lot of very explicit rules to follow to keep the procedure organized should the place get swamped with people with welfare checks or whatever. Take this form, sit here, fill the form out, stand up, walk here, wait, when called upon walk here, stand, wait, place the completed form on the counter, recite the alphabet backward, perform the Masonic handshake on the Resuscitation Annie lying on the table, then wait for further instructions from the Führer. Never being very good at this sort of thing, I botched the whole process repeatedly. There was no line this day, so I walked right in and said, "Excuse me, I—" "Did you fill out a form? Go outside and fill one out!" the sergeant major behind the desk bellowed. So I retreated back out the door, took a form from the stand, sat down, and filled it out. Then I walked back inside, and asked, "Okay, so I have a question—" "Wait outside until you're called!" he barked. Um, okay. So I stood outside the door. "Next!" he called. Trying to start over, I said, "Hi. I was wondering—" "Take off your sunglasses!" der Führer demanded. By this time, my cage was fairly rattled, and I felt like I was at boot camp again, a feeling I don't particularly care for. Because of my strict patriarchal upbringing, I sometimes have a tendency to switch into submissive mode when I encounter authoritarians, and when I catch myself doing it I get really pissed at myself for letting another quasi-father figure subjugate me. A lot of things ran through my head that I wanted to say. "Sergeant Major, I've been in the Army for thirteen years and I've been on this shitbird deployment for nearly a year. We're both NCOs and I don't appreciate you addressing me like I'm a basic trainee. So why don't you take this form I've so diligently filled out, put your little scribble on it or whatever, and send me on my way. And I'm gonna leave my sunglasses on and you're gonna like it, got it? Oh, and by the way, fuck off, you fascist fuck." I didn't actually say this, but instead I compacted it all into one handy phrase as I removed my sunglasses. "ROGER THAT." I handed him my form, he scrutinized it with a look on his face like I had filled it out with a pink crayon, he stamped it, then handed a stub to me and told me to see the sergeant at the payment window. "ROGER THAT," I told him again, hoping he'd clearly understand that I was saying, "FUCK YOU!"

I took the stub to the window, and the young black female sergeant asked me warmly and very deliberately, as if it were the first time she had ever asked it, "So how are you doing today, Sergeant?" I wanted to say, "Are you fucking kidding me? How am I doing? Your boss just made me feel like a piece of shit and now you think it's funny to rub salt in my wounds under the guise of friendly euphemisms? You're either more sadistic than your Nazi boss, or you're fucking retarded!" But she smelled good, and it made me wonder what her hair would feel like touching my nose and lips, and if she was the kind of girl who would let me stick my finger up her big ghetto booty while I made out with her. She had long painted nails that were nowhere near being within military regulations, but I imagined no one in her chain of command ever said shit to her about it because they were all trying to get into her pants, too. I can't stand nails like that, but I didn't really care, I'd just make her wear boxing gloves while we had our Oreo sex. I was already mentally through the first several weeks of the Marquis de Sade's 120 Days of Sodom with her before I caught myself and realized I hadn't answered her question yet. "I'm good," I replied perfunctorily. As she counted the money, a guy in civilian clothes on the other side of the wall from her teased her about something. She giggled because of him, and I felt a slight pang of jealousy. I hadn't even started chatting this girl up yet and I was already being cock-blocked. Damn.

The next stop was to get a few items at the PX and then to get a haircut. None of us four had swim trunks and there were limited options on the racks, so we actually had to coordinate who was going to buy which trunks so that we wouldn't be caught hanging out at the pool wearing the same shorts the way old married couples wear matching jogging outfits. Among us, we bought all the trunks available, some nonmatching towels, some slightly cold Gatorade, beef jerky, magazines, DVDs, and an assortment of other useless garbage, as soldiers always do when given the chance.

With bulging plastic shopping bags in tow, we made a stop at the barber in the same building. I had already administered a self-inflicted haircut two days earlier, something I'd mastered over the years as a way to save money and time and to prevent any girls from ever wanting to talk to me, but I accompanied the other guys as they got theirs cut. When Karl took off his uniform blouse in preparation to get his hair cut, my mouth literally went slack. He stood a good six foot three, about an inch taller than me, and the muscles of his back hung off his neck and shoulders like enormous cuts of beef brisket. His shoulders and arms were constructed entirely of long, lean muscles that were casually draped around his skeleton with an elegance of form that inspired in me acute feelings of fear and envy. The outlines of all this muscular mass tapered down into the waistline of his pants, making his torso into a trapezoidal shape, the likes of which I've seen only on He-Man action figures. It's moments like this in a heterosexual man's life when there is a staggering confusion that comes over him as he struggles to determine if he wants to *fuck* this guy or *be* this guy. But more important, how was I going to get any girlie attention when I was anywhere near this steroidal monster? Then a brief moment of pride came over me knowing that this guy with the amazing body was my buddy; he was with *me*. Wait, this is all totally gay stuff to think. I don't want to think this! Yuck! I repulse myself! But, Jesus, look at those muscles! I have to look away. I don't want to get caught staring. I can't help it, I have to look. Jesus! Would you look at that! Then I caught a glance of my reflection in one of the barber's mirrors, and I was brutally reminded that I have a fifteen-inch neck and that my six-foot-two frame weighs only 165 pounds. I sat down in one of the chairs in the waiting area and hoped that no one would notice the skinny kid in the Army uniform.

Once we had finished all the small tasks and had lunch at the dining facility—which if I had regular access to it would have caused me to become the fattest skinny guy in the Army—we headed over to the pool with our new towels, flip-flops, and trunks. None of us really knew our way around this base, and it took us a few trial runs to learn how the shuttle buses worked. But we finally got the hang of it after accidentally circumnavigating the base once. As we got off the bus and approached the pool area, we saw everyone standing around under cover of the building where the changing rooms were, as if waiting for something. We were really confused, so I asked one of the guys standing there, "So what's the deal? Why is everyone standing here?" The guy looked at me as if I were playing with my own feces while asking him this apparently ridiculous question, and it took him a moment to reply. He said to me without trying at all to disguise his feelings of contempt and incredulity, "We're at yellow." Oh, we're at yellow. Okay. That clears it right up. Thanks for the info, dick. So I asked the guy standing next to him, "What the hell does, 'We're at yellow' mean?" This guy was a little more patient and told us, "There was a mortar alarm. We won't be green until they give the all-clear." Okay, this made a little more sense. This base gets attacked often enough that they have a PA system to sound an alert when they receive incoming. I would later learn that the pool was one of the most desirable targets for mortar attacks because of the density of people. As far as terror goes, a mortar round landing in the pool would be pretty damn effective. The thought of bikini-clad bodies exploding everywhere and filling the pool with blood and gore is truly terrible. Not long ago a rocket was fired at this base and it struck the front of the PX, killing a few soldiers. Other than that particularly lucky shot, everything else has usually been a miss. What's ironic is the locals in my area believe that my base is protected by a force field (I'm not kidding), so they never attack it, but regardless, we have to wear full body armor all the time when we move around on the base. But this base gets hit with mortar fire multiple times a day, and nobody wears body armor and they actually run around wearing boonie caps instead of helmets. One time the laundry service got hit with a mortar, and soldiers didn't get their laundry back for over a week as there was a temporary strike when the surviving launderers refused to work.

By the time we changed into our new bathing suits, the "all clear" siren had blown. We shuffled over to an available white molded-plastic table with matching white molded-plastic chairs beside the pool. Once we sat down and got settled, we were able to properly survey this incredible landscape. Tits and ass *everywhere*. Out of respect for this truly holy moment and each other's madness-inducing starved libidos, we sat reverently enrapt for twenty minutes without uttering a word, our heads on swivels. Normally this scene would not have been that big a deal, but right now every athletic short-haired bull dyke and half-cute girl with small breasts and a huge ass was a priestess at the

Church of the Holy Need to Hump. And we weren't the only ones to sit and stare at the young girls like perverts on a park bench. Just outside the fenced-off area of the pool was a single-story building that some local laborers were listlessly working on. One of them, an Iraqi man with a red-and-white *shemagh* wrapped around his head, stood on the roof of the building, giving himself an unobstructed view of the pool. He was holding a rake and was as expressionless and unmoving as the farmer in *American Gothic*. I looked upon the land and saw that it was good, but I could only imagine what it must have been like to witness this scene through his eyes. The devil on my shoulder and the infidel on his gave each other enthusiastic high-fives.

Once we were able to return to earth and we started moving again, Karl and I hit the pool. There was a high-dive platform where all the guys performed feats of bravery and physical prowess, giving the girls an opportunity to judge who best to sexually couple with next. Karl and I split up and slowly paddled our way around the pool like wandering salmon looking for a place to spawn. Karl managed to get involved with one of the water volleyball games, and I cozied up to a group of girls while plotting a way to work a joke about "water sports" into conversation, just to see if they'd get it. Eventually Karl and I both got out of the pool, and we took turns testing our mettle with the high dive. After falling from the top platform for what seemed like a day, then falling a little more, I finally hit the water at which point half the pool was immediately forced through my nose. Once I decided I was done with all this tomfoolery, I made my way back to my chair and chillaxed for the next several hours, subsisting on nothing more than pure brainstem functions.

Without a doubt, the most relaxing and enjoyable part of the four-day pass, ironically, was the time spent at this pool before the four days in Qatar actually started. It felt good not to be wearing body armor and to finally let our skin see the sun. We all got pretty burned, but we really didn't care. And it was great to indulge in some quality people-watching. I was impressed by how bronzed some of these soldiers were. The pool itself was of immaculate construction, obviously not of Iraqi design. There were a few Americanized-looking Polynesian lifeguards with longish hair who, I had to deduce, had been contracted to work at the pool. They had the typical careless swagger that I suspect is taught at lifeguard school and they all had incredibly cute girls fawning over them. I had to hate them by default, knowing that they were hurting my chances of hooking up with a girl if they were skimming off the topmost layer by moving in on the girls who were both hot enough and confident enough to spend time at the pool in bikinis.

For soldiers who are traveling in and out of Iraq through this base, there are a series of tents with cots where you can crash before your flight leaves. It's not uncommon for flights to be delayed for days at a time depending on what the enemy activity is like. Days with a heavy rain of mortar fire and scattered showers of small arms fire could delay you a day or two. But on light days, you generally only stay overnight. After we were done with the pool and got our fill of chow, we retired to the tent we were assigned for the night. During our trip to the PX, I had perused the sizable and utterly predictable DVD section and purchased every single thing worth half a damn (*The Station Agent* and *Twin Peaks,* season one) and was looking forward to watching one of them before I went to sleep. DVDs are the primary source of entertainment for soldiers in Iraq, and we are generally able to buy pirated copies of just about anything from the local merchants. These discs are usually of exceptionally poor quality, and it seems that all the ones I ever buy crap out just before the end. I was excited to finally watch a real DVD all the way through, but my laptop battery died just before the movie finished. Figures. I'm really bad at remembering chronological details and usually forget how movies end anyway, so whatever. I put my laptop back in its battered Pelican case and called it a night.

Within the first few hours of meeting Karl, he told me in his heavy Puerto Rican accent, "Look, I just want to get laid. I don't care what she looks like. So if we meet some girls, I'm not even going to try for the cute one, I'll take one for the team and I'll fuck the ugly one." I couldn't believe what I was hearing. I knew if we met any girls they'd want him before me, but he seemed pretty dedicated to the idea of wanting a sure thing. I wasn't about to argue with him seeing as how this only benefited me.

The following morning after breakfast, we were consolidated into a large tent filled with benches, where we sat while we waited for our flight. Everyone who was going to Qatar was in the tent, and this would be the only time we'd all be in the same space. Karl and I slowly wandered around the tent, checking out all the girls. The eyes of every male soldier were darting around like sharks who smelled seal blood.

Statistically speaking, if you're going to get laid on pass, it's going to be with someone who is part of your group. I knew there would be soldiers already in Qatar and more soldiers showing up once we got there, and some of them would be female, but four days is not a lot of time to make something happen. Any female soldiers already in Qatar would have guys who had been working on them for at least a full day already before we got there, and any female soldiers who showed up with groups after us would also come with guys who had already been working on them since they left Iraq. You have to work fast; if you are to make any decent headway, it all has to start in this tent.

The average female soldier, by most standards, is totally unfuck-able. Take for example Lynndie England of Abu Ghraib fame. She is one fugly girl, but by Army standards, she is completely average. And when you haven't seen girls for as long as we hadn't, your standards shift dramatically. After you've been in combat for a few months, you'll find you're wearing beer goggles you can't sleep off. Additionally, you'll feel like you're thirteen years old again with regard to your sexual response to even the slightest flirtation. Once when I had to visit the medics on our base to get an anthrax booster shot, one of the female medics was lying on a cot on her back, napping. I had never found her attractive, but she was thin and petite. She was a few years older than me, and the skin of her face looked leathery from being in the sun. Her uniform blouse was off and she was in her T-shirt. Her breasts were small, and the outline of her bra was visible. Because she was lying down, the way her breasts sat made it so I could imagine how they must feel. Her trousers had ridden up and were tight at her crotch. While still lying down, she looked at me and smiled and said, "Good morning, Sergeant Hartley." I got an immediate erection.

The few girls in the tent who were the least bit cute already had guys chatting them up while small groups of other guys were standing nearby like vultures waiting for the jackals to finish. In the corner of the tent was a girl lying on a bench, resting. It was her hair that I noticed first. Beautiful blond hair combed neatly to one side across her forehead and tucked behind her ears. Her skin was perfect and smooth, her brows plucked into delicate arches. I couldn't find a single flaw—high cheekbones, a small straight nose, beautiful dark lashes, innocent pink lips curled slightly upward at the corners of her mouth. She was breathtaking. What in the world was *this* girl doing in the Army?

Karl and I sat down on a bench and discussed our options. There were actually a few fairly cute girls, and a few who were cute enough. But the blond-haired girl was far and away the most attractive. Karl said he didn't care who we talked to, whatever we could work out would be fine with him. I had to make a decision. I didn't know what the story was on the blond-haired girl, but it was obvious she was going to be getting the most attention for these four days and would therefore be the most difficult. Assuming sex was the priority, it would make more sense to shoot for one of the okay-looking girls, or better yet find one slutty enough willing to fuck more than one guy during the four days and just get in line. But I was already completely taken with this girl; I didn't even want to think about fucking slutty girls. I was instantly infatuated. I wanted to know her, I wanted to make her laugh, I wanted her to fall in love with me. I was already imagining what our kids would look like, what it would be like to wake up next to her for the rest of my life, how we'd still take romantic vacations to Paris after the kids had grown up and moved out of the house. It wasn't often I felt like this about a girl I had seen only once and whose name I didn't even know. I had to remind myself that I hadn't seen a girl this beautiful since I'd been deployed, and my twitterpation was unoriginal, predictable, and obviously irrational. But so what? What if she actually was an incredible person? What if we fell in love? It's not like getting laid by some stupid Army slut was in any way meaningful, why not just go for the gold and put all my energy into trying to get to know this girl? Besides, by taking the long shot, even if I failed miserably, I would at least be trying to accomplish something I could feel good about. Getting back from leave and telling the guys in my platoon I got my dick sucked behind a dumpster would be good for a laugh, but what the hell was the point?

The flight to Qatar was a drag. We rode in a C-130 and sat in the jump seats I remember sitting in as a paratrooper with my unit in Utah. The webbing seats are uncomfortable as hell, but they made me nostalgic. I really missed jumping. I fell asleep and when I woke up my ass was so asleep my balls were numb.

Once we landed, we had another orientation to attend, followed by a long bus ride to the base where we'd stay for the four days. When we finally got to the base and were assigned a place to sleep, it was well past midnight. The following morning there was one final orientation. After the orientation, they asked for those who had diarrhea not caused by nervousness to give stool samples.

For the rest of the day, Earl, Lawrence, Karl, and I all hung out together. We spent most of the time going from shop to shop, buying as much junk as possible—cheesy commemorative T-shirts and baseball caps, DVDs, CDs, magazines, toiletries, pizza, soda, junk food, Tijuana-quality Middle Eastern trinkets.

Karl and I were getting coffee from the coffee shop on post when the blond-haired girl walked in with another girl. Oh my god, she looked so good, even better now that she was in civilian clothes. They weren't with anyone else—the perfect time to talk to her! I totally froze up. I had absolutely no idea what to say. There was no use even trying to talk to her now. When I get like this, when I start giving a shit, it all goes straight to hell. I lose the ability to talk. I'm awkward, uncomfortable, and completely unfunny. I knew that if I tried to talk to her now all I'd do was make an ass of myself.

I was stirring milk and sugar into my coffee, hating myself for being such a loser, when I noticed that Karl had started chatting up her friend. She had short dark hair and looked a little butch. My heart was racing and I wanted to pee my pants. I finished stirring my coffee and casually walked over to where he was. They were speaking Spanish. She was Latin, too, and Karl had used this as an excuse to talk to her and bust out some of his Puerto Rican charm. I did my best to appear aloof and uninterested. He introduced us to the girls. The butchy one was Jess, and the blond-haired girl's name was Christine, but she said everyone called her Chris. The four of us talked for a few minutes, but mostly all I did was smile and laugh, trying to hide the fact that I was totally crushing on Chris. Karl and I said goodbye, as if we had something better to do, and walked out of the coffee shop. Somehow Karl had used his magical Latin powers and gotten them to agree to meet us for dinner later that night at Chili's. I wanted to kiss him. God I love Puerto Ricans.

Before we left for dinner, I took a shower and hung my favorite shirt—a black button-down with blue stripes—on the curtain rod to steam it. I was really excited. With Karl as my wingman I was golden. He seemed to get along pretty well with Jess, which would make it easy for me to talk to Chris.

Earl and Lawrence came along with us to dinner too. Lawrence looked like he was in his mid-thirties. He was a really nice guy with a quirky personality who still lived with his mom back home. He was a fuel specialist and he ran the fuel point where we would gas up our Humvees when we returned from missions. As we walked to the shuttle bus, I asked him how often soldiers said to him, "Lawrence? Lawrence what? Of Arabia? That name sounds like royalty. Are you royalty? Do you suck dicks? I bet you could suck a golf ball through a garden hose. I don't like the name Lawrence. Only faggots and sailors are called Lawrence!"

He laughed. "No. No one's ever said that to me. What's it from?"

I was shocked. "What's it *from*? Jesus god, man! It's from *Full Metal Jacket*! You've never seen that? I don't know if I can trust a soldier who's never seen *Full Metal Jacket*." His personality was fairly submissive. He spoke in a meek voice and was endlessly polite. I recalled him telling me how he lived with his mother and sisters, and the thought of him not having seen the movie started making a little more sense.

We got to Chili's a little early, so we sat down and made sure there were two places for Jess and Chris to sit. After a few minutes the girls showed up, but they went straight to a booth and sat down with some other guys! Unbelievable! I was totally crushed. Earl and Lawrence didn't give a shit, and Karl just laughed at me. Lawrence said, "Why don't we just sit at that table over there next to them?"

"Fuck that," I said. "Fuck her. She knows we were going to meet her here. I'm not gonna go beg for her attention. Those guys look like tools anyway."

"Damn. She's lookin' good tonight, too," Karl remarked, rubbing salt in the wound.

"I'm not even gonna look over at her. What do I care? Let's just eat." I was surprised at how much of a baby I was being. I knew I was being absurd, but I couldn't make the childish feeling go away. I tried my best to enjoy my non-pork dinner.

Before we finished eating, Chris and Jess came over and sat down next to us. The guys they were sitting with were from their unit. This made me feel a little better. Chris and Jess were fuel specialists, like Lawrence. We talked for a while and agreed to meet up later that night at the bar.

There are two "bars" at Camp Chili's. Both are basically just auditoriums that serve canned beer out of buckets of ice. Since there's a three-beer limit per soldier per night, you have to present your ID to a cashier, who sells you a ticket. Your ID is then scanned and entered into a computer system that is networked between the bars, foiling soldiers from getting three from each bar. One bar plays popular music and is where the younger soldiers hang out. The other plays classic rock and is where the hillbillies and middle-aged soldiers go.

When we got to the bar, Chris and Jess were already there. As to be expected, there were a bunch of guys hitting on Chris, but they were sitting at a table big enough for the four of us to still be able to sit down. Lawrence, god bless him, sat down on the other side of Chris and just started talking to her. Since they had the same job, he found all sorts of things to converse with her about. Between

Lawrence's innocent fearlessness and Karl's intimidating physique, the other guys scurried away after a few minutes.

We stayed at the bar long enough to drink our three beers. In addition to being a fitness nut, Chris was from Michigan and a huge sports fan. This sucked. I'm not exactly a gym rat and I know exactly jack squat about sports. After the bar we went to the coffee shop. Chris told us, without much conviction, that she was married. Her husband was a soldier as well, a National Guardsman also in Iraq, but part of a different unit. There were occasions when his unit would get fuel from her base—the only time they ever got to see each other. The longing, the sense of danger, the fleeting moments together—it had all the elements of a heartbreaking romance. I wasn't buying the story about their being married, but it was obvious she was in love with the guy and I'm sure they intended to get married, probably once they got back. I knew she was cool with me to the extent of having spent as much time with us as she had, but I sensed that telling me she was married was a load of shit and just something she told guys to make it as clear as possible that she wasn't single. I had to realize I didn't stand a chance with her, but it didn't matter. It was incredibly cool just to be spending time with someone as sweet and attractive as she was. We had almost nothing in common and she was in love with someone else, but now I was fascinated by how utterly wholesome she was.

Karl and I spent a day off post with a retired sergeant major who worked at the base and sometimes took soldiers around to see the sights. Qatar is one of the cleanest places I have ever been to and in a lot of ways it was very beautiful. But mostly it was depressing. We were in the capital city of Doha, where everything was sterile and Westernized. We drove around for a while, looking at the bay, the amir's palace, and one of the new opulent hotels. The sergeant major kept asking us if we wanted to go to his apartment to have lunch and maybe to take a nap. We politely declined the offer. I chose to ignore the nap comment. He asked us where we wanted to eat lunch. He said, "There's Applebee's, Fuddruckers, Bennigan's, Ponderosa. McDonald's, too." (Applebee's? Are you fucking kidding me?) Again, we politely declined and asked him if he could take us somewhere locals ate. He was reluctant at first, but then took us to a wonderful little hole-in-the-wall place with tasty traditional Middle Eastern cuisine. Doha is a phenomenally boring city, so after lunch we went to the mall. Were it not for all the men wearing man-dresses and the signs on the stores in Arabic, we might as well have been in the suburbs of New Jersey. All I wanted was to experience Qatar and the Middle East in a traditional way (that didn't involve combat), but I finally gave up once I saw Starbucks. At this point I knew resistance was futile, so I ordered a latte.

For the rest of the time we were in Qatar, Karl and I didn't see Earl or Lawrence that often. Lawrence was the kind of guy who liked to do his own thing and was content spending time alone, while Earl spent most his time at the massage place on post. The girls who worked there were all Filipinas hired by KBR. In fact, almost every worker on post was from the Philippines, apparently a favorite place for KBR to recruit.

In the evening, Karl and I would usually see Chris and Jess at the bar. It was virtually impossible to have conversations with Chris for more than a few minutes before some guy would interrupt. She was always polite and would humor these fools more than she had to. But I couldn't really complain, she humored me, too.

There was one group of guys in particular who Karl and I came to particularly hate. The ring leader was this arrogant prick with reddish-blond hair. He was the handsome one and he looked like a cut-rate

Craig Kilborn or Josh Homme. He always had two cronies with him. One was shorter and had large features—big nose, fat lips, big eyes, thick eyebrows. The other was tall and gangly with a droopy eyelid and was always completely expressionless, like an executioner on quaaludes. They were perfect henchmen. The three of them would stroll around the base with the swagger of combat grunts, each with a lip full of tobacco.

The cut-rate Kilborn and his two droogs spent as much time vying for Chris's attention as I did with Karl. It was always a battle to see who she'd spend the most time talking to. I had to give the guy props for one thing though. Even though he was hitting on a girl, he would still have dip in his mouth and spit into an empty soda bottle partially full of what looked like diarrhea.

On the last night before we had to return to Iraq, the battle for female attention was at its peak. It was everyone's last chance to find someone to fuck. Even if you found someone to hook up with, there was still the problem of finding somewhere to do the deed. There were bomb shelters at various locations on the base constructed of sandbags that were popular with those unafraid of animalistic copulation in the dirt. There were sometimes pillows or blankets already there from previous tenants. Sometimes, if you were lucky, an empty room could be found. I saw a mattress on the floor in a janitor's closet.

I had made the conscious decision to put all my efforts into the cutest girl in Qatar—one that I don't regret—but it didn't work out, and now it was *way* too late to try and find sex. What few girls there were had their pick of the litter and had long ago paired off with the Adonis of their choice. Mr. Strawberry Blond had set his sights on the same girl I had and didn't seem willing to take no for an answer too easily. He was one of the alpha males of our rotation and probably could have scored with most any of the other girls, but he didn't want to settle, either. I can't blame him for trying.

He talked to Chris for a good forty-five minutes. Afterward, she came back to where Karl and I were hanging out with Jess. Karl probably would have slept with Jess if given the chance, but she wasn't into guys. The three of us talked about this for a while. (In Spanish, Jess confided to Karl how incredibly hot Chris was naked.) The fact that she couldn't serve openly was ridiculous. There will be a day (hopefully soon) when the military will finally realize how embarrassing, stupid, and wrong their policy on homosexuals is.

The four of us hung out the rest of the night. When the bar closed, we went to the coffee shop and talked while we shared pizza. The blond prick and his two shitbirds were never far away, but they eventually gave up and walked back to the barracks. I have to admit this was enormously satisfying for my ego. It was a hot night, hotter than any in Iraq (if you can believe that), but a nice way to end our time on pass.

We flew back to Iraq the next morning. Once we got back, everyone was in the big tent again, sitting on benches, but this time we were waiting for transportation back to our various bases. The vehicle that would take Karl, Earl, Lawrence, and me showed up, and the driver told us to hop in. Chris was sitting on the ground, leaning against the tent post. Even in uniform she was heartbreakingly beautiful. I knew I'd probably never see her again. All I could do was look at her one last time and take a mental picture. Her hair was pulled up like it was the first time I saw her—off her collar (per military standards), combed to the side, and tucked neatly behind her ears. She looked up at me, smiled, and waved. I waved and said goodbye.

THREE DAYS OF COMBAT

Day One: Operation Salt Lick

Iraq has one major highway, and from it there are two roads that run to the logistical support base in Balad. These two intersections are an obvious favorite spot for insurgent assholes to attack coalition convoys. This day's attack was a remote-detonated car bomb. Basically a few 155mm artillery rounds were primed, connected to a cell phone as the trigger device, then placed in a car parked off to the side of the road at one of the intersections. In this kind of attack, someone will watch the intersection and when the next tasty target drives by— *Boom!*—mayhem ensues. This car bomb was an old Volkswagen taxi. There is a spot near this intersection that has become a small landfill due to the fact that Iraqis seem to love to dump their garbage *wherever*. When the taxi blew up, the landfill ignited delightfully from the explosion, filling the area with a hazy drift of smoke to make the whole scene a bit more apocalyptic. Nice touch, insurgent assholes!

This convoy was mostly Air Force, and one of their guys took some shrapnel to the shoulder from the blast. Our medics fixed him right up and called in a medevac chopper. His wound wasn't life-threatening, and he ended up being okay. And as per usual, this attack made a big mess of the highway and injured more innocent bystanders than coalition forces, both of which are more of an inconvenience to Iraqis than anyone else. Keep up the good work, insurgent assholes!

Later that night . . .

Our battalion commander had an idea. We would put a cargo trailer by the side of the road and kill or capture anyone who tried to steal it! Brilliant! And this goatfuck . . . er, genius plan needed a good name. So he chose to call it . . . OPERATION SALT LICK! The trailer was driven to the designated spot on the highway and left just off the side of the road as if it had been abandoned. Sometimes when huge convoys have major problems, trailers or vehicles that they cannot recover in a timely manner will be abandoned. By the time someone can be sent back to recover them, the Iraqis will have either stolen them or picked them totally clean like vultures. You almost have to forgive the little thieving bastards because they consider this completely acceptable behavior, like picking up a nickel from the sidewalk. The battalion commander and his flunkies then waited in the bushes (or whatever) for the evildoers to take the bait.

One thing you can count on in Iraq is for Iraqis to take anything that isn't cemented into the ground, even huge tractor trailers. Sure enough, once it got dark some people with a truck pulled over and tried to hook the trailer up. That's when the battalion commander and his boys popped out of the shadows and nabbed the would-be thieves! Ha HA! It was at this point that my platoon, still on QRF, was called to the scene to help with security and the removal of the detainees. So far things were going brilliantly, just as the battalion commander had planned!

But this was where it all started to go a bit sideways. First, there was some confusion about getting a truck there to tow the trailer back. Once a truck was finally sent down, it turned out to be the wrong kind of truck and would not be able to tow the trailer. Then there was some more discussion as to what *kind* of truck was needed and if one was available. No one could seem to figure out where the truck was that had originally dropped the trailer off. Then a brilliant sub-plan was hatched to send a truck that could tow the thieves' truck, which in turn could tow the trailer.

After a few hours of unbelievable nonsense and some hilarious radio traffic about the different makes of military tractor trailers, their capabilities, and their current availability to us, plus a decent helping of the battalion commander gnashing his teeth, we were finally ready to leave.

While the battalion commander was on the radio trying to find himself a truck, we did some traffic stops. Any chance we get to pull vehicles over, we take advantage of. The more random the occasion, the better. The less predictable we are about traffic stops, the more effective of a deterrent it is for insurgents who use the highway to transport their evil wares. And you won't believe some of the stuff we find this way. On this particular night, we found a car that had a large cardboard box completely stuffed full of stacks of Iraqi cash. The car's occupants claimed the money had something to do with the Olympic soccer game. (Winnings perhaps?) There was nothing else incriminating in the car, and the passengers didn't seem very scumbaggish, so it was decided to just let them and their money go. Our night was already deep into the realm of clusterfuck and no one was eager to fill out all the witness statements that this amount of cash would require.

Yo yo yo. One good thing did come from this day. While we were medevac'ing the wounded Air Force guy, I found on the road part of the grill with the VW emblem on it from the car bomb (quite a ways from the point of detonation), which I now sport as a necklace, ghetto-fabulously.

September 7, 2004

THREE DAYS OF COMBAT

Day Two: The Head

One of the best things about taking something over is you get to change things. Like when you marry a girl, you get to change her last name, or if you buy someone's house, you get to turn the spare bedroom into a game room. Sometimes the changes made are good, and sometimes they aren't. Sometimes the changes take, and sometimes they don't. When my battalion moved into forward operating base Lion, north of Baghdad, the first thing we did was change the name to FOB O'Ryan. Our unit is known as Orion, but it was decided that we would use the spelling O'Ryan, the name of the decorated officer our unit was homophonically named after. I prefer the Greek over the Irish, and this book is my fiefdom, so I am hereby changing the spelling of our base to FOB Orion. Isn't arbitrarily wielding power fun?

FOB Orion needed a lot of work and most of the physical changes we made in the time we were there were pretty good. For example, plywood shitters with poop barrels that needed their contents burned regularly were replaced with a port-o-john-type service. Sometimes the Iraqis who ran the port-o-john service and their families would be killed by insurgents, and it would take several days before replacement workers could be found, so we'd have to go back to shitting in burn barrels temporarily, but regardless, the port-o-johns were an excellent change, a definite improvement. Another improvement was the gym that KBR, a subsidiary of Halliburton, built for us. They took an old ammo bunker, cleaned and painted the interior, installed air conditioning, put down a sectional rubber-mat floor, then brought in some exercise machines and free weights. It wasn't fantastic but it was pretty damn decent. And it only took them six months and eighty thousand dollars to build. I am not exaggerating when I say that my platoon could have done the job in two days, five at the most, absolutely free of charge. After all, it was the soldiers who wanted the gym, not the overfed, beer-bellied KBR guys. But, hey, who am I to say how American tax dollars should be spent? Thank god for combat zone tax exclusion, because if I were paying taxes I would be *pissed*. Speaking of which, have I ever mentioned the KBR truck drivers I talked to who said they didn't know of one single driver who didn't fudge the hours they reported having driven each month? I love how the truck drivers would confide things like this to soldiers.

The most vital changes to FOB Orion were those that involved security. When we first came to our FOB, a smallish but somewhat sprawling collection of concrete and earth bunkers, there were a handful of insurgents who were living in and operating out of one of the remote bunkers. Concertina wire and berms were put up around the entire perimeter of the base, and the unexploded ordnance that littered the place (a draw for insurgents because this is what they use to make their improvised explosive devices) was cleared.

After the basic level of perimeter security was improved, there were ongoing changes to base security, most really good and some a little more superfluous. The buildings that housed our tactical operations center (TOC) and the administrative and logistics office were strong, but not what one would consider "hardened." Tall concrete barriers were eventually put up around these buildings, a definite improvement. In an effort to further protect these buildings, a massive berm was installed in a location between the front gate and the TOC. I don't know the exact reasoning behind the installation of this monstrosity of earth we dubbed "Hunter Mountain," a name in honor of the battalion moniker of "The Hunter," the professional title of the legendary Orion, but it just seemed a little excessive. If the insurgents had tanks, they would not have been able to directly attack the TOC because of Hunter Mountain. In that sense, it was a successful improvement. But the insurgents *don't* have tanks, so it was just a big dumb pile of dirt with a wall of dirt-filled barriers across the top like the Great Wall of China.

Another security-related aspect of our base that was constantly being improved upon was our front gate area. There were barriers forming entrance and exit lanes for both civilian and military traffic. There was a parking lot and a vehicle search area. There was a machine gun bunker that overlooked it all but that had nearly useless fields of fire. No one could seem to come up with a solution for the area that was truly effective, but there were certainly plenty of attempts to do so.

The most recent improvement was to completely change the entrance and exit for military traffic. Long, serpentine Jersey barriers were installed, with the entrance and exit lanes located in the almost exact opposite places as they were before. In my humble opinion, the change was stupid and unnecessary, but again, not my call. It was dumb to start with, then changed to dumb-but-different.

The day this change quietly went into effect, my platoon had QRF and CASEVAC duties. Since the job of CASEVAC is to act as an ambulance escort, anytime there was a routine need to transport a patient, be it a soldier or a local, from our base to the hospital at the major base ten minutes up the road, CASEVAC would be called. We had a routine patient transport to perform late in the afternoon, so when the time came, we mounted up and met the field litter ambulance at the front gate.

Once we got the go-ahead and we left our base, the lead vehicle noticed that the barriers outside the gate had completely changed. A dump truck with a load of dirt in it was being used as a makeshift outer gate to deny entry to any would-be attackers who might consider bursting through the entrance to our base with a car bomb. But with the new configuration, it was not immediately clear if the truck had to be moved for us to leave. The guys who were supposed to man the truck weren't always *in* the truck. So the fact that there wasn't anyone in the truck at this time made the exit route even less obvious. There were multiple paths ahead of the lead vehicle, so the driver of that vehicle chose the one that he thought was the exit. Once our four-vehicle convoy had snaked a good way down this tight path, it became apparent that it was a dead end.

The guys who were supposed to be in the dump truck had returned (from wherever) and were getting ready to pull the truck back to reveal the new exit, but our vehicles were in the way. None of us knew yet what the proper way to exit the base was, but we knew that the way we had chosen was definitely the wrong one. For at least one full minute everything was frozen. We could have asked the guys who worked the gate which way we were supposed to go, but we didn't have direct radio communication with them. To talk to them, our conversation would have to be channeled through the TOC, and no one was going to be the one to ask, over a channel everyone listened to, where the exit was. I reached into my assault pack, rifled around through my extra magazines, 40mm grenades, and classic Nintendo cartridges, found *Blind Man's Humvee Tetris*, blew out the dust, popped it into the Nintendo entertainment system and hit Start.

First, someone who thought they knew how to get out started to move his Humvee. Then someone else would think they knew how to get out or just wanted to follow suit and would start to move *his* Humvee. The guys in the dump truck, knowing their tardiness was the catalyst for all the confusion, just wanted to move their vehicle so they could look like they were doing something. I was in the fifth and last vehicle, so I started to back up my Humvee. Everyone in my truck had a perfect view of the madness but we hadn't the foggiest idea where to go either. There was just enough room to move the vehicles around to make it even more of a confused mess. A vehicle would move, it wouldn't work, another vehicle would move, another would move out of the way, and so forth. Guys got out of vehicles, some tried to take charge, there were short discussions and arguments, guys got back in vehicles. This was repeated several times. It eventually became apparent to me that the exit was behind the dump truck, and the only way we were going to be able to leave in the correct order was to completely back up all the vehicles one by one, let the dump truck move, then drive off the base like we knew what we were doing. Someone else figured this out too and called over the radio to back up and continue to back up. Back in line and with the exit before us, we hit the road, fifteen minutes from the time we had initially left. Thank god this was only a routine CASEVAC mission and not an urgent one.

On the way to the base up the street, the lead vehicle noticed some debris in the road. It was nothing big, nothing that could really be used to hide an IED, but we stopped briefly to check it out, cleared some of it out of the way, and drove on. Once we got to the big base, the ambulance dropped the patient off at the hospital, then we escorted the ambulance back to our base. The entrance for military traffic was now in a completely different place, but the lead vehicle found it on the first try. Good job!

Later that night after a shift rotation, I was on QRF. We drove to chow, ate some yummy pork and/or chicken, then drove back to the staging area. Back in my hut, I put my laptop on my cot, sat on my small folding stool, and popped in a DVD. I've never watched so many DVDs in my life as I did in Iraq. Honestly, any soldier who complains about their quality of life in Iraq needs to spend a moment and consider the days of pre-laptop combat.

I think I was near the end of watching *The Rules of Attraction*, a film I can't seem to get enough of, when *BOOM!*, one of the loudest explosions I've ever heard shook the hell out of my hut. Then

BOOM!, a second explosion, no more than a second after the first, both of them powerful enough that I felt them in my chest despite being in a heavily sandbagged shelter. I thought to myself, Holy fuck! That was fucking close!

I ran outside to see if anyone knew what was going on. Sometimes EOD performs detonations and the word doesn't always get to everyone. But they almost always do this during the day, never at night. Most everyone at the staging area was outside now, trying to find out what the story was. I saw my platoon sergeant. I said to him, "That was fucking close. You don't think it's EOD, do ya? Was there a net call about EOD activity?".

"No way that's EOD," he said. "That had to be just up the road. Gotta be one-fifty-fives, at least two or three each."

Radio traffic on the battalion net was uninformative. No one seemed to know what was going on. Truthfully we didn't need to know details yet; it was fairly obvious that they were IEDs, it was now just a matter of waiting for the TOC to send us on our merry way. Everyone started getting geared up and ready to roll. Then *BOOM!*, there was a third explosion, just as massive as the first two. Someone yelled, "Oh, we're *definitely* going now. No fucking doubt *that* was an IED. What the fuck is the TOC waiting for?"

We weren't going to wait any longer for word from the TOC, so both QRF and CASEVAC mounted up and drove to the front gate. EOD and the medics in their FLA (field litter ambulance) met us there.

The radio squelched, "Hunter QRF this is Hunter X-ray. Over."

My platoon leader didn't waste any time with the radio banter. "This is Hunter QRF. We're leaving the gate at this time. We have with us CASEVAC, EOD, and an FLA. QRF out."

Blind Man's Humvee Tetris. Player Two up.

There was a different crew of guys in the lead vehicle this time from the earlier CASEVAC mission, and they made the exact same mistake trying to exit. They drove down the dead end and stopped. There were some attempts to turn, back up, turn again, and so forth. It was an almost perfect repeat of what had happened the first time. Someone got out of a vehicle, ran up to the lead vehicle, pointed, shouted, pointed, shouted, then ran back to his vehicle. It still required a bit of orchestration to unfuck, this time in just a little over five minutes.

As we rolled out the gate, more details came through. There was a huge convoy up the road that had been hit with the IEDs on its way to the base. At least one vehicle was down. A portion of the convoy didn't stop after the attack and continued on toward the base. A unit of engineers from our base who were out when the attack took place were already on the scene. There were wounded soldiers, and the engineers needed CASEVAC at their location immediately.

This was no small convoy. It was all military vehicles, probably twenty or thirty, mostly the multiuse heavy-duty trucks that can carry fuel or large equipment. Near the front of this row of vehicles were two craters, side by side, in the dirt shoulder of the road. Not far from the first two was a third crater. A few hundred meters ahead were more vehicles from the convoy, along with the vehicles of the engineers who had responded. CASEVAC and the FLA continued on to the vehicles ahead, while QRF and EOD stayed back with the other group.

Once we dismounted from our vehicles, I noticed that one of the heavy-duty vehicles had driven off the road and was several hundred meters away. There was a small fire in the cab of the vehicle, and it looked like some of the engineers were working on putting it out. A lot of the truck drivers had dismounted and looked wide eyed and shocked. Transportation guys always look like this, but tonight it was especially pronounced. The stereotypical Army truck driver in Iraq is a middle-aged National Guardsman with a mustache, a sizable gut, a hillbilly accent, a disheveled uniform, and a too-big helmet with a loose chin strap, crooked and cocked to the side. These guys looked like confused children, holding their aging M16s, a weapon that looks like a silly oversize toy in comparison with the tidy little M4s we carry. I always felt bad for transportation guys. They have just about the most dangerous job in Iraq because they are the easiest and best target for IEDs and they are the least suited to deal with them. Their vehicles lack decent armor, and by virtue of their job they lack decent combat training, but they have to deal with situations that would be stressful for a well-armored, well-trained tank platoon.

While EOD investigated the craters, the dismounted QRF guys spread out and did a quick sweep of the area. An M16 was found on the street in three pieces, covered in blood. In the same area were a few bloody chunks of flesh. These items were policed up and put in plastic bags. EOD was able to confirm that each detonation was approximately four or five 155mm artillery rounds and were remotely detonated by a wire that ran into the huge open field next to the road.

CASEVAC was working on a wounded soldier and had more information about what had happened. The first two blasts went off directly in front of one of the trucks in the convoy, sending huge chunks of shrapnel through the windshield. The driver was killed instantly. We later learned it was his rifle we found in pieces. The truck commander (TC) of the truck was badly wounded, but still alive. The blast had broken both her arms, both her legs, and her jaw had been blown off. I inquired later about her jaw having been "blown off," but couldn't get anyone to elaborate on what that meant—if her jaw was literally removed or just merely destroyed. Didn't really matter. She was fucked up.

Once the driver was killed, the truck swerved off the road and drove far into the open field. It coasted for approximately four hundred meters before coming to a stop. Once the vehicle stopped, the wounded TC got out and proceeded to crawl back to the road *with her weapon*. She carried her rifle almost the entire way, but finally ditched it in the field after a few hundred meters. She made it all the way to the road, where the engineers found her.

Back at the craters, several of us from the QRF spread out across the road and started to trace the wires into the field. The terrain there was flat, irrigated farmland. There weren't any crops being grown at the time; the ground was a series of hardened dirt furrows. Walking across it wasn't easy, and in the dark it was virtually impossible to run across. It's times like this when your typical infantryman yearns desperately for the enemy. I wanted there to be an engagement but knew that if we came under fire now it would be a very difficult movement. The insurgents know they can't beat us in a force-on-force kind of fight, so the chances of anyone still being at the end of that wire were slim. Regardless, we continued to follow the wire, getting farther and farther from the vehicles.

The wires used in attacks like this are usually communications wires, the kind used for field telephone systems. This particular wire was just like all the rest we'd found attached to IEDs, most likely an American wire, the kind that come on big spools. And this one was long. *Really* long.

After following the wire for approximately eight hundred meters, we came to a dirt road that ran alongside a deep canal. There was a defilade between the road and canal. The canal was old and dense with overgrown rushes. Even if you stood a short distance away during daylight hours, it would not have been apparent that there was a depressed area on the other side of the road. The wires ran over the road, then ended in the defilade.

This canal road ran at an angle to the main road where the convoy was, but didn't connect for more than a kilometer away. In the other direction, the road connected with a few other dirt roads. At eight hundred meters from the main road, the enemy was outside the range of all our weapons except the machine guns. But given the lack of visibility, hitting targets in the open at that distance would have been nearly impossible, let alone ones that were behind cover and that could easily have blended into the background of the rushes. The ground was too rough for a Humvee to approach directly, and even if a Humvee in the convoy knew exactly where the enemy was and knew exactly what roads to take to get to them, the enemy would still have plenty of time to escape with multiple routes of egress. In short, this was the best enemy firing position I had ever seen.

I was with my lieutenant and the EOD sergeant as we searched the area around the firing points. The EOD sergeant explained that given a wire of this length, a car battery or something larger would have to have been used for there to have been enough charge for detonation. We found no discarded battery, and since it was highly unlikely that the person or persons who made the IED went far with it on foot, we figured that there was most likely an escape vehicle. There were two firing points, one where the first two wires ended, and one a short distance away, where the third wire ended. There were at least two distinct sets of footprints clustered around these areas, one of which looked like soccer cleats. This was a shoe print we agreed we had never seen before. In fact, I don't recall having ever seen any kind of cleats worn by anyone in Iraq. Most insurgents wear the same bullshit shoes everyone does, crapola plastic sandals or blown-out loafers, shoes that make Payless look like Bruno Magli. But this guy knew he might have to run through dirt and he came with the appropriate footwear. Whoever these guys were, they seemed to know what they were doing.

My lieutenant and I, along with the rest who had ventured out this far, continued to follow the dirt road to see where it led. Normally when it's this dark and we're this close to our own base, we're able to get the mortar guys on base to fire illumination rounds over our position. But because of certain restrictions involving the possibility of aircraft being in the area that night, we were denied an illumination mission. Frustrated, my lieutenant asked me if I had any illum rounds for my 203. I told him I had three. He said, "They won't give us illum? Then we'll make our own fucking illum." Our biggest concern at the time was the field on the other side of the canal. It was impossible to see anything out there, even with night vision, and there was at least one building we wanted to have a better look at. I opened the tube of my 203, pulled a long white illumination round out of the pouch on my left leg, loaded it in, closed the breech, guesstimated the best direction to fire in relation to the breeze, removed the safety, and *Doonk!* fired the round into the night sky. *POP.* Suspended from its small parachute, the round ignited and cast a faint white light everywhere. The illum rounds are not that big, but on a night as dark as this one, they make an enormous difference. After it burned out and fell to the ground, my lieutenant told me to fire again. This one didn't hold in the air quite as long and fell to the earth before it finished burning. He told me to fire my last one, so I did.

Our platoon sergeant was out in the field with us and came jogging up to our location. He looked pissed. He explained to the lieutenant that things going "pop" right now were not a good idea when there was an entire convoy of jittery truckers with guns still on the road. The lieutenant conceded.

When we came to the end of the canal, we saw where the road connected with a few others. We had been following the cleat prints and saw that they ended at a set of tire tracks in the dirt. We realized at this point there was nothing more worth looking for, so we began the walk back to the Humvees. The second flare I shot a few minutes before had started a small fire in the brush, which provided some illumination, making the walk back a bit easier.

By the time we got back to the Humvees, my small brushfire had become an enormous brushfire. I could imagine some poor Iraqi farmer waking up in the morning to find half his field charred black, and to be completely honest, I couldn't have given a shit. A part of me wishes every time we were attacked we'd just kill the ten nearest civilians. Sooner or later the math would start to sink in with the insurgents and they'd stop attacking us, right? Then I remembered that in most cases, anytime there's an attack, a handful of civilian bystanders are usually killed anyway, either from shrapnel or crossfire, so I suppose there would be no real need to implement the Overwhelming Math doctrine.

The rest of the convoy had finally moved on, and those of us who had followed the wires were gone for quite some time, so I figured once we got back to the Humvees we'd be leaving shortly. But back on the street, I noticed everyone searching for something along the sides of the road. I walked up to Dan, who had been in the vehicle ahead of mine, and asked him, "What are we looking for?"

"A head."

"What?" I half laughed.

"A head. We're looking for a head." Dan loved to explain things without explaining anything.

"Um, okay," I responded blankly. "Whose head?"

More impatient than I think he had the right to be, Dan looked at me and said curtly, "The driver. They can't find his head. We're looking for it."

I think the next thing I said was "You've got to be fucking kidding me." For the briefest of moments I wanted to think this was funny. I immediately thought about the movie *Eight Heads in a Duffel Bag*. If we couldn't find the head, would we try to find another head? God knows there's plenty of them in Iraq these days. But this moment passed quickly. What if someone who didn't care for Americans in this area—i.e. anyone we weren't handing a wad of cash to—found the head before we did? What if the people who *did* this found the head first? I thought of this soldier's mother. Then it started to really bother me. That was when it really sank in. There was no way to dismiss this or laugh it off. We had to find the rest of this soldier's remains.

The sun had started to come up. This was good, because I knew once morning came we would be able to make a more legitimate and concerted effort to recover the remains. I had been up all night and was exhausted. I wanted badly to go to bed. But I knew that if it were my mother, I'd hope that for her sake those trying to recover my remains would never stop until everything was found. I think we had been searching for a little over an hour when word came down that there were no longer any remains missing. I almost felt disappointed. I wanted to be able to confirm personally that we had recovered everything. I felt so intent about the search and asked why we were giving up. I was told that we most definitely were not giving up; we would have searched all day and all night if it were thought that any remains were missing. It turned out nothing was missing; it just took a while for the hospital to confirm this.

There are two things my platoon never did unless we absolutely had to: talk on the radio and perform after-action reviews. But this time when we all got back to our base, our lieutenant had everyone gather around and we discussed what had just happened. We talked about the driver who was killed. We talked about the incredibly tough female soldier and what she had done. The lieutenant assured us that if anything ever happened to any of us we would never be left behind the way she was by her convoy. We talked about what we did well and what we could have done better. But mostly we just talked and listened to one another.

Three Days of Combat

Day Three: Baby Chickens

When we first got to Iraq, we assumed and hoped we'd be fighting an enemy the way we'd always trained: they shoot at us and we shoot at them. Those who took part in the initial invasion of Iraq got to do this, as did those who were in certain areas such as Samarra and Fallujah. Our area of operations is mostly rural, a little north of Baghdad. After the midway point of our deployment, we started coming to terms with the fact that direct contact with the enemy wasn't going to happen that often, if ever. There have been a few incidents where soldiers in our AO have been shot at, but in most cases it was either farmers firing warning shots at patrols of soldiers, thinking them to be thieves in the night, or other units. There have been a handful of such friendly-fire incidents, which resulted in some really close calls, but thank god no injuries. The farmers aren't always so lucky.

Something that there has never been a lack of in our area, however, are IEDs. Almost every day there is an IED, either discovered by us and then destroyed, or exploded by insurgents. There have been lulls in enemy activity in our area at times, but they rarely last for more than two weeks. The EOD guys have been earning every cent of their paychecks.

In most cases the IEDs are placed somewhere on the main highway, and the attacks usually take place at night. After the first few months we got a feel for the areas along the highway the insurgents liked to use. Our AO has an abundance of vineyards and orchard, and there is an extensive system of irrigation canals. The techniques used to employ IEDs are almost always the same. A wire is run from the IED to a remote location several hundred meters away, usually over at least one major canal. The systems used by the Army to jam IEDs that use radio and cell phone trigger mechanisms must be working pretty well because almost every IED we've encountered is wire-detonated.

With a decent set of data on the locations and times of the attacks, our company has been able to plan feasible counter-IED operations. Our area of operations is huge, and choosing a spot to sit on all night in hopes of running into the enemy is usually a total crapshoot, but it feels better to be *proactive* about these attacks than endlessly *reactive*. Plus, even if we never see a single bad guy on these operations, the time spent becoming familiar with these areas is invaluable. One of the major advantages the enemy has over us with the IED attacks is their intimate familiarity with the areas they are attacking us from. We know the highway as well as the streets in our own neighborhoods— we drive up and down it almost every day—but we don't know a lot of the back roads worth a damn. So given the event where we have to react to a future attack, we are only helping ourselves by becoming more familiar with the areas where these have a tendency to take place.

In the U.S. Army, there is a very specific set of doctrine on how to perform an ambush. These procedures are in many ways unlike any of the other battle drills performed by the infantry. For example, an ambush is one of the few times where you are encouraged to *not* aim. (Apparently this is because it is less psychologically traumatic for the soldier doing the shooting.) Generally speaking, an ambush position is set up along a road or a known avenue of enemy travel, preferably at a bend or turn where a machine gun can be aimed in such a way that it has access to the entire length of the road without the gun's having to traverse much. Positions for individual soldiers are established with very specific fields of fire. Left and right limits are established, usually by putting sticks or stakes into the ground, which physically limits how far to the left and the right the soldier's rifle is capable of shooting. Upper and lower limits are established as well, sometimes by attaching a string between the two stakes, which acts as a guide for the upper limit. These limits are set up in such a way that the field of fire is focused tightly on the specific area of the road established as the "kill zone." Once all the positions are prepared, the soldiers lie in wait for the enemy to come down the road. When the enemy enters the kill zone, the soldier who has been chosen to initiate the ambush will wait for the optimal moment and then will throw a hand grenade, detonate a Claymore mine, or fire the first shot. Once that signal has been given, everyone lets loose with everything they have, firing blindly but thoroughly across their sector of fire. Some guys will fire their weapons on full auto, some will fire on semi-auto, more hand grenades, more Claymores—the idea being to maintain a constant volume of fire without any breaks, even while magazines are changed and fresh belts loaded. This is called "the mad minute." After the order to cease fire is given, the ambush team sweeps across the kill zone. All enemy weapons and equipment are consolidated and destroyed, then the ambush site is left hastily.

We call the counter-IED missions we run "ambushes," but they are nowhere near being textbook ambushes. An area is chosen where there have been attacks in the past, and we look at spots that give us access to nearby roads and intersections. We further study maps of the area, make an educated guess as to which roads a bad guy may use to get to and from a likely firing point, then determine a good place to camp for a while. Jeff says this is called an "area ambush," but what we look to do isn't even that. We will usually perform a movement to and from the place where we want to sit, and would be happy if we made enemy contact during the movement. It's more a matter of looking for a fight than anything. Part typical patrolling, part ambush. I don't know if there's a name for it.

For the first ambush I went on, I was part of a five-man team.

Since the areas these missions were in had a lot of vegetation, we always wore green uniforms and green face paint for ambushes. A team of Humvees dropped several ambush teams off at different locations, then the Humvees were staged at a location several kilometers away. On this particular night we had a short movement to our chosen location that involved crossing a canal. The canal was a typical cement one, about fifteen feet wide with a forty-five-degree slope on each side and a flat bottom. The canal was less than half full of water, but what we didn't plan on was how slippery the sloped sides would be. Once in the water, getting out was nearly impossible. We could have crossed the canal at one of the small bridges, but Jeff, the leader of this ambush team, wouldn't hear of it. If there is water or mud to be crossed, Jeff will find a reason to cross it. He claims it is unsafe and against all principles of the infantry to cross at bridges. He's right, but getting stuck in canals also goes against all the principles I know. Jeff was the first to go in the water, and once he realized how difficult it was to get to the other side, he removed all his gear and body armor and put it on the ground on the other side along with his weapon. He was then able to climb the slope and help the other guys up. While the others were getting help from Jeff, I tried to do this on my own. If someone were waiting to attack us from anywhere along the canal in either direction, now would have been the time and we would have been fucked. I thought of this as I tried to climb the slope. After a few attempts, I finally made it up unassisted and with all my gear on, but I had to use the reserves of energy you only normally tap into when you know your life is in danger. By the time we had all made it over the canal and began the short movement to our ambush location, I was already completely exhausted. I noted to myself that I would never do that again unless I absolutely had to. There had to be a better way.

Our most recent ambush was in the same vicinity as the last, and we'd have to cross the same canal again, but this time we came better prepared. Rubin, one of our platoon's squad leaders, is a master at building things from scrap wood and he made for us a sort of ladder-bridge we could place across the canal. On the night of the ambush, we rode in the back of a cargo Humvee with the "assault bridge," and once the Humvees had dropped us off, we carried the ladder with us to the canal. On one end of the ladder we tied a rope for the purpose of lowering the ladder across the canal. We practiced this a few times before we left, but when it came time to do it for real, we couldn't keep the ladder balanced while lowering it without it falling into the water. I was pissed that we were still having trouble with the whole canal-crossing thing, so I got into the water and set up the ladder-bridge by hand. The team crossed, and I climbed out. At least only one of us had to get wet this time. I wasn't too excited about being covered in slime again, but I refused to let anyone think about using the bridge we had noticed about fifty meters away from us. If Jeff says we're not using bridges, we're not using bridges! If we're going to go through all the trouble of building and carrying a stupid assault bridge—which was pretty damned heavy by the way—we were going to use it, dammit! Once on the other side of the canal, we hid the ladder in the weeds and continued on.

The movement for our last ambush was fairly short, so for this one Jeff had chosen an ambush location well over a kilometer away from where we were dropped off. A movement of a little more than a kilometer is not much of a distance by any standards, but given the terrain we were in and the weight of all our gear, particularly the ceramic body armor we were all wearing, this short walk quickly became excruciating. (I asked Jeff a few days earlier if we could ditch the body armor for ambushes, but he just laughed at me.) The area we were in was a patchwork of vineyards and orchards. All the growth made it easy to conceal our movement but made walking a slow and arduous process.

The vineyards weren't that bad for guys who were really short, but if you were taller than five eight, it was a serious pain in the neck, literally. Taut wires were horizontally strung between the rows of vines, usually at least five and a half feet from the ground, but never more than six feet. In the summer, the vines would grow and create a lush, shady canopy across the wires. But at night, with the diagonal support wires hidden from lack of moonlight and the ground uneven with irrigation furrows, walking through the vineyards was no easy task, especially since night-vision goggles ruin your depth perception. The most comfortable way for me to walk was standing mostly upright with my head bowed, but I couldn't see anything other than my feet when I walked this way. The only way to move through tactically was in a crouch, but given the weight of all I was wearing, I couldn't keep this posture up for more than a few minutes before my thighs started to burn.

We moved at a snail's pace. Jeff was on point, and finding a route that was both concealed, navigable, and not directly on any actual trails or roads wasn't easy. Sometimes we'd go a short distance, realize it was not possible to continue due to fences or foliage, backtrack a bit, then try a different route. We had maps of the area, but they weren't as detailed or as up-to-date as the maps we were accustomed to using in the training areas of U.S. military installations. Also, the scale of most the maps we had were intended more for pilots than grunts. So when routes were planned for missions such as this one, we knew there would be a lot of improvising when it came to actual execution.

We were only a little more than halfway to our destination before a couple of the guys started to complain that they needed to take a breather. I was carrying ammunition for two weapons, being the grenadier of the team, but I had one of the lightest loads. Sean and Jimmy were both carrying SAWs, and Rich was carrying the radio, but we were all just trying our best to keep up with Jeff.

Jeff is a staff sergeant in his late thirties, a heavy smoker, and I don't think he's exercised once since we've been in Iraq. But there is no end to his energy. He's one of those guys who's so ugly he's handsome, like Willem Dafoe or Christopher Walken. He's tall, skinny, and incredibly hairy. His teeth are darkened from his unending consumption of coffee and cigarettes. He always wears black-rimmed Ranger glasses strapped to his face with green parachute cord, the ends of which have been melted to prevent fraying and are knotted in ways that sailors would consider unholy. He's just plain salty. His field craft and technical expertise as a soldier are second to none, something that came from his having spent several years in a Ranger battalion. But what makes me truly love Jeff is the fact that he's just a little bit nuts. In my opinion the best soldiers are the ones who are slightly crazy, guys who can embrace the chaotic nature of soldiering and revel in it. And on this night he was completely in his element.

I ran up to Jeff and asked him if we could stop for a few minutes. He seemed a little disappointed but agreed to take a quick break. I took the radio from Rich, who seemed to be struggling with it. Then, after about three minutes, we started moving again. We had finally made it out of the vineyards and orchards, but then found ourselves wading through dense brush and deadfall. The terrain was at its most ridiculous when we wandered into a grove of tall bushes that seemed to naturally grow in the shape of giant mushrooms. I had to remind myself that this was Iraq, though I half expected to see a talking caterpillar smoking a hookah on the top of one.

We backtracked a short distance and looked for a better way around. Jeff told us to hold our position as he walked over a small hill. As I watched his silhouette disappear over the crest of the hill, Jimmy fell backward and lay on the ground unmoving. I walked up to him and bent down close to his ear. I whispered, "You okay, man?" He looked at me and said, "That's it. I'm done. I can't move. Can we just stop here?" Then I heard Jeff call me on the radio, telling me to bring the rest of the guys over the hill. I called back, "Roger. Be advised codename Jimmy is, um, stuck at this time. We'll be right over. Over." After a little consoling and coddling, I convinced Jimmy to get up, telling him it was only a little bit farther and that I knew he could do it, that he was a big boy and I was really proud of him, that he was doing such a good job and as soon as we shot some stuff and blew some stuff up we'd go back to our bunker and I'd give him a bubble bath. Jeff yelled over the radio, "Get the fuck over the hill now!"

At the top of the hill was the road we were interested in watching. There were a number of depressions that made for decent positions to occupy. It had taken us an hour and a half to move to a location only a little more than one kilometer from our drop point. We were all exhausted. Except of course for Jeff.

In theory, ambushes sound like they could be a lot of fun. But in practice, having to lie in the same spot for hours as quiet and unmoving as possible sucks. And if you haven't gotten enough sleep beforehand, it can be incredibly difficult to stay awake through it. Falling asleep in an ambush position is very bad. So anytime there's been an ambush planned, I've always made sure to get as much sleep as possible the afternoon before the mission.

As we lay in our positions, I felt tired but alert. My job was to keep an eye to the rear of our positions, while the other four guys watched the road. I knew it was highly unlikely someone would sneak up on us through the field I was watching, but I scanned the area actively. From our slightly elevated position, I had a decent view of the area and wished someone with an RPG or an AK-47 would be unlucky enough to happen upon us. It's virtually impossible not to daydream in situations like this, and I did what I could to keep my mind occupied without completely zoning out, so I spent most of my time imagining all the different things I would do in response to different attacks. We lay there in our positions for several hours.

It was nearing time to leave. Our plan was to be picked up by the Humvees at the same place where we had been dropped off. The contingency plan, in the event of an emergency or the need to be extracted immediately, was to run down the dirt road we were watching, out toward the main road, and be picked up where the two roads met. It's standard infantry doctrine to never use established roads or trails as routes for movement, so this plan wasn't going to be executed unless it was truly necessary. But I knew the guys weren't going to want to go back the way we'd come, and, frankly, I wasn't sure it was really worth it.

I was trying to think of a way to persuade Jeff to go with Plan B when we heard shooting in the near distance. More than a dozen shots were quickly fired, all the distinct report of 5.56mm rounds. It was clear one of the other ambush teams was shooting at something, but we didn't know at what. I had given the radio back to Rich earlier, so I was unable to listen to the radio traffic about what was happening. Jeff then told us there was a van that had stopped at the side of the road, directly in front of one of the other teams, that a man had gotten out and appeared to be dropping what looked like artillery rounds on the ground next to the road. Something we've suspected about IEDs is that different people will perform different parts of the task rather than a single person or group doing the entire thing themselves. We guessed that one person dropped the explosives at the side of the road, another ran the wire through the field, then another would explode the IED by connecting the ends of the wire to a battery. Shots fired by the other team were intended to disable the vehicle.

Moments after the series of shots was fired, there was another burst of shots, this time about twice as many and twice as rapid. After listening to the radio for a moment, Jeff yelled out, "They're trying to drive away! Let's go! We're going to intercept them on the road!" We all jumped to our feet and started jogging down the dirt road in the direction of the main highway. After running for only a few minutes, we came to the cement canal, this time several hundred meters from where we'd first crossed it. I could see roughly where we'd been dropped off, and it was depressing to think that we'd just run in three minutes most of the distance that it had taken us an hour and a half to walk. A dirt road ran parallel to the canal, and not far from us was a bridge running over it. The highway was about fifty meters from us. I was in the lead and wanted to get over the bridge, but Jeff yelled for me to wait. We had gotten pretty spread out, and Jeff wanted us to tighten the group up a little before we went any farther.

A few vehicles had gone down the highway over the last minute, but they all seemed to be eighteen-wheelers. We saw another set of headlights coming down the highway toward us. There was no other traffic. I couldn't make out what kind of vehicle it was yet, so I yelled back, "Is this the van?! Is this the van?!" I knew there was a chance that the vehicle had already passed us. Everyone was up to the canal now, and we stood there watching the approaching headlights. I went down on one knee. As the lights got closer it became clear that the vehicle was something that looked like a Volkswagen bus. It was nearly in front of us, and I yelled again, "Is this it?!" All our weapons were aimed at the vehicle, and through my NVGs I could see all our lasers on the van. No one moved or said a word. Half a second passed. Then Jeff shouted, "FIRE!"

I began squeezing the trigger of my rifle as quickly as I could. After the first few rounds I fired, my NVGs inexplicably shut off. I continued to fire, aiming now by watching my tracers as the steady stream of our bullets pelted the speeding van and the road around it. I expended my entire thirty-round magazine at the van as it flew by. It was nearly out of sight now and Jeff was yelling to cease fire. Frustrated that the van was getting away, I removed the safety on my 203, used the Force to guesstimate an angle of trajectory, and—*Doonk!*—fired a grenade, a total Hail Mary. My forty millimeters of high-explosive love disappeared over the treetops that lined the road. It was completely quiet, now that everyone had stopped shooting. That wonderful smell of just-spent rounds hung in the air. My heart was pounding, and I felt an exhilaration like none I had ever felt. I thought to myself, Oh my god, I could do this every day! Then I immediately started to second-guess my decision to fire a grenade, and my moment of ecstasy began to pass. This was the first time I had fired a live grenade in combat. I wasn't sure if I was even allowed to shoot a grenade in a case like this. Fuck, I hope there weren't any houses on the other side of the road. There was no explosion yet. The round seemed to sail through the air forever. Maybe it won't explode. Maybe it was a dud. Maybe no one even noticed I'd fired it. There was still no explosion. Then, *BOOM!* Shit, that was really *loud*. I didn't remember grenades being that loud. Well, maybe in all the confusion no will notice or remember the explosion.

"Oh my god, dude, that was almost the coolest thing I've ever seen!" Sean said excitedly. "Your grenade only missed hitting the back of the van by four feet at the most! If you had hit it, that would've been worth an extra life! That's like getting a green mushroom!" Sean's Super Mario Brothers analogy was making me feel better about the grenade when Jeff came up to me and said, "Congratulations, you've just become a permanent member of the strike team," then he laughed, half maniacally. So I guess the grenade was okay after all.

A minute later, the Humvees sped past us down the highway. It didn't take them long to catch up to the van. The man driving the van had pulled into the driveway of a house just off the highway and went inside looking for help. One of the bullets had hit him in the lower back, barely missing his spine, and there were a few wounds to his legs, either from bullets or bullet fragments. Matt was with the Humvees that night, and began giving the man aid for his wounds while they waited for CASEVAC to arrive. How the people in the house were involved, or if they knew this man at all was unclear, but it was decided they would all be brought in just to be sure.

While the situation with the people and the wounded driver was being handled, the van was inspected. Much to everyone's astonishment, the entire cargo area was found to be stacked from floor to ceiling with crates of baby chickens. No explosives or any IED-related materials were found.

Back at the canal, our team and the other ambush teams met at the extraction point, where we waited for the Humvees to pick us up. Those guys had their hands full at the moment, so it gave the rest of us a chance to talk. We should have continued to be tactical, sitting silently behind cover and concealment while we waited to be extracted, but given all that had just happened, noise discipline went out the window. Our biggest concern was being shot at by passing convoys, who would not be expecting to see friendly troops off the highway in the bushes, so we all sat in a depressed area near the canal, which provided us with cover from the road.

I sat down next to Ray, who had been part of the team that fired the shots intended to disable the vehicle. He was complaining about how he thought it was stupid to try to disable a vehicle with 5.56mm rounds. We discussed the series of events from the time he shot at the van to the time my team shot at the van. He said, "Yo, when I heard that 203 go off, my dick got hard."

One of the unfortunate things about being an infantryman, and therefore at the bottom of the information totem pole, is it's not always easy to follow up on events to learn of their outcome. It was a few days before we learned the story behind the chicken van and what the man driving it was doing that night. From our perspective, all we saw was a man stopped at the side of the highway in the middle of the night in an area notorious for IEDs and messing around with something that looked like artillery shells. Apparently the man driving the van needed to transport the baby chickens but couldn't do it during the day because the cargo area of the van would have gotten too hot. The average temperature during the day is over 120 degrees, and prolonged exposure to that kind of heat would have killed the chicks during a long drive. So he thought he'd transport them at night, while it was cool. But his van was a piece of shit, and partway into his trip he noticed that the engine was starting to overheat. Since the highway is littered with empty water bottles discarded by soldiers in convoys, he thought he could drive until he found a discarded bottle that still had some water in it. When he pulled over, he took a box out of the van, perhaps a place to put water bottles, then started picking up and putting down bottles on the side of the road. A lot of the bottles used by soldiers have a shape almost identical to artillery rounds. So when Ray's team watched this man through their infrared scopes, what he was holding looked to them like artillery shells.

There are some who were never convinced of the man's innocence. If it were an elaborate ploy—the story of the chickens and the overheating engine—an excuse to stop a vehicle on the highway during the wee hours of the night in prime-IED territory, it would have worked very well.

Once I'd learned the man we shot at was most likely just an innocent guy with really bad luck, I am a little embarrassed to say it did not diminish for me the excitement I felt. I will forever be relieved and happy he didn't die and that most of the chickens survived the van's aeration, but I have to admit that a part of me still wishes that grenade had hit the van.

The van was towed back to our base, and the man driving it went into surgery. The bullet that struck him had gone through the van, through the back of his seat, then into his back, and was lodged in his gut. The surgery to remove the bullet was a success, and the man recovered very well. His van was held at our base (for several days in sweltering heat) until someone came to pick it up. All the chickens died.

September 10, 2004

By Far the Most Breathtakingly Stupid and Embarrassing Thing I've Ever Done in My Entire Military Career

One day while I was with the QRF, lounging around in one of the four-man huts in our staging area, we got a call that farmers had found some mortar rounds and wanted to turn them in. This was not an unusual call. Locals often report unexploded ordnance because they want a reward for finding it. It wasn't an urgent call, but we quickly mounted our vehicles and headed toward the front gate of our base.

Before leaving on a mission, each soldier will have a ritual he goes through to be sure he has everything he needs. We've been on so many missions now, the method I've developed is I will subconsciously check to see if anything *feels* different. For example, when working with the QRF, my chemical suit and assault pack with extra ammunition would already be loaded into the Humvee. Then, when a call came, I'd don my body armor, strap on my vest that had all my ammunition on it, put my helmet on, grab my CamelBak and weapon, and get into the Humvee. In my mind I wouldn't consciously be thinking, "I need to put my armor on." I would just know that there was a certain feeling that putting on my armor gave me. Specifically, I was looking for the weight of the gear on my body. Once in the vehicle, my hands were always occupied because they would be holding my rifle. The way I know I have my weapon is by the feeling of having my hands occupied.

When we got the call, I was in the middle of cleaning my sunglasses. I have 20/40 vision, which is what I like to call the Vision of Optimists, because at a distance, everyone is good looking. I don't particularly care for wearing glasses because I hate having anything on my face. I've always been able to pass my rifle qualification without glasses, but I usually do this by using the Force. Three-hundred-meter targets are virtually impossible to see when you have the Vision of Optimists, but if you memorize where the target is and have someone call it out when it appears, or if you can see the sun glint off the target as it pops up, you can sometimes hit it. I can hit targets at two- and three hundred meters without glasses, but there's no way I can positively *identify* targets at that range. There are never innocent or friendly targets on a normal rifle range, only targets you're supposed to shoot. Real life, obviously, isn't the same. Accidentally killing the wrong person is a big fear of mine, so I didn't mess around and made sure to get both regular glasses and prescription sunglasses for this deployment, which meant that something I did on a daily basis was clean my glasses. The moment we got this call, I was in the middle of giving them a good cleaning, so I continued to do so while we rolled up to the gate.

Before leaving the base, the leader of the QRF would check in with the Tactical Operations Center to let them know we were about to leave. This process usually took only a few minutes, then we would be sent on our way. I finished cleaning my sunglasses and put them on my face just as we started to leave the TOC. Now my hands were unoccupied. Why are my hands empty? Why aren't they occupied? Why isn't my weapon in my hands? Holy Jesus god! Where is my weapon?

My eyes scanned the interior of the Humvee frantically. I knew that if my weapon wasn't in my hands, it probably wasn't in the Humvee at all. I didn't see it and didn't waste time looking for it—an M4/M203 is not something that can drop out of sight between the seats like a pen or a coin. I had to accept the fact that I had left it hanging on the hook on the wall of my hut at the staging area.

We hadn't left the base yet, and there was still time for me to get it. The staging area was less than one minute away. We could drive to the hut and drive back to the gate in two minutes, tops. But there would be no way around explaining to the rest of the QRF why my truck had to drive back to the huts.

In the Army, and especially in combat arms units, your reputation is the most important thing you have. It is how you are judged by the other soldiers in your unit. Anytime anyone does something stupid, word spreads instantly. What usually happens is one or a few guys will interpret and assess the event, share this interpretation, and then an opinion is spread along with the story. The same process takes place anytime someone does something noteworthy as well. This is, for the most part, how a soldier's reputation is generated and propagated.

Even if I attempted to make up a convincing cover story for going back to the huts, there was no getting past the fact that I had forgotten something really important. If we went back, I saw no way to hide the fact that I had forgotten my weapon. My mind raced. Then I noticed that there were two spare SAWs in the Humvee.

My position in my Humvee was usually in the passenger seat, where I would man the radio. This position is called the "truck commander," or TC. The term TC is borrowed from tankers; in a tank, the guy in charge is called the TC for "tank commander." On this day I wasn't the TC; I was in the seat behind the driver. Orlando was driving and had his SAW next to him. In the turret on the machine gun was Cesar, with his SAW lying at his feet next to me, along with his ammo vest.

I didn't want to humiliate myself by letting anyone know I had left my weapon in my hut; the only truly important thing was that once we got outside the base, I had a weapon. I assumed no one would think it even remotely possible to forget your weapon, so I decided that if we had to get out of the vehicles, I would just put Cesar's ammo vest on and carry his SAW, since the only reason he'd have to leave his position in the turret would be if the Humvee were destroyed, since the machine gun he currently manned was the most important weapon we had. Besides, it wasn't completely uncommon for us to use one another's weapons in certain situations, so I knew I could get away with it.

When we first came to Iraq, standard procedure for us was to keep the windows rolled down, with the barrels of our weapons pointed out of them. Once we finally realized the chances of our engaging an enemy out the window of a Humvee was zero, and something blowing up next to the Humvee only a matter of time, we changed our procedure and kept the armored windows up at all times. Since I didn't have to put the barrel of any weapon out the window, there was an even better chance of my being able to pull this off without humiliating myself. Since everyone would be occupied with scanning their sector, I knew I had a reasonable chance of making it out of the woods.

The drive to the farmers and their mortar rounds was a bit of a trip, so it was decided that along the way we'd check in on some areas that tended to have a fair amount of enemy activity. While we drove, I had some time to reflect. Granted, I was the only one aware at the time of the breathtakingly stupid thing I had done, but, frankly, my opinion of myself was the only one that really mattered in the long run. I tried to remember the last time I had felt this embarrassed and stupid. The first thing that came to mind was when I was fourteen and sang "Orange Crush" by R.E.M. with the "band" my friends and I had at a "Battle of the Bands" contest at a local skating rink in Utah. I was horrifically off-key and forgot some of the lyrics. A girl I had a life-altering intense crush on was in the audience, as were my parents. That was really embarrassing. I think the worst part of that was the endless amount of internal embarrassment I put myself through every time I thought about it. It took years of maturing and innumerable recountings of the story before I ever really got over it. I thought about an incident where I accidentally farted during a math class in tenth grade. It was so loud the teacher stopped teaching just to say, "Wow. That was *loud!*" I was sitting next to two of the cutest girls in the school when that happened, of course. The worst part about doing something embarrassing and stupid is the effect it has on your reputation or "coolness." When you're a teenager, although your reputation is of little consequence in the grand scheme of things, it seems like the end of the world when it takes a serious hit. One of the worst hits my self-image took was when I met my biological father for the second time. I've always had father issues, since I never got along very well with Jim, my adoptive father in Salt Lake, so when I finally met George, my biological father, it was important to me on a deeply meaningful psychological level to impress him. This went straight to hell when I met him for the second time at the age of twenty-one. My sister, Dayna, had just gotten her associate's degree from the university she and I attended, and George had flown to Utah to celebrate with us. After dinner, we were going to see the premiere of *Batman Forever* at a local theater. Dinner wasn't agreeing with me, and in a moment of desperation, when I couldn't find a bathroom in the mall where the theater was, I shat on the floor in a remote area, where all the shops were closed. As luck would have it, when the long line for the movie was formed, it snaked around and went right down the hall where I had left my Jackson Pollock masterpiece. God, it's all so Freudian. The anal stage of psychosexual development is, what, the second stage? The child derives satisfaction from the ability to control his own bowel movements. The whole father thing was explained by Jung, but I simply don't recall how it all works. Now, here I was in combat, and my life and the lives of the guys I was with depended on my ability to make the men I worked with and was in charge of feel safe and in good hands. How could I ask anyone to have confidence in me when I couldn't even have the confidence in myself to remember my fucking rifle?

Now the QRF team was in a sprawling area of gravel pits, where the terrain was cut deeply by roads, ravines, and streams. We briefly dismounted, so I put Cesar's ammo vest on and grabbed his SAW. A few guys noticed my change in weapon, but they assumed I was just being hooah carrying a heavier weapon for a bit.

We got back into the Humvees and drove out to where the farmers were. Sure enough, there were a few tank rounds. The explosive ordnance disposal guys did their thing and loaded the rounds into their truck. Once again we dismounted, me with Cesar's SAW, and spent some time looking around the area. This time most everyone noticed my new weapon and had a comment for me about it. "Yeah, I thought I'd check it out," I told them. They all bought it.

Most all our SAW gunners, at one time or another, complained about the weight of their weapon. Cesar had his vest rigged so there were two two-hundred-round drums in the front pockets and a two-hundred-round drum in each side pocket. With a hundred-round pouch on the weapon itself, I was carrying seven hundred rounds, a typical load for a SAW gunner. With most the weight of the rounds in the front, and with the additional weight of the SAW itself hanging down in front of me from its sling, I quickly realized that this setup was in fact incredibly fucking uncomfortable. I felt like a pregnant woman. I could either never be a SAW gunner or I'd have to figure out a different way to carry all the ammunition.

I told Cesar, "Man, you weren't kidding. This thing really *is* quite heavy. And uncomfortable as hell." "No *shit*," was all he said and laughed.

Once we were done collecting the ordnance and giving the farmers a few bucks, we headed back to our base. I was virtually home free. All we'd do now is clear our weapons at the gate, drive back to the staging area, park the vehicles, and go back to lounging around in the huts. No one need be any the wiser. So long as no one had gone into my hut while we were gone—which no one had any reason to do— I'd be set. I would be the only one who had to know what I had done, and could learn to start living with that. Maybe I'd tell someone someday, most definitely after we returned from Iraq. Maybe just Willy. But his opinion is important to me, so maybe I wouldn't tell him. Come to think of it, I probably should just keep the whole thing to myself.

After we got back to our base, we cleared our weapons, but then a wrench was thrown in my plan. It was decided that we would go straight to chow first, then head back to the huts. Since the QRF always had to move as a group in case we got a call, I had no choice but to go to chow. This meant I would have to endure my current level of anxiety a bit longer. I didn't like this. I just wanted to be reunited with Wazina. I felt like such a piece of shit. But, whatever. I had no choice but to go to chow.

The QRF staging area is also used as a staging area for the CASEVAC escort. The way CASEVAC works is nearly identical to QRF. Should anyone need an ambulance, the CASEVAC vehicles escort a field litter ambulance to wherever it needs to go. While the QRF was out, the CASEVAC guys were still at the staging area, and Rubin, one of the squad leaders in the platoon, decided, for whatever reason, to check in on the QRF huts.

While I was waiting in line for chow, Rubin bursts into the chow tent and announces, "Who the fuck is weapon number twenty-four?!

Who's fucking weapon twenty-four?!" Jesus Christ Almighty. I make it through the whole mission, all the way back to base without incident, and now this? A little mercy would have been nice. Pull me aside, privately confirm to me that I am in fact the world's biggest asshole, then give me a shitload of extra duty for the next few days and allow me to retain a little dignity. But, no, Rubin was intent on making it a public whipping. A reputation, like politics, is a relative thing, and an easy way to improve your own is to discover ways to damage the reputation of others. And the gossip factor is a plus. I'll admit, 99 percent of guys take gleeful enjoyment in being the first to discover something fucked-up about another soldier and sharing it with everyone as quickly as possible. I can't cast the first stone. I like doing it, too. Oh well.

"Rubin, I'm twenty-four. It's mine. I took the SAW out today," I tell him. I don't know why I even tried to act like I'd meant to take the SAW and not my own rifle. No one would ever buy that story, and no one did. "Never leave your weapon in the hut!" he lectured me. He went on for a while, and all I could say was, "Roger. I know. You're right. Roger. Do you have my weapon? May I have it now? Thanks."

When we finally got back to the huts, I lay down and took a nap. I had the worst dreams of my deployment that afternoon, all a variation on the theme of forgetting my weapon.

I slept with Wazina in my bed that night, and the next day I gave her the most thorough cleaning I've ever given a weapon. For the next three days I pulled a record-breaking number of guard shifts. It actually made me feel a little better, being allowed to be punished like a soldier.

September 12, 2004

The Compassionate Combatant

It was September 11 and we had an ambush planned that night.

Three years ago on this same date, I was asleep in my father's Lower Manhattan loft when the phone rang. I was living there with my friend Tim, who was the manager of my father's photography studio that was part of the loft space. It was Tim's grandmother on the phone, and she asked me, "Is Tim okay? Is he safe?" Still half asleep, I told her, "Yeah, he's okay. I guess, he's in the other room." She seemed upset, but I had no idea why she wanted to know if her grandson was all right. "Okay, I was so worried. I just wanted to be sure he was okay." I hung up the phone and immediately fell back asleep. A few minutes later the phone rang again. My friends know that I have a strict policy to never call me before noon. I picked up the phone and answered with an aggravated hello. "Is Jason there?" It was my friend Felix, one of the guys from my National Guard platoon. I answered, "Felix, it's me. What's up?" "Hey man. Terrorists just flew an airplane into the World Trade Center. I don't know if they're gonna call us up or what, but I just wanted to call you so you knew." Felix, like most the guys I know, has a tendency to say ridiculous shit on the phone as a form of greeting, but it was way before noon and I wasn't in the mood for jokes. Exasperated, I told him, "You call me and wake me up just to tell me some ridiculous shit about terrorists? Dude, never call me this early again." I hung up the phone and went promptly back to being unconscious.

I wasn't asleep for more than a few minutes when I woke up again to the sound of the TV. Tim was standing in front of it watching the news. I got out of bed and walked over to him. "Can you believe this shit with the World Trade Center?" he said.

Both towers had already been hit by the time Tim and I started watching the news. We were looking at the TV and seeing the same massive plume of smoke rise over downtown Manhattan that we saw when we looked out the window.

The loft was a few blocks east of Lafayette, and I knew there was a good view of the Trade Center towers from West Broadway. As I got dressed, Tim gathered some camera equipment. We both left at the same time. Tim wanted to see how far downtown he could get. I wasn't eager to head downtown because I didn't want to get in the way of what I knew was probably an already very chaotic emergency effort. We were both driven by impetus, he as a photographer, I as a soldier. I knew I'd most likely be called by the National Guard and would see what was going on soon enough. We agreed to meet back at the studio in a few hours.

By the time I made it to the intersection of West Broadway and Spring Street, the street was full of people, most in business attire, many with briefcases in hand, some covered in ashes, all headed uptown. I could see only one of the towers, and it was burning. There was so much smoke I concluded I couldn't see the other tower because of that. I felt guilty standing there, little more than a lookyloo or a tourist. I saw the people standing in the windows on the floors just below the fire. The towers always seemed so big, larger than anything I could comprehend. But when the people jumped from the windows, they looked too big to be people. It made me realize how close the towers were, that they weren't nearly as tall as I was convinced they were. I said, "Oh god," and instinctively wanted to reach out and catch the falling people. I felt so helpless. A woman next to me gasped and covered her mouth and started to cry.

I hated that I didn't know what was going on. I wanted to hear what was being said on the news. Not wanting to stand there helpless any longer, I started walking back, hoping to find a bar with a TV or to go back to my father's loft to get assurance that the fire was under control and everything would be okay shortly. As I crossed Broadway, I felt and heard a great rumble. At first I thought it was a subway train passing under the street, but I knew this rumble was much louder than a train. I quickly walked back to West Broadway. When I looked downtown, all I saw in place of the towers was a clear blue sky.

Dumbfounded, I stood there and stared at the blankness. The thought never occurred to me that the towers could fall. They have always been a mental anchor for me, the way I determined which direction was downtown when I came out of the subway, the first place I always took friends when they came to visit me so they could see from the top how truly incredible New York City looked.

Everyone from our infantry company had been called that afternoon and told to meet at our armory in Midtown. As we got off the bus near Ground Zero that night, a city bus Willy had commandeered for us from its route earlier, it was suggested we pray. The soldier who was asked to give the prayer was Muslim. The prayer given that night, asking god to watch over his troops in New York City, was in Arabic.

In the eleven days we worked at Ground Zero, I experienced more than I could really process. For twelve hours a day, I sat between buildings Four and Five, as a perimeter guard of sorts—a painful job, really, having to turn away all the people who insisted they wanted to help in the recovery effort. One day a group of firefighters who had driven from Montana asked to help.

I'd always thought the island of Manhattan to be more an international community than just simply a part of America. You can walk the streets on any summer afternoon and hear dozens of different languages being spoken, you can eat food from nearly any part of the world, and you can buy items from just as many foreign locations. Why attack the World Trade Center? If the attack was meant to be against America, why not attack something with a name like the

American Trade Center? How many citizens from countries other than America were killed that day? What also seemed sadly significant to me was that the number of people initially estimated to have died that day exceeded the number of Americans killed during the American Revolution. While I sat there pondering what I was witnessing, I knew I'd probably be wearing my uniform a lot over the next several years.

The movement to our ambush site would be a short one, but it turned out to be no less difficult than the last. Late that night, our Humvees drove down a dirt road and we were dropped off next to a vineyard. We crept through the wires and the vines. A dog barked wildly near us. As we continued to walk at a half-crouch, concerned the dog was giving away our position, we came unexpectedly close to the house in the center of the vineyard. A man sat outside smoking. To avoid detection, we moved quickly to the edge of the vineyard and exited the tangled mess.

We were less than a hundred meters from the location we intended to occupy, but between it and us was an open field, muddy with irrigation water. Jeff was leading this mission. I tried to telepathically persuade him to go around it, but that would have put us too near a large dirt road, the one we were going to be watching. He took a step, sinking deeply into the mud, and began to trudge to the other side. Given that there was neither cover nor concealment as we crossed the field, we went one at a time, waiting until the man in front was at least halfway across the approximately fifty-meter field before the next man went. The guys with the machine guns had it the worst. Jimmy, who was carrying a SAW, fell flat on his face into the mud twice. The mud was incredibly deep, up to our crotches at times.

The spot we were occupying put us close to a lot of houses and farms. We lay down near some small hills and ravines along a dirt road that was near a bridge that crossed a very large canal. All night we watched as people walked and drove by us. It was a little unnerving being so close to so many people, but we had night-vision systems, and they didn't. And given that we were now all the color of the dirt, we blended into the environment nicely.

It was amazing to me how many local men were out that night driving and walking around. Everyone seemed suspicious. For an area that survived almost entirely on farming, there sure were a lot of people who didn't keep farmers' hours.

So much of a soldier's job involves sitting somewhere doing basically nothing. Sitting in an ambush site is not exactly doing nothing, but it does give one ample opportunity to ruminate. The temperature that night was perfect. We're trained to lie on our stomachs in the prone position in situations like this, but I've never liked how difficult it is to see anything when I'm lying like that. I had found a nice spot to lie on my back, where I could position the gear in my butt pack to make a good backrest. I was low to the ground and I had an excellent view of the field behind us. I'd go so far as to say I was comfortable. There was a slight breeze, and for the first time in several months I wasn't sweating profusely. I was glad that we had chosen this date to go on an ambush. It seemed appropriate, and I felt a sense of satisfaction and participation. The greatest comfort I'd felt from working at Ground Zero was being able to participate in what was going on. I have always hated having to sit at home when horrible injustices are taking place the world over and not be able to do anything other than watch them all through the distorted channel of information known as television. If there were an organization that responded immediately to human rights crises, a group who would never ask what's in it for them and on principle would go in by force to places like East Timor and Rwanda, I would join that organization. One of the only ideas I believe in with all my soul is the preservation and protection of basic human rights. For me to entangle myself in the argument of whether or not I should be in Iraq is now irrelevant. We're here, good or bad. What matters is what happens next. As just one person, one soldier, I know my impact is minimal, but I feel a certain degree of satisfaction being able to participate in a process that is otherwise intimidating and inaccessible.

Sitting there in the ambush position, I asked myself, How can I contribute positively? It's a difficult question to answer. There are so many things to worry about that I wish I could do something about. The ancient and interminable conflict between Israel and Palestine. Russia's gradual decline away from democratic values as they try to cope with the inhumanity of Chechen separatists. Pakistan and India's potential nuclear dispute over Kashmir. North Korea and Iran, places with horrible human rights records, possibly becoming nuclear powers. And, of course, the process of establishing democracy in Iraq. While I personally cannot have much of an impact on these situations, the United States government can. I can't be certain that my government will contribute positively to the resolution of this conflict, but I have to have faith that it can. Others may disagree with me, but the organization that can do more for the protection of basic human rights than almost any other is the U.S. Army.

I give regularly to Amnesty International, the International Campaign for Tibet, and the American Civil Liberties Union. Does my check for twenty bucks really do much to give political and religious autonomy back to Tibet? Not really, but does my vote for the president of the United States or the mayor of New York City really make that big a difference either? The Dalai Lama, President Bush, Mayor Bloomberg—these men don't know me. But I will put my two bits in when given the chance.

My nominal contribution to world issues took place when I reenlisted in the National Guard. My first enlistment was just something to do, my first adult decision during high school, something that I knew would piss off my parents. Plus, the opportunity to play GI Joe for a few years was appealing. I tend to believe that people *join* the military mostly for dumb reasons. I mean seriously, what the hell did I know as a seventeen-year-old? But I believe people tend to *stay* in the military for good reasons. I work with guys who have pretty diverse personalities and beliefs, but the most common value we all share is a sense of duty. Our country needs a military. Somebody has to do this job, and it might as well be me. Who else is going to do it? You?

The chances of my personally capturing Osama bin Laden are slim, but I'd like to do something a little more than just simply being in the Army and sometimes sending money to the ACLU. This is something I think about a lot, and it was something I thought a lot about that night on the anniversary of the most egregious affront to human decency I had witnessed in my life, sitting there by that road as I scanned the field in front of me.

Anytime I think about this I always come to the same conclusion. The best I can do right now is to plant seeds, to treat people the way I would want to be treated. I can think of nothing more important than compassion. I am not a pacifist nor am I a conscientious objector, but I believe there must be a way to be an infantryman and still be able to preserve a sense of compassion. I have tried my best to be honest with myself about my apparently instinctual desire to fight and commit violence, but I also feel unafraid to express my innate desire to bring comfort to those around me. I realize these are diametrically opposed forces, but in combat, an environment fertile for violence, there is still a need, and an opportunity, for compassion. So if the closest to a tangible contribution I can make right now is to live by example, to try to foster compassion by simply following the Golden Rule, I am content with that.

September 11 then quietly changed to September 12.

September 19, 2004

Combat is so one-sided when you're a soldier. You never really get to know exactly what happened from any perspective other than your own. There's always loose ends, non sequiturs, and red herrings. I'm not a reporter and I can't go interview insurgents in hopes of painting a fuller picture, so instead I made up (!) a whole story to explain a few things. Yes, that's right, the following story is total hogwash. Well, some of it's true. Anyway, the thing is, I'm fucking sick of writing stories about combat. There are only so many adjectives to describe explosions, ya know what I mean? So here's the story of Raed, the fictional Iraqi. I wish I could meet him.

Raed

I left Baghdad University a month before the Americans invaded my country. The government wouldn't let the school officially end the semester early for this reason, so an announcement was made that the semester would be accelerated and final exams held a month early so a longer period of time could be used on the much-needed renovations that were scheduled to take place on the buildings. The university did need to be renovated. The plaster on the walls sometimes fell off in chunks, and the plumbing rarely worked properly, but not one worker would ever step foot into the school. The renovations were announced in the newspaper, and posters were plastered on street walls for a five-block radius. They trumpeted the prosperity and well-being of Baghdad and how the university would herald the continuing success and ongoing improvements to the country of Iraq over the next several years.

The professors were never openly critical of our country's leaders, and the students would discuss the regime only in private, with close friends. We were all proud to be Iraqis, we also had no illusions about the impending invasion. Most of us wanted to be with our families, and in many cases this meant leaving Baghdad. Although it went unspoken, we all knew the professors and administrators were of the same mind. The day we were first told of the truncated semester, it was not a surprise, nor was it discussed at school. The professors soberly delivered the message at the beginning of morning classes then continued on with their lessons.

Every evening after classes, my brother Abdullah and I would meet in the dorm room shared by our two friends, brothers Barak and Kaliq. Normally we would show up at different times and drink tea for an hour or longer while we conversed casually about our day. But when the announcement for the shortened semester was made, we all showed up for tea at almost the exact same time. Unable to talk openly about it in school, we were eager to discuss what our plans were going to be. It was something we had been talking about for several weeks already, but this was the catalyst that finally made it all seem real.

"Kaliq and I are going to return to Baqubah the day we finish our exams," Barak told us while Kaliq began making the tea. "Our mother will need the help, and we want to be with our sisters." Their mother was a grocer, and it was her money that paid for them to attend the university. Their father had been in the army and was killed when the Americans attacked the first time, in 1991. He was a tank commander and died doing what he considered defending his country. Barak and Kaliq understood why the Americans had attacked, but they never forgave them for their father's death.

Abdullah and I grew up in the Salah ad Din province north of Baghdad. Our mother and her sisters lived in a small village outside the town of Ad Dujayl. When our parents had first married they lived in Dujayl, where their three sons—me, Abdullah, and Dawud—were born. In 1982 an assassination attempt was made against Saddam when he drove by our town. Dujayl is a mostly Shia town, and there was no love lost on Saddam and his Baathists, but there had been no talk of anyone planning an attack. The assassination was unsuccessful, but the repercussions were brutal. Farms were razed and plowed under with salt, making them unfit for crops. Anyone thought to be involved with the plot was put in jail. More than a hundred men were slaughtered by death squads sent into town by the regime, more than a thousand people were held without charge for sometimes as long as four years, and countless women were brutalized, raped, and sometimes even mutilated in front of their children. Our father, a barber and dentist, was a popular man and well known by many of the people in town. Assuming he would know better than anyone the gossip of town, the death squads killed him in his shop. When our mother heard of our father's death, she did not shed a single tear. She immediately packed some clothes for me and my brothers, and we left for her sister's small farm home in a village several miles to the south. I was five years old.

Our mother was indescribably stolid and self-reliant. I never once saw her mourn in front of us, but there were nights when my brothers and I could hear her quietly sobbing, usually on occasions like our father's birthday or on their anniversary.

Our mother remarried in less than a year to a kind but quiet man who owned several acres of vineyard. He lived in the same village as our aunt and had never been married. He was born with a club foot, which seldom put him in favor with any of the fathers whose daughters he tried to court as a younger man. He was in his late forties when he married our mother. His two nephews, Essam and Ferran, lived with him on his vineyard along with their wives and children.

My brothers and I grew up walking to a small school several miles from our home during the day and helping with the vineyard and animals when we came home in the afternoon. We had become quite attached to our stepfather, and we begged our mother to not make us go to school, but to let us spend more time at home and with him in the vineyards, the same as all our friends. Our mother would become furious anytime we asked her this. She told us it was her wish and the wish of our deceased father that someday we attend the university in Baghdad. Despite the beatings that would accompany this speech, we still would ask her permission to quit school at least every two months.

After being married two years, our mother and stepfather had a baby girl. She was named Amirah. As Amirah grew up, she quickly proved to be as stubborn and precocious as her mother. My brothers and I doted on her and defended her jealously from other boys in the village.

To the east there was a vineyard that bordered ours where a family lived who had a girl Amirah's age, named Zia. Zia and Amirah first met before they could even talk, but they took to each other immediately. Sometimes Zia's mother would visit our mother, and the two of them would play while the mothers talked. Anytime the two were separated they would both cry incessantly. As the two got older this never changed, so each mother eventually decided to take turns watching the other's daughter, usually for days at a time. Zia became as much a part of our family as Amirah became a part of theirs.

For years our family stayed at a pleasant status quo. Our stepfather struggled at times with the vineyard and to provide for our family, but with the support of the other families in the village we got along well enough.

As my brothers and I got older, we were able to do more work in the vineyard. Then our stepfather's health began to deteriorate, and we helped keep the family financially afloat by working harder. Sometimes I think my mother was jealous of the loyalty we had for our stepfather and would tell us anytime we suggested quitting school that it was too much manual labor that made a man get a club foot. It wasn't until we were nearly adults that we learned you couldn't "catch" a club foot from working too much.

When we were in our teens, I noticed that an affinity had developed between Abdullah and Zia. I didn't notice the bond they shared for a long time and mistook his concern for her as the protectiveness we always exhibited for Amirah and Zia. But it was one afternoon when a group of boys on bicycles had ridden by teasing Zia that Abdullah yelled at the boys, as we always would, then mildly scolded Zia for attracting too much attention to herself. I saw him touch her hand slightly. It wasn't anything inappropriate or really that unusual, it was just the *way* he did it that struck me. There was an affection to the way he looked at her now and a certain tenderness in the way he touched her. And instead of the usual scowl the girls would give us when we told them to avoid the boys, there was a demure look on Zia's face and the slightest of smiles. I was unable to acknowledge it to myself that day, something I recorded to memory then promptly put out of my mind. Zia, by all accounts, had become our sister, and I rarely thought of the fact that we were not at all related to her.

In 1990, soldiers from the Iraq army came to our village looking for conscripts. At thirteen and fourteen, Abdullah and I were considered too young. But Dawud was sixteen and old enough to serve. A week later he was put on a truck bound for a base in southern Iraq. We never saw him again. He was killed a year later by the Americans, part of a fleeing convoy of vehicles on the highway south of Baghdad. We learned of his death a month later from a friend of his who served with him who had survived the attack. Dawud died the day before his seventeenth birthday.

Once we were old enough, Abdullah and I started going to a secondary school in Taji, a town twenty miles south of our village. For years our mother had searched for other mothers who had similar intentions to educate their sons. By the time we were old enough to attend, she found two other families who were willing to share the cost of a car to drive us to school each day. This arrangement was very unusual for people who lived in our area. Our mother put up with a lot of mockery from the women in other families. She was accused of being a harlot, a thief, and an Iranian, among other jealous epithets. But her determination to educate her two remaining sons was unflagging.

In the vineyards it was common to have small shelters where seasonal workers would sleep. These shelters also were a place to keep tools, wheelbarrows, and other common items used in the vineyards. Since both Zia and Abdullah spent a lot of time working in their respective family's vineyard, these sheds became a common meeting place for them as their relationship grew more intense. Zia was the second youngest daughter of thirteen. The sisters who were too young to be married lived at home, and most who were married lived with their husbands in homes nearby. Zia's family's vineyard was larger than my family's, and all the women continued to work in it. The men of their family all had jobs away from their homes, and the vineyard was run exclusively by the women. Abdullah would work on our family's property every day, but would find time to visit Zia in secret at least once a week. There was no way this would have gone unnoticed by Zia's sisters. I had to conclude that the sisters were actually protecting the clandestine affair.

In Zia's family all marriages were arranged, and it was no secret between our families that Zia's sisters hated this tradition. Those who were married tolerated it, and those who weren't yet married resisted it. Their father was well respected because of his extensive property, and he openly told anyone who would listen that he felt it his pious duty to adhere to the tradition of arranged marriages.

The week before I was to graduate from secondary school, Zia's father introduced her to the man she would marry. He was in his forties and already had five wives and twenty-three children, many older than she. He was a very wealthy man who owned several homes and properties in the Salah ad Din province. Zia was introduced to him just before the family sat down for their evening meal. After the meal, Zia's father allowed the husband-to-be to spend a short period of time alone with her in one of the rooms of the house. Again, this was not an official tradition but something that was common in the area to let the soon-to-be husband become acquainted with his next wife.

For years Abdullah didn't tell me what happened that night. All anyone knew was that the "meeting" had gone very poorly and the marriage was called off. The wealthy man never showed his face in our village again, and Zia's father did not arrange another marriage for his youngest daughter. For years, I prodded Abdullah to tell me what had happened, but he always told me he didn't know. Finally, just this year, when Abdullah started school at the university with me, he told me that apparently the man had wanted Zia to use her mouth for something other than talking, and she bit him badly. The potential humiliation for the man over what he'd done and for Zia's father for allowing it to happen in his home was tremendous. Zia made a deal with her father that she would never speak of the incident so long as he never again spoke a word to her of any arranged marriages.

After I graduated secondary school, I moved to Baghdad. Our family's money had gotten me to that point but would never be enough to pay for a university education. Once I had been in Baghdad for a year, Abdullah graduated from school and moved into my apartment with me. The first and only time we ever discussed Zia was when he first moved in and I asked him what he intended to do about his relationship with her. He didn't seem shocked that I knew and he answered without hesitating, "I want her to be proud and I want her to live well. We have agreed to marry once I have graduated from the university."

I never brought the subject up again. We went to classes during the day, studied at night, and about once a month we would borrow a car for the weekend and drive home to see our mother. Zia's sisters, forever the protectors of the secret, made sure she was able to spend time in private with my brother when we came to visit.

Although Abdullah and I lived together, the friends we spent time with began to diverge over the years. There were times he would bring friends to our apartment who would express religious and political views that were very anti-West.

When we left the university and moved back in with our mother, Abdullah began spending a lot of time at the Al Sadr office in Dujayl. He had made a lot of friends who were associated with members of the Mahdi Army, who sometimes spent time at the office. I spent most of my time at home, helping my mother with the vineyard. Our stepfather had died a year earlier, and his nephew Essam, with help from my uncle, kept the farm and vineyard going.

After the invasion, things were very chaotic. Two of Zia's sisters were killed in separate incidents, one in a crossfire and the other after her vehicle was mistaken for enemy by Americans. This only gave further fuel to the fundamentalism Abdullah was embracing. While in Baghdad, the two of us wore typical Western clothes, usually jeans and T-shirts, but now that we were back home Abdullah was dressing in traditional garb again.

One night after the evening meal with our family, Abdullah told me that Zia's father was becoming suspicious and that her youngest sister was threatening to tell him about the relationship if she didn't end it. Her youngest sister was blind in one eye from when a dog bit her as a toddler and she was jealous of the attention her sisters gave Zia. Abdullah's anxiety was noticeable when he told me this. He also confided in me that he had been having doubts for quite some time with regard to his religious and political beliefs. He then told me of his plan.

The Madhi Army would give anyone a thousand U.S. dollars who killed an American soldier. The American Army was also offering a thousand dollars for information that would lead to the arrest of any leaders of the Mahdi Army. Abdullah's plan was to put a bomb on the side of the road and if he was able to successfully kill an American, he would take it as a sign from Allah that his convictions were true. If it failed, he would tell the Americans what he knew about the Mahdi army. He said that, either way, he would take the money and use it to marry Zia and move back to Baghdad. I tried to explain to him that his plan was ludicrous, but he refused to listen to anything I told him. His desperation was apparent. He told me he had already arranged a day for the attack with a friend of his, and he begged me to be with him. I knew my brother needed someone with him he could trust, so I agreed. I had no intention of hurting anyone and I most certainly would not let him go to the Americans, so I decided to help him because I knew once his attack failed—I knew he had no desire to kill anyone—he could abandon his fundamentalism.

When the day came for the attack, I met Abdullah's friend, but never learned his name. He was shorter than the two of us and was young, but had a full, dark beard. He had a tendency to stare at me when he spoke, his brow furrowed, and he spat out his words with conviction. He had with him the materials to make a pipe bomb. He explained to us how to make the bomb, how to set it, and how to explode it. We were told that the Iraqi National Guard would be setting up a roadblock on the highway nearby. There would be an ING soldier standing next to a small hole that would already have been dug. Abdullah was to start a conversation with the soldier and drop the pipe bomb in the hole. Then, later tonight, two men would meet us outside the gate of our property with further instructions. Abdullah listened intently. After his friend was done giving us the instructions, we told him goodbye, and we took the materials to the shelter in our vineyard and got to work.

As we worked on the bomb, I realized I had no idea how to assemble it properly. Abdullah told me he had been told that it was important that he be the one who actually assembled it. While we were talking, our uncle came to the shelter. I quickly tried to hide the materials, but Abdullah told me it was okay, he had told our uncle everything. Before I had a chance to be furious with him, our uncle greeted us. He told me to give him the materials for the bomb. Abdullah handed them to him and our uncle looked them over. He then handed them back to Abdullah and explained what to do.

An hour after nightfall, the ING set up a roadblock on the highway near our home, just as we had been told. Abdullah took the bomb with him to the intersection and dropped it in the hole next to the soldier, just as he had been told. Everything was going well so far.

For several hours Abdullah and I tried to stay busy around the house, always keeping the gate in sight. Our uncle kept us busy with tasks and he also kept an eye on the gate with us. After all the women and children had been put to bed, we locked the chain around the front gate and went out to the road through a side gate through the vineyard.

For two hours we waited at the gate, talking with my uncle while he smoked. He told me stories I had never heard. How he was once part of the outlawed Dawa party in Dujayl and about all their failed efforts to muster support against Saddam's regime. I dared not ask him if he was in any way involved with the assassination attempt on Saddam, but I had to assume that he at least knew about it.

When the two men showed up, one of them was carrying an AK-47 and the other had an RPG. I was used to seeing assault rifles—almost every home in the area had an AK-47—but this was the first time I had seen a rocket. It made me very nervous. The demeanor of the men was stern and cold.

The two men explained that a wire had been attached to the

bomb Abdullah had placed and it ran to a grove of trees that they would lead him to, several hundred meters from the highway. Abdullah was to wait in the grove of trees until the next American convoy came down the highway and explode the bomb somewhere in the middle of the convoy. The two men would be a few hundred meters farther up the road and would fire their rocket at the nearest vehicle once the convoy had stopped.

My uncle chuckled. He said, "You may be too late. You may not have noticed, but there hasn't been any traffic on the highway for some time. The Americans may have already found your bomb." He was right. The highway was a good distance from us, but I hadn't heard any vehicles for at least the last half hour. The two men cursed. One of them tried to blame Abdullah. He then put a flashlight in Abdullah's hand and told him to walk up the trail closer to the highway to see if the Americans had found the bomb.

"Wait, that's not smart," I said. "It's a full moon out, he doesn't need a flashlight. That will only make him stand out even more. Abdullah, don't take the flashlight."

But the man was shaking his head. "If you are stopped by the Americans, tell them you are looking for a cow. You need to not look suspicious. A flashlight will make you look less suspicious," he told Abdullah. I still thought it was stupid, but Abdullah took the flashlight without argument and began walking toward the highway without saying a word.

"Be careful," I told him. "Just go far enough to see the highway, then come right back." He looked back at me and smiled.

I was tense and I think my uncle could sense this. He offered the men cigarettes. While the three of them smoked, my uncle made small talk. I had a bad feeling. I was starting to regret having gotten involved. I was thinking how I should never have let it get this far and how I should never have let Abdullah fall into these counterproductive ways of thinking. My uncle continued to talk, but I wasn't listening. In the direction Abdullah was walking, a dog began to bark. One of the men was laughing now. My uncle was good at putting people at ease. I tried to smile.

Suddenly a deafening amount of machine gun fire erupted extremely close to us in the direction of the barking dog. I saw the bright flashes of the guns then found myself facedown on the ground with the wind knocked out of me. I was never more confused or terrified in my life. I stood up and began to run in the opposite direction. I heard the AK-47 shooting. I ran for a few minutes. I remember nothing else.

When I woke up, I was in a hospital in Baqubah. Barak was next to my bed. He explained that I had been shot in the chest and brought in by two men who were friends of Abdullah's. He said I had given them his name and address. He told me it was important that I stay with him in Baqubah for a few months. I asked him where Abdullah was. He told me he didn't know.

I returned home after two months. My uncle hadn't fled, and when the Americans who shot at us searched our house, they took him and Essam away. Essam was later released, but my uncle had been sent to the Abu Ghraib prison. The Americans claimed they had proof he'd made the bomb.

Abdullah had disappeared after the shooting. It was assumed he was safe and staying with friends, as I was, but two months later his body was found in an abandoned shack a few miles from our house. He had a bullet wound in his head. The day his body was found, Zia hanged herself from the roof of her house. The two were buried on the same day.

Jason

The rest of this story is true, from the me-sided point of view.

We had another ambush planned, and I was excited. We were getting more adept at the planning and execution of ambushes. Jeff would usually choose the spot where we'd be dropped, find a good location that overlooked a few roads and intersections, then plan a primary and secondary location for the pickup. For months we'd been performing operations that mostly involved being in the Humvees. This wasn't bad work, but it wasn't what we had been trained to do. We were all light infantry and we were most comfortable being on foot, moving across the terrain, looking for a fight. Since the ambushes allowed a short movement, we were finally being afforded the chance to do this. Additionally, we were operating in small teams, usually with five men, which made movement easy to coordinate and made us extremely mobile. After the incident with the chicken truck, we were eager for more action but wanted more than anything to engage actual enemy. I had fired my weapon only twice now, both times at people who were quite arguably not combatants. Regardless of whether or not we ever were to directly engage any true enemy combatants, it felt good to be performing light infantry tasks.

The team I was always a part of was run by Jeff. He liked to refer to the team as the "strike team," apparently from watching too many episodes of *The Shield*. The strike team consisted of Jeff, me, Rich, Jimmy, and Sean. Jimmy and Sean both carried SAWs, and I carried the M203. Because of my ability to fire grenades, I was always given the job of rear security, the logic being that I could shoot over the heads of the guys in front of me if the need arose.

Normally, Sean would be a part of the strike team, but since he was one of the few guys in the platoon who was qualified to man the .50-caliber machine gun and since the guy who would normally have been in the turret of the Humvee where it was mounted was on leave, Sean had to stay with the .50-cal and wasn't able to be with us for this ambush. For this mission our lieutenant replaced him.

The evening started the way it always did when we performed ambushes. The Humvees drove us down a dirt road, not far from the highway, we got off and laid low, then they drove away to their staging area, several kilometers away. We were getting good at the infil/exfil parts of these missions, now only taking a few seconds to be dropped off and less than a minute to be picked up.

Once the Humvees were out of sight, we picked up and started the movement to the ambush site. This time we were not going to be crossing any canals. I think it had finally sunk in that crossing canals was way too much of a hassle and a security risk. This movement was also going to be across mostly open fields, no vineyards or orchards— another improvement. The only comfort in moving through the vineyards was that it necessitated our staying close to one another. When you are in the dark, there is a natural tendency to want to be close to the guys you're with. Now that we were moving across open fields, I had to resist the impulse to follow too closely behind the guy in front of me. Since I was in trail, it sometimes got a little disconcerting when I couldn't see Jeff, who was always on point.

The phases of the moon become something very important when you are an infantryman. For this ambush we had a lot of visibility because of a nearly full moon. But it also meant the enemy would have more visibility, too. Given the environment (open fields, minimal foliage, few houses) and the time of night (zero-dark-thirty), there was little reason for anyone to be out unless their intent was questionable.

There was a lot of radio traffic. There were engagements at other locations in our AO, but not near us. This put everyone on top of his game for the night. We knew the bad guys were out.

As we crept through the field, I saw a bright streak stream across the sky. Through my night-vision goggles it looked like a rocket, a large tail of continuous flame. I hadn't heard a pop or an explosion from a rocket's being fired, and as it flew overhead it made no sound. My heart started to pound. I said, "What's that?!" but no one responded. At first I thought maybe it was a flare, then maybe a mortar. But I knew mortars weren't self-propelled, so that wouldn't explain the tail. It must be an RPG. I waited for the impact and the explosion, but it never came. I flipped my NVGs up and looked up at the sky and then toward the horizon in the direction of fire. I saw nothing, whatever it was seemed to have just disappeared. I was baffled. I asked again, "Did anyone see that? A flare or something, overhead." I got puzzled looks and head shakes. I didn't get it. Then it hit me. It was a shooting star. The streak would have made very little visible light, but through the NVGs, with the tail and all the infrared light it must have been emitting, it looked huge. No one else had seen it; I just happened to have been looking up at the time it was above us. This made me relax a little, but I was still on edge.

In the distance, there were a few homes and a couple of clusters of trees. A lot of these homes had flickering lights coming from them, probably small fires used for illumination. The light was barely visible to the naked eye, but was easily visible through our NVGs. Sometimes when people would walk by the flames, a shadow would block the light cast on the nearby clusters of trees. Most of the homes were several kilometers away from us, but the shadows made it clear that there were people still awake.

The movement was basically flawless. We got to our ambush site in a minimal amount of time without any major setbacks or obstacles. We immediately settled into our normal positions: two men were located where they could overwatch the road we were next to in one direction; two others watched the other direction; and I kept an eye on the field behind us. I had brought along a helmet-mounted infrared viewer that our company had purchased for the sniper section. None of the snipers like it, so I have had possession of it for a few weeks now. I always take it with me on ambushes, and alternate between scanning the field with my NVGs and scanning with the infrared viewer, keeping it detached and using it the same way you would use binoculars. The military has been trying to develop a system that integrates IR capabilities with the NVGs. I hope I am still in the infantry when this device is released because it would be really cool to be able to use both types of systems simultaneously.

The overall sense of imminent danger slowly waned as we sat in our ambush site. Whatever conflicts were going on in our AO seemed to be resolving themselves, and all was quiet where we were. It was another pleasant night for an ambush: comfortably cool, with a slight breeze. I knew I had to enjoy this while it lasted. In the coming weeks the temperature would dip down into the range where sitting in ambush positions would require cold-weather gear. This meant either wearing more layers or bringing along an extra jacket or blanket.

As with all the ambushes we had performed, we sat in our positions for several hours without event. I knew it was highly unlikely that we would make contact with the enemy, and I had given up on the notion a long time ago. At the very least this was good exercise and good training. We were getting better at navigating at night, at moving tactically despite the weight of our gear, and we were all becoming intimately familiar with these areas along the highway that were favorites of the enemy for IEDs.

It was nearing our exfil time, and we prepared to move back to the site where we had been dropped off. As we were preparing to move, we were informed that there was a suspected IED on the highway, near the intersection the Humvees would need to use to get to the extraction point. With a suspected IED being reported, I hoped we might stay a bit longer on the ambush, but it had come to our planned time of departure, and it was decided that we weren't going to deviate from the plan.

The movement to the extraction point was going to be fairly quick, but on the way out, Jeff found some trails that followed a canal that were low enough that we had cover and concealment in almost all directions. To stay out of sight and to have the ability to be mobile and move quickly was more important than following typical infantry doctrine, which would have kept us on our original path. This is just one of many things we had been slowly learning; it was too bad that we didn't learn them sooner, because I believe we could have been more productive in the time we had spent thus far in Iraq. (By productive, I mean we could have found and killed more bad guys.)

The trail we were on met with the dirt road on which we were to be picked up. The intersection where the trail met the road would have left us too exposed, so we sat just far enough down the trail so that we had a lot of protection but could still be easily seen and picked up by the Humvees.

On the road, a dog began barking incessantly. This could compromise our security, but there was nothing we could do. To shoot it would announce our presence to anyone within miles. But its barking also made it obvious to anyone listening that there was someone nearby. A few of the guys shined the IR lasers from their weapons into the dog's eyes. There are two settings in the PEQ-2 lasers we had mounted on our weapons: low and high. Low is essentially used for training, and high is used for combat. The lasers are incredibly powerful. The distance they are visible at night is remarkable. The PEQ-2s also have a floodlight that is unbelievably powerful. It is invisible to the naked eye, but blazingly bright when viewed through NVGs. The high setting is physically disabled during training, because the danger of blindness to soldiers is too great. Knowing this, there have been many occasions where soldiers have shined the lasers into the eyes of animals at night. I can't say I like it when guys do this, but I'm not going to be the one to tell them to stop. This perhaps is a failing of mine: I am not prone to stopping guys from being cruel. I'd like to think I'd prevent any crimes against humanity, but I can't get excited at the thought of being tagged a member of PETA for asking the guys to not blind any dogs.

The lasers didn't seem to have any effect on the dog, or at least it didn't make it stop barking. We gave up on getting the dog to go away and continued to wait. Because of the suspected IED, we knew there would be a delay in the Humvees' getting to our location.

While we waited, I noticed a faint light coming from the direction of the highway. It was moving—bobbing, actually. I wasn't sure what it could be; it was probably two hundred meters away or more. The more I watched it, the more it seemed to be someone carrying a flashlight. We knew there was a suspected IED in that direction, and to see someone with a flashlight coming from the same direction was definitely worth paying attention to. I tried to get the attention of Rich, who was nearest to me, but he and the other guys had started to move closer to the road. I wasn't sure why they were moving; we were already in a pretty good spot. I also didn't want to lose track of the guy with the flashlight. The dog was still barking, and it was pissing me off that I had no way of getting it to shut up. I wished that I had a crossbow or a silencer. The dog was about seventy-five meters away. The man with the flashlight seemed to be on the same road we were on, and he would be near us soon. I got up and moved with the rest of the guys, being sure to keep at least one of them in sight.

We crept up the trail a short distance more, until we were on the road. I was a good distance from the other four guys, but they were well within sight. I kept my eye on the bobbing flashlight. Then, without any warning, all four of the other guys started shooting. I was completely at a loss. I had no idea what the hell they were shooting at. My first reaction was to think that they were performing a recon by fire—that is, shooting in the direction of a suspected enemy to see what happened, to see if he ran, shot back, shouted, whatever. It can be an effective thing so long as you aren't afraid to give up your own position in the process.

My thought process in trying to determine why they were shooting lasted for only a split second. All I knew was that we were shooting now, and there was no reason not to kill the dog. I put the bright green dot of my laser on its chest, moved the selector lever on my rifle to fire, and squeezed the trigger. *POP!* I had hit it, but it was still alive and yapping, so I just kept shooting it. *POP! POP! POP! POP!* It had started chasing its own ass, trying to figure out, I supposed, what was biting it. I couldn't believe it hadn't died yet. *POP!* The last round went through its chest, and it dropped to the ground. I had rapidly fired six rounds, four of which had hit it. It broke my heart to do it, but I had to stop the barking. The dog went down hard. I was proud of it.

"Get the 203 up here!" Jeff yelled back to me. I ran up to the four who were online together across the road. I took a knee and fired a few rounds in the same direction they were firing. I still had no idea what we were shooting at.

I yelled, "Give me a distance and direction!"

The lieutenant yelled back to me, "Twelve o'clock, seventy-five meters! By that gate!"

"Roger!" I had a round of HEDP in the tube. I removed the safety from the 203. Because of all the dust and smoke, our lasers were highly visible now. I pointed my rifle so that the laser was parallel to the ground and aiming at the chain link gate, then raised the angle slightly. I squeezed the trigger of the 203. *Doonk! BOOM!* The round detonated shortly after being fired.

Jeff yelled, "Keep firing!"

"Roger!" I yelled back. Shit, that's all you had to say. I opened the breech of the 203, and the smoking casing from the fired round fell to the ground. While I was loading the next round, I asked what we were shooting at. I think it was Rich who said, "There's a guy with a fucking RPG! He was by the gate with a bunch of other guys!" Jesus. I loaded the round, then aimed, this time a bit farther, aiming the laser a bit higher. *Doonk!* A slight pause. *BOOM!* About 150 meters away this time. I opened the 203, and the spent casing clattered to the ground. I loaded another. When firing indirect weapons like mortars, we're taught to "bracket" the enemy, firing far then near, far then near, or left to right, left to right. I was thinking I should do essentially the same with the 203, to at least try to fire in as many different spots as possible in the same general vicinity as the first. *Doonk!* Pause. *BOOM!* This one about a hundred meters. The spent casing falls; I load another. This time I thought I'd try to bring it in a bit closer, maybe fifty to seventy-five meters. I put the laser right on the gate this time. *DoonkBOOM!* There was virtually no pause from the time I fired to the time it detonated. It hit the road in front of us no at more than twenty-five or thirty meters. The minimum distance a 40mm grenade can be fired where the arming mechanism allows the round to detonate is supposed to be thirty-five meters, but that was thirty-five meters at the absolute most. They say that in heated situations like this there's a phenomenon that takes place called "auditory exclusion," where your ears sort of shut off a bit and you don't hear how loud things are. The two times I had fired my weapon I didn't have earplugs in, and my memory of the firing was nothing more than a popping sound when I shot, not the incredibly loud *Crack!* that there normally is. The first three 40mm rounds I had fired didn't seem loud—just a muffled boom and a bright flash of light. This fourth round, however, was noticeably loud. *Really* loud. Jimmy must have thought the same thing, because he shouted, "Too close!"

I started loading another round in the 203. I yelled, "Do you want me to keep shooting, or are we going to maneuver?" Once I got the round in the tube and was ready to fire, Jeff said, "Hold your fire. We're gonna throw frags, then we'll maneuver." Frags? I thought. No need for frags, these guys are either dead or long gone. And if they were on the run, I wanted to get moving. Whatever. While Jeff and the lieutenant got their hand grenades ready, I got down behind the shoulder of the road. Frags make me nervous. If you fuck up and drop them or don't throw them far enough, you're gonna be in a world of hurt. Plus, they send shrapnel in all directions at once. You better have some pretty good cover when one goes off. I got as low as I possibly could. I could see Jeff and the lieutenant standing on the road. Jeff yelled, "Frag out!" and they both threw in unison, then got down off to the side of the road just ahead of us. BA-BOOM! Both frags exploded at almost the same time. I looked up and saw that the cloud of dust from the grenade the lieutenant had thrown was close. Then I heard him yell, "I'M DOWN!" Oh god. This is why I hate frags. The grenade must have gone off right next to him. Rich and I ran over to where he was. I didn't need to see his injury to know that we would need an immediate medevac. I looked at Rich, who had the radio, and I said, "Call a nine line, NOW!" (A nine line is the report you call in when you have casualties.) Rich looked stunned, but started the call. Then I heard the lieutenant's voice again. "I'm good, I'll be okay. Don't call the nine line." When I got to where he was, I saw that he was up to his head in water, and Jeff was in the process of taking his own gear off to try and help him out. There was a canal that ran under the road, totally invisible to us. It was heavily overgrown around the sides with rushes. The canal wasn't very wide, but seemed to be at least eight or ten feet deep. When the lieutenant had thrown his grenade, he jumped down to a spot by the side of the road for cover, but instead slipped into the canal. He went in over his head. The current of the canal had taken him under to where the water flowed under the road, so when he came up for air his helmet hit cement and he wasn't able to get a breath. He then pushed himself off—from what I'm not sure—back against the current and out from underneath the road. Once he was able to breathe again, most likely in a slight state of panic, he yelled that he was down. Our lieutenant is a pretty athletic guy and he was doing what I thought was impossible, which was treading water with all his armor and gear on.

He seemed to be okay, and Jeff was doing his best to help him out. I looked at Rich again and said, "Tell the Humvees to get up here *now*. Tell them to get a tow strap ready, and the second they pull up to use it to pull the LT out of the water." Almost all the Humvees had either a tow bar or a tow strap, items that could be used to tow other Humvees or vehicles if they broke down.

I kept looking back up toward the gate where we had fired. I wanted so badly to maneuver, but knew I couldn't with only two other guys and with the lieutenant possibly in the process of drowning. I cautiously moved a little closer to the gate.

It was several minutes before the Humvees got to us, but once I could see them approaching, I brought Rich and Jimmy up with me to the gate. One of the Humvees had stopped at the canal and was helping Jeff with the lieutenant. I came up to the gate and saw that it was locked with a chain and padlock. There were a couple houses on the other side of it, and I wanted in. I considered shooting the chain, but was concerned about shrapnel from the bullet. As I was contemplating this, Dan was flying up the road in his Humvee then stopped next to me.

He yelled, "Do you want me to ram it?"

Ram it? Yeah, that sounded good! "Yeah! Go, go, go!" I yelled back to Dan. I stepped aside, and he hit the gate. It burst apart and collapsed. Dan drove over it. As soon as the Humvee stopped moving, I yelled for his dismounts. I now had four guys, enough to at least start clearing the structures on this side of the gate in front of us. Sean was in Dan's truck on the .50-cal, something that gave me a lot of comfort. As we passed him, he told me, "I've gotcha covered, Jason."

The first building we came to was smallish and had an open door. It looked like nothing more than a pump house. It was empty, other than a few pipe joints coming out of the ground. We moved on to the next building.

This one looked like a home, a typical mud-brick house. It was on the other side of some dense brush and a small canal. We slowly circled around to the far side of the house and down the dirt road that ran alongside it.

As we came around the corner of the house, we saw what I expected to: an enormous family. By now the rest of the dismounts were behind us, along with my platoon sergeant. We found a walkway that crossed the small ditch and began searching the buildings. There were two men and more women and children than I could count, probably a dozen or more. The men were immediately pulled to the side while we searched the area. All we found were animals and more kids. As we searched, we consolidated all the women and children into the open area in front of the buildings. There were some makeshift tents in the same area, with more sleeping children. How children could sleep through the explosions was beyond me. One of the women was holding a child who looked dead. I tried to ask her if the baby was okay. She didn't understand me, and I didn't understand her. I pointed to the baby, and all she did was hold it out for me to take. I didn't want to take her baby; I just wanted to be sure it was okay.

For the next two or three hours we searched the area around the house extensively. There were vineyards everywhere. We had mortars set up at the location where the Humvees had been staged, and they were prepared to fire if we needed them. This would have been an excellent opportunity for them to fire high-explosive rounds, but our engagement was too close and too brief. So as we searched, we asked them to fire illumination rounds over our area. Rich called the fire mission in, since he was the one on the radio. The first shot was perfect. In radio communication, you never use the word "repeat" if you want someone to repeat the last thing they've said. You use "say again." The reason for this is "repeat" means "shoot again." Since the first shot the mortars fired required no corrections, I told Rich, "Look, you gotta say 'repeat.' The mortar guys must love that. It'll make them so happy if you just say it. Go on, say it." Rich called the next shots in by only saying, "Repeat." Maybe mortar guys don't think this is that big a deal, but I thought it was cool as hell to finally get to hear "repeat" used appropriately.

We searched the canals, up the road, the path the men would have to have used to get away—we searched everything. We didn't find any weapons, no RPG, not even any blood. One of the illumination rounds had started a small brushfire, but it didn't burn the entire country of Iraq to the ground as I had hoped it would. It was so frustrating. There was simply too much to search and too few guys to do it properly. We had already spent way too much time on the objective, and we needed to leave.

The lieutenant had been pulled out of the water and was fine. He spent probably ten minutes treading water before someone with the tow strap came to him. I have no idea how he did this, I would have sunk in five seconds. I now have a greater appreciation for why Rangers make it a habit to carry rope with them on missions.

I asked Rich and Jeff what exactly they had seen. They told me there was a group of guys standing around near the chain link gate, smokin' and jokin', one with an RPG (rocket-propelled grenade) and one with an AK-47. Something we all have dreamed of is finding someone with an RPG. There is absolutely no good or legal reason for anyone to have an RPG, and it is one of the few situations where you have advance permission to kill whoever is holding one. So as soon as they saw this guy walk by while we were waiting to be picked up, they moved into a better position to engage them from. They said the guy with the AK-47 returned fire briefly before he bolted, and that they hit at least one of the guys because he spun around like he had been hit in the shoulder.

I never actually saw any of these men, another thing that frustrates me. And what scares me is that the four grenades I fired were directly in line with the house with the huge family. The house was on the other side of a slight incline behind some growth and was not visible to us at the time, probably two hundred meters from where we fired. At least one of my rounds exploded about 150 meters out, not far from the house. Had I aimed any higher, I could easily have hit the family. The road we had fired down turned slightly and was not straight, as we had at first assumed. We thought the grenades were being dropped along the road and in the direction the men had run. But in reality, once they had escaped the area we were hammering with rounds, they would have been in the clear for the most part.

Once we concluded our searches and reconsolidated everyone, we moved out. We took the two men with us to the big base up the street from ours and ran some tests. One of the men tested positive for having recently handled TNT.

I think about that night constantly. There's so much I wish we could have done differently, but given the situation we did what we could. Two months later another company in our battalion found in that same area a body, dead with a gunshot wound to the head, lying on a bed in an abandoned building. The medics estimated he had been dead two months. We wanted to believe that this was one of the men we shot at, but I knew someone with a head wound wouldn't have been able to run away. Even if he was carried by the other men, why wouldn't they have buried him immediately, as was the custom?

Although this was without a doubt the most exciting experience of my life, recounting it has been one of the most boring. We did this, we did that, blah blah blah. I haven't read a single book about the military in my life, unless you count *Catch-22*, yet here I am writing one. I'm not trying to record history or be a news source. Those both require research and fact-checking. I'm trying to record events the best I remember them, but it's not reliable. Take for example the grenade my lieutenant threw. I was right there when it happened, and from what I saw, for a few seconds I would have sworn he had blown himself up.

I spent a lot of time trying to decide how to tell this story. You can write the same stories about ambushes only so many times before they quickly become repetitive and dull. I'm not Richard Marcinko or Tom Clancy; I couldn't turn this into hero-porn even if I wanted to. There just wasn't enough action with satisfying results, and besides, it would just be too nauseating. I thought maybe I'd include dwarves, mermaids, and synchronized dancing and singing. The mermaids would have explained how our lieutenant was able to tread water for so long, the dwarves could have scampered away with the bodies of the men we'd shot, and I could have interpreted the firefight as a musical. That would at least have made the act of retelling the story a bit more interesting. But I don't want to make something as significant as the first time we actually directly engaged bona fide enemy something so escapist. It would have been nice to know how all the details fit, for there to be a resolution. So I decided it should include a family of women, a benevolent man with a clubfoot, and a tragic romance with a girl named Zia.

THE TAO OF SOLDIERING

I. Learn to suffer
II. You are not special, Know your place
III. Release your attachments

THE TAO OF SOLDIERING

Today is the birthday of the Monastic Order of Infantrymen.

Soldiering is difficult. But for soldiers with the proper attitude, there can be great fulfillment from this work. To find peace and contentedness from a job that may seem intuitively chaotic, you simply have to find the tao of soldiering and embrace it.

For soldiers who are nauseated by terms like "embrace," "peace," and "contentedness," and don't know how to pronounce "tao" (it's like "dow," as in Dow Jones, and can be translated loosely to mean "the way") let me put this in terms a grunt can understand. Being a soldier is to live in a world of shit. You're constantly surrounded by assholes; you have to endure an unending amount of bullshit from your leadership, military regulations and paperwork, and stupid training missions; and in the end, you'll most likely get shit on by your own government sooner or later when they fuck up your pay and benefits. And to top it all off, you might actually have to go into combat at some point, which also means you'll spend a lot of time in another world of shit (i.e., Iraq) and possibly get your balls blown off by some insurgent asshole who is too afraid to fight you face-to-face so he explodes jury-rigged artillery rounds next to your Humvee while he's outside the maximum effective range of most of your weapons systems. Soldiering just plain sucks. From the pogues who cook the food and do the laundry to the Apache pilots and the Green Berets who do all the Hollywood stuff, soldiers' lives are in a constant state of suck. But there are soldiers who have found a way not only to endure it all, but to enjoy it. Contentment, happiness, fulfillment, reward, peace, meaning, purpose, Zen, the way, the middle path, nirvana, the big nothing—whatever you want to call it, it's there if you are unafraid to see it.

Learn to Suffer

Most everything a soldier does entails discomfort. As a soldier, you will discover an encyclopedic number of ways to suffer. The suffering is physical, psychological, and emotional. It can also be financial, legal, marital, and any other word you can give the -al suffix to. There is nowhere you can go to avoid suffering. There is no reprieve, no solace. It is unavoidable and inevitable. You can either cry about it, or you can just learn how to suck it up.

One of the first things an effective soldier learns during basic training is that physical endurance has nothing to do with physical ability. Your body gives you the illusion that you are able to do only what is within your physical limitations. Say, for example, your muscles are strong enough to do only fifty push-ups. This limitation is very convincing. You believe that you can't do more than what your muscles and bones are physically capable of doing. In reality, the only limitation is the will of the soldier. You probably think that if you lift weights and make more muscle, you will be able to do seventy push-ups. This is true, but you aren't able to do more push-ups because your muscles are stronger; you are able to do more push-ups because your stronger muscles are a convincing illusion to allow yourself the will to do more. The truth is, with will alone you can do seventy push-ups, or ten thousand for that matter. Accomplishing more than you physically should be able to is referred to as "using the Force." If the Jedi metaphor for describing "will" doesn't work for you, then use the Christian one. In the New Testament (Matthew 17:20), Jesus says that with the faith of a mustard seed you can move mountains. So whether you're raising an X-Wing fighter out of a swamp or parting the Red Sea, the concept is the same: you simply need the will.

It is not necessary for the novitiate to buy into any of this. But when he's into the twelfth mile of a forced road march carrying nearly his own bodyweight in gear, a soldier learns that there is a landscape of pain he never knew existed. Once you've learned that there is no real limit to what you can endure, you're on your way to understanding that you can do just about anything so long as you allow yourself to have the will to do it. And the easiest way to learn this concept is to suffer and realize you can endure it. Then, as you reach a new level of painful experiences, you are able to begin working on the next level. Eventually you learn that there is virtually no end to the kinds of pain mortality can make available to you, and you continue to learn that there is no discomfort you cannot overcome. The process of learning to suffer is always ongoing. No matter how much you've suffered, there is always more to suffer.

You Are Not Special

As Americans and Westerners, we value individuality more than just about anything else. Individuality is at the core of our concepts about freedom. The protection of the individual is vital to a free society. But while the civilian is the "individual," the soldier is the "protection."

As a society, we've gotten really good at fostering individual development. As a soldier, the idea that individuality must be discarded is usually a very hard thing to accept at first. Because of basic psychological instincts for self-preservation and a million beliefs that have been socialized into us from the moment of our birth, we protect our "ego" more than anything. You are who you think you are. You spend your life developing an image in your head of who you are. You have a name, you live in a certain place, you have a certain profession, you have tastes, opinions, preferences. In terms of a capitalistic society, we are nothing more than consumers. So we define our individuality by what we consume. (Sometimes the consumer becomes disillusioned by this, so he simply adjusts his tastes to something that will identify him as an individual. "I'm not into Metallica anymore, they're too mainstream. I'm into the Mars Volta now.") There are eight million individuals in New York City. I was one of them. Like in college, where the second question asked after "What's your name?" is "What's your major?" in New York City the only two things anyone wants to know when they first meet you are "So what do you do?" and "Where do you live?" I was a paratrooper and a computer programmer who lived in Nolita. I doubt there has ever been anyone who could say that. So I'm an individual, right?

One thousand years from now, no one is going to know who you were. Right now, even while you are living, you don't really matter. You live in Ohio, you work at a hardware store, you drive a Saturn, you have two kids, you send your mom a Mother's Day card every year, you have a beautiful lawn. You're the CEO of a Fortune 500 company, you have a loft in Chelsea and a summer home on Fire Island, you come from old money, every Christmas, you visit your mom, who lives in the home where you grew up an only child in New England, you were on the cover of *Forbes* and *Out* in the same month. Does any of this really matter? Someday you're going to die, and they'll throw dirt on your grave just like everyone else's. Someday the sun will expand and consume every living thing on earth. Someday the universe will collapse in on itself then explode into a brand-new universe. Even these events don't really matter; they're just things that happen. So whether you prefer creamy or chunky is of such absurdly little consequence, the near meaninglessness of it is mind-boggling. Accept that you are of no consequence, that you are essentially nothing. In a universe of infinite universes that will ultimately return to the singularity from whence they all came, you are as inconsequential as my peanut butter preference.

Know Your Place

As a corollary to knowing that you are not special, you must also know your place. Unlike the private kindergarten you attended in Woodstock, where everyone was special and equal—even Timmy in his wheelchair and Tyrone the black kid—in the military there is a hierarchy because it is the easiest way to get things done. I spent an enormous amount of my military career as a private. I took out the trash and mopped the floor. Now that I'm a sergeant, I want you to shut the fuck up and continue sweeping, is that clear? Everyone has a job and a role, and by staying in your lane, work can be accomplished more efficiently. Imagine if your car's fuel injection system decided it wanted to start managing the antilock braking functions. The compartmentalization of tasks exists so you can be free to concentrate on your own set of tasks. When I raid a building, I know how I'm going to breach the door, I know how to clear the rooms, I know how to handle detainees. While I'm doing this, there are Apaches circling overhead. I don't know how to do their job, and that's okay. I need air support, and they provide it. The intelligence guys interrogate the detainees and come up with more targets for my platoon to raid. Remember, you are Soldier Nobody, not General Patton. Concentrate on your job and you will be able to perform it well. As an infantryman, your job is to shoot people. Don't worry about Abu Ghraib, Fallujah, or Michael Moore. If your target is moving, remember to lead your point of aim a bit.

Release Your Attachments

Attachments cause suffering. The sooner you accept this, the sooner you will learn how to overcome suffering. As Americans and Westerners, we love our stuff. How much did you love Christmas as a kid? I remember thinking that the entire purpose of life was Christmas. That's when I got a whole new batch of toys. As a kid, all that mattered to me were toys. To this day, the feeling Christmas gave me is one without parallel. But toys break, they get lost, and eventually you lose interest in them. As an adult, what is more of a pain in the ass than your car? Or the upkeep of your house? You can get a lot of satisfaction from stuff. I won't deny how much I love going to Barnes and Noble or to the music store. But you don't get real happiness from material possessions.

And attachments go well beyond the things you can own. Relationships you have with people can be attachments. There are more relationships in the world based on insecurity and attachment than on love. And the ultimate attachment is your own ego. Your sense of "self" is something you cling to. The linchpin to the tao of soldiering is freeing yourself from your attachments. The less you own, the better. The more stuff you own is more stuff to worry about while you're deployed. The girl you were dating isn't going to wait for you for eighteen months, so just get over her and move on. Even if you are in a healthy and strong relationship with your wife, your marriage will not be the same when you get back. It won't necessarily go bad, but it will certainly be different. There are several guys in my platoon who missed the births of their children. This affected them, and I'm sure it affected their wives. And in turn it will affect their marriage. Crappy marriages don't handle this sort of thing well, and they will end. Good marriages will weather it but will evolve into something different. Either way, guys who are attached to the way things *were* will be miserable. And whatever you thought about yourself, ideas you cling to that you consider part of your identity may very well change after you've been around some good ol'-fashioned death and destruction.

I like being a soldier and I love being an infantryman. There are a lot of things that truly suck about being in Iraq, but none of it's really all that bad. This is the most interesting and exciting thing I've ever done. War is a horrible thing, and I hope that as a human culture we can find a way to completely put an end to it, but I have to admit I like combat. I'm not sure how this is possible, but it's how I feel. When guys discuss when we will be sent home, I get sort of depressed. I don't want it to end yet.

October 27, 2004

THOUGHTS ON IRAQ

Last night three IEDs were detonated next to a small convoy, disabling two Humvees and injuring six soldiers from my company, one seriously. The explosives in this case, as in most, were 155mm artillery rounds, munitions that seem to grow on trees in Iraq. In the case of last night's IEDs, the wires used to detonate them ran over a cement irrigation canal, an obstacle that is virtually impossible for dismounted infantry to traverse on foot. In addition to being on the other side of the obstacle of the canal and concealed by foliage and vineyards, in typical fashion the firing point was outside the maximum effective range of most of our weapons systems.

This attack took place at the same location as last month's ambush, where we engaged the men with the RPG. What is especially frustrating for us now is knowing that the men responsible for last night's IEDs are most likely the same we couldn't seem to kill a month ago.

I like combat. Most of my life has been a suburban daydream where I've floated along the peaks and valleys of minor triumphs and minor failures. Now I'm beginning to see things in hues more saturated as my time in Iraq quietly reveals how life is precious and sublime. I'm not a warmonger, I'm not blood-thirsty or trigger-happy. I am not anti-Muslim, anti-Arab, or anti-Iraqi (although the temptation to slip into these ways of thinking is seductive). I am not hateful. I make it a point anytime we've detained someone to share a cigarette with him. I suppose it's just a way of saying, "We are enemies and it happens I won this round—now let's enjoy a moment of repose together the only way we can." But know this: As an infantryman in Iraq, everything that I am and everything that I hope to accomplish is concentrated on killing the people who behead contractors and film it, who execute their fellow Arab Iraqi Police and Iraqi National Guard en masse, and who injured friends of mine last night.

Thirteen years ago, as a junior in high school, when I enlisted in the Army, I decided in advance that going into Iraq, or any conflict, would be a superb idea. I have renewed that decision every time I've reenlisted. Before I reenlist is the *only* time for me to ponder the overall politics of my job. After I enlist, it's my job. Command-detonated 155mm artillery rounds, clearing the kill zone and establishing a casualty collection point, maneuvering on likely enemy egress routes—as a soldier, these are the things that concern me. For you, a concerned citizen of the Earth trying to better your understanding of the big picture, you do what you can to expand your thoughts and actions on the matter *outward*, like a blanket of empathy, as it should be. If this describes you, I commend you; you are what is good about this world. For me, the "big picture" doesn't go beyond the tactical environment I am in. From there, my thoughts on Iraq continue *inward*, a contemplative introspection, as it should be.

October 28, 2004

SEGUN FREDERICK AKINTADE

A large hidden cache of weapons and explosives had been found in a remote desert area in the western part of our area of operations. Rather than immediately seize the items, snipers from our battalion were put in an overwatch position at the cache site to see if anyone would come to it. The following morning, two men and a boy came to the site and were detained.

Guys from my platoon were the QRF on this day and they were called to retrieve the detainees and bring them back to our base. The road back from the cache site was long and unpaved, rife with mogul-like potholes and large mounds of gravel. The five-vehicle convoy was only a few hundred meters away from the main highway when an IED detonated on the left side of the third vehicle. Jeff was the TC of this vehicle and said that the explosion filled the inside of the Humvee with sparks and smoke. He called over the radio that his vehicle had been hit. Yanko was behind the wheel and continued to drive another hundred meters or so until the Humvee died and came to a stop. The explosion and the shrapnel had rocked the vehicle hard enough to cause the transmission to fall out.

The convoy stopped, and soldiers began to dismount. Our battalion commander was out of his vehicle and firing at something to the south. Sean was in the turret of the lead vehicle behind the .50-cal and fired in the same direction as the battalion commander's tracers. The IED was on the north side of the street, and bursts of automatic fire were coming from the same direction. Other soldiers returned fire to the north as well. Jeff quickly checked the guys in his vehicle to see if everyone was all right. Jimmy was in the seat behind Yanko and his door took the brunt of the explosion, but the armor of the Humvee left him unscathed, if a bit shaken. One of the detainees was in his vehicle, and Jeff yanked him out and pushed him flat to the ground off to the side of the road. Pressing his knee into the detainee's side, Jeff yelled at him, "If you move, I'll fucking kill you!" Everyone was out now except Akintade, who was still in the turret. When Jeff looked back into the vehicle, he saw a waterfall of blood coming from the ceiling under the turret and covering the radio. With the help of Yanko and Jimmy, Jeff pulled Akintade out of the Humvee and off to the side of the road, where they began assessing him. Their vehicle had all the possible armor available. It was an up-armored Humvee with a second layer of armor on all the doors, and there were additional armor plates that surrounded the turret to protect the gunner. Despite all the extra armor, a piece of shrapnel struck Akintade in the back of the head, just below his helmet, entering at the base of his skull.

Yanko and Jimmy administered an IV and began CPR. Johnny-O was in the vehicle behind theirs and ran up with his combat lifesaver bag to help while they waited for the medevac chopper to arrive. Yanko found a pulse for Akintade, but it quickly faded. A breathing tube was inserted into his airway, and for twenty minutes they continued CPR until the chopper arrived.

Akintade was put on a stretcher and moved to the awaiting Blackhawk, which had landed on the road. As they were preparing to load him in, the medic on the chopper said, "Is this guy dead? We don't fly dead guys. We only fly wounded guys." There was a short and heated argument that Jeff ended by shouting, "YOU'RE FUCKING TAKING THIS GUY!" Moments later, the chopper took off with Akintade.

While the QRF from my platoon was retrieving the detainees from the weapons cache site, I was on a mission to recon a building for a raid later that night. Another platoon from my company had a few tasks to perform in the town, and I was tagging along to get photographs of the raid site and to get a feel for the streets in the area. It was late in the morning as we drove into town when the call came in about the QRF being hit.

We temporarily abandoned the mission we were on and sped to the site of the attack. As we flew down the highway, blowing by traffic with our horns blaring, details of the attack began to come in. We were told the convoy had been disabled by an IED and there were sporadic bursts of small arms fire. Then word came that there was a U.S. casualty.

Another unit from our battalion had also responded to the attack and had already secured the immediate area. Since the vehicles were now relatively safe and the small arms fire had ceased, the group I was with seized a nearby building and put a sniper team on the roof. There were four Iraqi men at this house, probably in their early twenties, three of whom sported typical Western clothes and haircuts. One of them had an ID card from a U.S. base for some sort of security force I wasn't familiar with. The men seemed nonchalant and glib, chuckling to each other as if they were sharing an inside joke. We took them out of the building, separated them, and made them sit against the outside wall of the property.

I helped search the property, and in the backyard I found a bucketful of clothes. Underneath the clothes were pipe fittings and other miscellaneous garbage. There was a white plastic box with a metal dial that looked like some sort of timer, a cell phone faceplate, a large 12-volt battery, and the battery tube handle of a flashlight. These were all items related to IED triggers. I went back to the front of the house, where the men were being watched, and told another sergeant about the trigger materials. I didn't want the guys we were watching to know what I had discovered yet, so I left the bucket in the yard where I'd found it.

John was also there, and we briefly discussed the attack. He told me he had heard they were doing CPR on Akintade. This was a really bad sign. If someone is receiving CPR on the battlefield, it usually means they're a goner. I tried to put this out of my mind.

There was a lot going on and I hadn't had a chance yet to tell anyone in command about the trigger materials I'd found. After a short wait, all the guys who could be spared were gathered together to begin a sweep of the field where it was believed the men who had detonated the IED had been located. There was a lieutenant from another platoon who was part of this sweep, so I informed him about what I had found.

As we searched the field, we found a location concealed from the road by tall rushes growing out of a muddy canal, with what looked like a map drawn in the dirt. The map seemed to depict the road with the IED, the highway where the road connected, and the power lines that were directly over where the blast occurred. IEDs are remotely detonated, usually from a great distance, and it's believed that the tall poles of high-tension power lines are often used as reference points by the insurgents for them to know when to trigger an explosion. Beside the map were footprints and tire tracks over recently trampled weeds. We continued to comb through the field but found nothing else.

We came out of the field and back to the road. I saw the spot where Akintade had been worked on. There was a small puddle of blood, and the ground was littered with latex gloves, IV bags and needles, field dressings, and other spent medical supplies. We were letting traffic through now, and I noticed that people were slowing down to gawk at the medical garbage and the blood. Before going back to my vehicle, I quickly picked up as much of the garbage as I could and threw it out of sight into the weeds and kicked dirt over the blood.

For the rest of the afternoon we raided house after house in the area behind the field. We believed the men who had detonated the IED must have fled in the direction of the houses we were searching. The raids were tedious and fruitless. Every house seemed to have an improbable number of women—no telling who were the wives and who were the daughters—and there were always scores of children. It felt good to be doing something, to be making some sort of effort to find the attacker, but I knew the chances of our stumbling onto a wild-eyed man hiding out in a barn, sweaty and breathing heavily with a red-and-white *shemagh* wrapped around his face, still clutching a metal box with an antenna and a big red button with "Acme Remote IED Detonator" emblazoned on it, was highly unlikely.

I kept thinking about Akintade, hoping at any minute we would hear that he had been stabilized and would be all right. I was eager to hear news of him, but at the same time I was afraid of bad news.

●　　●　　●

After Akintade was medevac'd, the QRF convoy continued back to the base. The disabled Humvee was in bad shape, but it could still roll, so it was towed by another Humvee. One of the rear tires was torn apart from the explosion and had quickly begun to deteriorate. After a few miles on the highway, the rim was scraping the road, gouging a crease into the asphalt. I don't know if it was the sparks flying from the scraping rim or the friction from the destroyed transmission, but the back of the Humvee being towed suddenly burst into flames. Orlando was in the vehicle right behind the burning Humvee, so once they stopped the convoy, he took the fire extinguisher from his Humvee and began putting out the flames. Everyone was eager to get back to the base and could ignore the damage being done to the road, and the further damage being done to the disabled Humvee, but a Humvee engulfed in flames was enough to make them decide that maybe it was time to get a proper tow vehicle out to do the recovery. There was another unit from our base on the highway at the time, and they stopped to help. After the fire was put out, the charred Humvee and the one towing it were left with the other unit to wait for the tow truck. As the convoy with the detainees was about to leave, someone from the other unit asked, "Hey, are you gonna take that guy with you?" There was still a detainee in the burned Humvee everyone had completely forgotten about.

It was almost sunset, and the group I was with needed to continue our original mission. We came up empty-handed from the houses we had raided, and we were exhausted. Everyone returned to their vehicles, and we made our way back to the town. We were about a mile away from town, on a quiet road without any buildings, when our commander ordered that everyone stop and get out of their vehicles. Everyone except the gunners got out of their Humvees and gathered around the commander, who said he wanted to speak to us. Once the group was silent, he looked around at everyone, then said, "Akintade is dead."

I don't remember much else of what he said except that Akintade had been pronounced dead on the medevac helicopter and that we should direct our anger constructively, not destructively. As he spoke I couldn't stop thinking about the word he chose: "dead." Not passed away, not lost, just dead. I was so uncomfortable. How are you supposed to act when you've just been told someone you've known for years has been killed? Was I supposed to keep my eyes on our commander while he spoke? Was I supposed to look at the ground as if in deep contemplation? Do I look around at the other guys to see how they are acting? Was I supposed to be thinking about revenge? I didn't feel hate, but I thought maybe I should. I was having trouble comprehending that I'd never get to see him again.

After our commander was done speaking, we got back in our Humvees and continued the mission. The kids in town were just as annoying as they always were, and I had absolutely no patience for them whatsoever. I was afraid that if any of them pushed me hard enough, I'd end up beating him senseless. Thankfully, none of them bothered us that much. While I was standing in the street, I looked over at John, who was standing by his vehicle. Our eyes met, and I was wondering what he was feeling. I imagine he was probably thinking the same thing about me. I couldn't even look at him, and I certainly didn't want to talk to anyone. I felt drained and listless. I got the photographs of the house I needed and we returned to our base.

October 29, 2004

Akintade had been dead for only a few hours, but I had to put it out of my mind. It was my first time leading a raid and I was nervous as hell. I wasn't the actual leader of the raid—I wasn't in command—

but since I had done the recon for the mission, I was in the lead Humvee of the convoy, directing the vehicles into town on the route I had chosen during the planning of the mission.

The intelligence we had was very explicit. We had the name and a photograph of the man we were looking for, and an informant had confirmed from a photograph the exact gate of the target house. It was in the center of town, a typical urban environment, dense with buildings. I knew the streets fairly well where the target house was, but I wasn't completely familiar with the road we would be taking to get there from the main street of the town. During my recon I had noticed a large tree at the corner of the street where we needed to turn, and I knew its exact GPS grid location, but despite all this data I was still worried I'd miss the turn.

It was early in the morning and still dark, and from my seat in the Humvee, my view of the landmark tree on the other side of the street would be obscured. I was obsessively watching the grid numbers on the GPS, and judging from them I knew we were getting close to our turn. The intersections were pretty close together, and the numbers on the GPS were changing rapidly. I knew it would be easy to make a mistake if I went solely off those numbers. At the next street I asked the gunner in the turret, "Is there a tree to your left—a really big tree?" The tree I was looking for was tall but it was behind some buildings. The gunner said, "Tree? What? Uh, yeah, there's a tree." He had no idea what I was talking about, and I couldn't see anything. Fuck. I told the driver to take the turn and then I realized it was the wrong one. Fuck, fuck fuck. The whole convoy was snaking behind us. I started to panic. I had no idea where we were. "Fuck! This is the wrong turn. Um, keep going," I told the driver. At the end of the road there was a T-intersection with a building that had a long horizontal fluorescent light on it. Wait, this looked familiar. I recognized the light from the photographs. The house we were looking for was on the same street as this building. I was relieved. But this meant we'd be approaching the house from the opposite direction from the one I had planned. The sergeant who would be leading the teams in was in my Humvee. I told him the mistake I had made and that we'd be hitting the house from the opposite direction. He told me, "Don't worry about it, it's fine. We can adjust." His simple reassurance helped me get my mind back on track.

This was the first mission Willy and I had ever been on together. He and Kirk were the breach team and would be breaking down the door to the house. Without any more wrong turns, we arrived at the target location. A hook and chain was attached to the top of the gate, and the gate was pulled open by a Humvee. Once the double doors of the gate had burst apart, the teams quickly filed into the courtyard. The entrance to the house was a heavily reinforced metal door that Willy and Kirk immediately started pounding away at with the breach tools while the teams lined up alongside it and waited anxiously.

On a perfect raid, the front door is breached in only a few seconds. This particular door was stronger than any I had seen, and it looked like Willy and Kirk had a ways to go. Then the family who lived there started to come out a side door we hadn't even noticed, probably to see what the hell was going on. This kind of tunnel vision is a common mistake made during missions, where you get so fixated on one thing— in this case, breaching the front door—and you fail to see alternatives.

The family was corralled into the courtyard and the house was searched. This was one of the nicest houses we had been in. We found no weapons other than one AK-47, clean, well oiled, and legal for them to have. The man of the house was a doctor and certainly not the man we were looking for. Hitting the wrong house is, unfortunately, a common mistake made on raids, so I double checked everything. I went out to the street and looked at the front gate as well as the address on the wall. I went to the nearest Humvee and checked the grid location on the GPS. This absolutely was the house we were supposed to hit. Mike was in charge of this raid, and once he realized this was not the man we wanted, he asked me tensely, "Are you *sure* this is the right house?" I looked him in the face and said, "I'm *positive.*"

My only guess is that someone purposely gave us bad information, perhaps envious of a family who had money, knowing we would break into this man's home and detain him until we got things sorted out. This was not a happy time for us, and getting negative results on an otherwise well-planned raid was totally frustrating. It had been less than twenty-four hours since Akintade had been killed; he was our company's first casualty. It was still not real to me, someone I'd known for years suddenly just . . . gone. I wanted a moment of reprieve to think about it, and to grieve, I suppose, but we had been working nonstop since it happened.

October 31, 2004

REMEMBERING AKINTADE

The memorial service held at our base for Akintade was really good. A company formation was held outside our tactical operations center in front of a small platform with a display of boots, a rifle, and a helmet to symbolize a fallen soldier. Ceremonies held in a combat zone are usually an undisciplined mess, but this one, for the most part, was a rare and touching exception.

Shortly before the ceremony began, two helicopters landed with the brigade commander, the brigade sergeant major, and their entourage. The moment the helicopters landed, several soldiers rushed out from them and formed a perimeter around the helicopters, all down on one knee with their weapons at the ready. (This security detail never ceases to amuse me. The helicopters with the brigade leadership land on a U.S. military base, but they still deploy their own security team.) After the imperial guards were in place, the leaders majestically stepped off the birds and were followed by a motley band of mismatched soldiers—some short, some fat, some female—all carrying strangely shaped black cases of different sizes.

As we stood in formation waiting for the ceremony to begin, the brigade sergeant major took a moment to check us out. Sergeants major are usually the torch bearers for standards, and they take uniformity very seriously. This one was no exception. Every time he visited us he wore knee pads, elbow pads, and yellow-tinted ballistic glasses. We were required to wear knee pads and ballistic eyewear for every mission—something that was a never-ending source of complaints from soldiers who wanted to configure their gear at their own discretion—but elbow pads were optional, and no one ever wore them. But this sergeant major was a stickler for maximal protective gear. For any other formation we would have been wearing our typical combat gear, where each soldier might look a little different—some with goggles on their helmets, different styles of modular pockets to hold ammunition on their vests, various types of slings on their weapons, and so forth. But for this formation we made sure each soldier looked as uniform as possible. One of the things we had done was to remove everything from our helmets except for the black plate on the front where night-vision goggles are mounted. After the sergeant major informally looked us over, he stood in front of the display on the platform. He then pulled our first sergeant aside and told him that we were not uniform. Everyone in formation had the black plate for their night-vision goggles on their helmets, but the helmet on the display to represent Akintade didn't. The sergeant major insisted that either everyone in the formation unscrew and remove the plates from all their helmets (not a simple task considering the number of screwdrivers we'd need) or we affix one to Akintade's. I couldn't believe that he was serious. I wanted to murder him on the spot. To play this game any other time was one thing, but to do it at our friend's memorial service was tactless and tasteless. I was furious. I *knew* these clowns were going to ruin this. The memorial was in honor of Akintade, but it wasn't really for his sake, it was for *us*, the soldiers—something you do to get a sense of closure and to begin the process of accepting the loss. Psychologically I needed this ceremony. The loss of Akintade was so abstract to me, and something about a memorial made me feel better—that his death was now something official and concrete. It felt good to have a chance to formally show my respect for him, and in a sense to say goodbye, and now this guy was fucking with it. Before I had a chance to murder the sergeant major, someone found a spare night-vision plate and it was hastily glued onto the display helmet.

A pair of speakers had been set up along with a microphone and a lectern for those who would be speaking. I was pretty sure we didn't have a bugler in the battalion, and I felt it unfortunate that taps would probably be played over the speakers from a CD. Ray told me a story once about when he was on a funeral detail. At the end of the ceremony, when it came time to play taps, the CD was queued to the wrong song and reveille was accidentally played instead. I hoped this wouldn't happen.

When the ceremony began, the chaplain gave a prayer and read a few words, as did a few of our leaders. Two soldiers from our platoon read eulogies for Akintade, one of which I was proud to have helped write. There was also a well-executed twenty-one-gun salute led by Chris. The soldiers who were part of the salute had practiced the procedure for hours the day before, despite the fact that when it was performed at the ceremony they were behind barriers and completely out of sight from everyone in the formation. I found this gesture to be particularly thoughtful. To insist on doing something well even though no one is watching is the definition of integrity, and appropriate to symbolize the life of Akintade.

During the moment of silence, I couldn't stop thinking about how of all the soldiers to be killed, it was sadly ironic for it to have been Akintade, because he was more empathetic toward the Iraqis than any other soldier in our platoon. There have been times when I've witnessed locals treated without as much respect as they deserved, and I am a little embarrassed to say that I never spoke up. It's not easy to tell another soldier, "Hey, go easy on that guy," for fear that your sympathy will be seen as weakness. But Akintade was unafraid to insist that everyone be treated with dignity.

Taps began to play, and it was beautiful. I was standing at attention with my eyes fixed on the horizon, and I thought, Wow, those must be some incredible speakers because if I didn't know better I'd say it was being played live. I glanced toward the sound of the music and was shocked when I saw a complete five-piece brass section, including a tuba! (The imperial guards had now formed their defensive perimeter around the musicians.) It was such a bizarre sight, but what made it especially surprising was that the musicians were phenomenal. After taps, they played "Amazing Grace." The performance was sublime. There was a slight breeze that carried the music, and I didn't want it to end.

I had known Akintade for years, but I didn't know him very well. He was a very private person and kept much of his personal life to himself. Very few people (including me) knew he had a fiancée. He was an immigrant from Nigeria and had the last name Okiwobe (oh-kih-WHOA-bee) when I first met him. It was a difficult name to remember, so most the guys called him "Obi Wan." When he changed it to Akintade (ah-kin-TAH-dee), his mother's equally difficult maiden name, I thought it was pretty funny. So I made up a short song for him that I loved to sing when he was around, even though he hated it:

Akintade (Sung to the tune of "Istanbul [Not
    Constantinople]," by They Might Be Giants)
Akintade was once called Okiwobe
Why he changed it I can't say
Maybe he liked it better that way

Something that always bothered me a little is that Akintade
thought I didn't like him. During the first few months of our deployment, while we were still at Fort Drum, I was having a hard time getting the respect I needed from some of the soldiers in my squad and
platoon, and it was making my life very difficult. One morning, after
I had just woken up, I was standing in the hallway outside my barracks
room door in a particularly bad mood, contemplating how I was only
two months into what would be an incredibly long deployment with
a platoon full of know-it-all assholes, when Akintade walked by,
slapped me hard on my ass, and said in his jolly, booming voice, "Good
morning, Sergeant!" He had a habit of sometimes doing this when he
walked by me. He would usually do it pretty hard, which made for a
nice loud *SLAP!* and it would always scare the bejesus out of me. Since
I had just gotten out of bed, the only thing protecting my ass was a
thin pair of Kermit the Frog pajama pants. Normally this wouldn't
have bothered me—I've always found ass-slapping to be hilarious,
something I like to do a bit of myself—but on this occasion his
timing was really bad. The slap was loud as hell, I might as well have
been bare-assed, and there were a lot of sniggering witnesses. For the
past week I had been trying to wean him from slapping my ass so
much, but this time my patience was depleted. I shouted down the
hall at him to drop and give me twenty I'll-stop-slapping-your-ass-
sergeant push-ups. I was pissed, and it was apparent to him. I usually
avoid publicly punishing soldiers, but since the ass-slapping incident
was public, I made the punishment public. I felt horrible doing it, but
I thought it important to curtail the notion that I was someone

whose ass could be slapped. Later in the day, a few guys from his squad told me he thought I hated him. This just made me feel worse. I wanted to apologize to him, but I couldn't. To apologize to a soldier for disciplining him is patronizing and wishy-washy. I had to stick to my guns. The more I thought about it, the more I couldn't believe I was spending so much time thinking about something I should never have given a second thought. He never slapped me on the ass again. He also hardly ever spoke to me again.

Something I learned from Akintade is that when you get frostnip on your toes, it's best to warm them on the stomach of someone who is a little flabby. Our company was at a weapons range late one freezing night at Fort Drum, and a lot of guys were starting to get cold-weather injuries. My feet were colder than they had ever been before, and I couldn't feel my toes. A lot of guys were in the same boat I was, so Joel, our medic, made us go into a small heated room, take off our boots and socks, and place our feet on another guy's bare belly for twenty to thirty minutes. I wasn't very excited about putting my feet on some dude's stomach, but I got over it instantly once I realized how well it worked. Joel knew he wasn't going to get many volunteers for belly duty, so he would go outside and grab the nearest innocent bystander and command him to surrender his belly. I was given one guy for a little while, but when Joel checked my feet he said they were not warm enough yet. Rather than use the poor guy who had already endured twenty minutes of my stinking frozen feet, he grabbed Akintade to pull the second tour of duty. Akintade had an incredible physique, and I always swore that if I had a body like his I'd be a merciless womanizer. The first guy had been a little on the soft side, and my feet had sunk nicely into his pillowy gut. But Akintade's abs were lean and flat, which made for less surface area for my feet. He wasn't very comfortable with this duty and kept laughing nervously. But every time he'd laugh, his stomach would take on the shape of a cobblestone road, making it even less effective for feet warming. I told him to stop laughing and to relax his stomach because his stupid chiseled abs weren't warming my feet very well. This just made him laugh more. I eventually gave up, relieved him of his duty, and put my boots back on.

I didn't see Akintade the morning he died, so I had to think for a while before I remembered when I had last talked to him. The night before he was killed, I was at my bunk sitting in front of my laptop when Santo, one of our platoon's machine gunners, came over to ask me a question. While we were talking, Akintade also came over to ask Santo something. Santo and Akintade were the two primary machine gunners for our platoon, and I had always found it very humorous that they also both possessed, by far, the largest penises in the platoon—something that was a common topic for jokes among the guys. Even though Akintade slept on a bunk less than twenty feet across the room from me, this was the first time he had ever been at mine. It was also unusual for Santo to come over to my personal area, so I held my arms out and announced, "To what do I owe this pleasure of having the two biggest cocks in the platoon at my bunk?" Akintade laughed his loud, distinctive laugh, and Santo put his arm around me, saying in his nearly unintelligible Dominican accent, "Aaaaaww, you know we luh you, Sar'n Hartley." This was the last time I saw Akintade.

November 21, 2004

WORRY WEEK

At the beginning of our tour it was a brigade policy that approximately 60 to 80 percent of soldiers from each company be allowed a two-week period of leave. Our company gave the first available dates to soldiers who had special situations, such as newborn children or sick family members. For the rest of the available dates there was a lottery for the order in which soldiers would be chosen to go on leave. My name came up as one of the first allowed to go, but I traded my slot with another soldier who had one of the last numbers.

It felt good to sacrifice my chance to go on leave so a younger soldier would be able to, but in all honesty I did it because I didn't want to leave Iraq. One of the ways to cope with being in combat is to go crazy just a tiny bit and learn to enjoy the work. I was cognizant of the fact that the comfort I felt in being in Iraq was somewhat illusory, and something I probably couldn't maintain indefinitely, and I was afraid that if I left, it would be difficult to get back into the "combat is fun" way of thinking when I returned.

About midway through our tour, the leave policy was changed to 100 percent of soldiers being allowed to go. I asked if it was possible to decline going on leave, but was told it was an order and not an option. Since my name was now near the bottom of the list, I would go during our second-to-last month in Iraq.

The unit who was going to relieve ours would be moving into our base soon, and the process of handing our workload over to them would be in full swing by the time I returned. I knew when I got back I'd have to tag along on certain missions as our unit trained the new guys, but I had convinced myself that there was a slight possibility I wouldn't have to. I rarely thought about my upcoming leave date, and the idea of getting killed or hurt was something I never worried much about either, but this changed when I realized I had only seven days left before going on leave. Given that this was possibly my last week of combat, the idea of getting hurt made me just as nervous as if it had been my first week.

For the first mission of worry week, I was in the lead vehicle of a convoy into town to set up concrete barriers around the police station. After a massive car bomb had detonated in front of the city council building the day before, it was decided that barriers would be put up around important structures. The explosion had left a deep crater in the street and collapsed a large portion of the outer wall surrounding the grounds of the building. An Iraqi National Guard soldier who had been guarding the front gate was killed in the blast, as were a few civilians who had been on the street when it happened. Most of the car bombs we'd seen were remotely triggered and usually destroyed only the car, doing minimal damage to the road and buildings. If the attacker was lucky, the blast sent enough shrapnel outward to damage a coalition vehicle and kill or injure a few people in the area. But this most recent event had been a suicide car bomb, and the explosion was tremendous. The bomber's body was scattered everywhere in messy pieces that were mostly unidentifiable, except for a section of his ribs and spine in the street, and his head, which had landed in the backyard of a nearby home.

The mission was pretty straightforward: we were to escort some flatbed trailers carrying the concrete barriers and construction vehicles into town and protect the engineers while they set up the barriers. Being in the lead vehicle, I had the job of scanning the sides of the road for bombs. This is the job of everyone in a convoy, but especially so for the first vehicle.

We were just outside of town, on a road with little traffic, when I noticed off to the side a cinder block with a wire going into it. My heart rate instantly doubled. This wasn't something typical of IEDs, but wires going into anything on the side of the road were never a good sign. I called over the radio to halt the convoy, trying unsuccessfully to not sound jittery. Whiskey was part of the convoy and had gotten out of his vehicle. I pointed out to him the wired cinder block. Then we noticed on the opposite side of the road an identical cinder block and wire. I wasn't sure what to make of this, but I sure as hell wasn't going anywhere near them. Whiskey crept closer to check it out, despite my suggestion that he not do so. He discovered that it was a power line that went under the street and to a nearby house. The cinder blocks had been placed there to protect the wire where it came out at the shoulder of the road. I felt relieved that it wasn't an IED, but now I was really on edge.

Once we got into town, the engineers went to work putting the barriers in place. We established a security perimeter around them while they worked, then we waited. Our company had done more than a hundred missions like this, but for the first time, I was actually worried. I knew this day was no more dangerous than any other I'd spent in Iraq, but just when I had almost gotten myself calmed down, intelligence was received that there was a high likelihood of another suicide car bomb attack in town, this time with two cars. We were given descriptions of the cars: one was white and the other black. Great. More suicide car bombs. I'm standing around here on a small city street and I'm supposed to defend myself against exploding cars? We knew it was common for suicide car bombers to use dead-man triggers where the detonation occurred when a button or lever was released, as opposed to pushed. This meant that if a carful of explosives came barreling down the road toward me and I shot and killed the driver, not only would the car still be coming right at me, but when his dead hand released its grip on the trigger, the bomb would go off.

I hated how helpless I felt defending myself against a car bomb. Normally I would never load a grenade in my M203 while in town due to the high density of civilians, but I knew a 5.56mm bullet was no match for a car bomb, so I loaded a grenade anyway. I knew a 40mm grenade probably wouldn't be much help either, but I was determined to use all available force to defend against an attack, even if it improved my chances of survival only marginally.

I spent a moment deciding what my response would be to various hypothetical threats. The obvious threat would be a single adult male driving a car fitting one of the vehicle descriptions, ignoring our road-block, and speeding toward us. I would not hesitate to engage this vehicle. But what if there were two men in the vehicle? Or a woman? Or an entire family? I briefed the gunner in the turret of my Humvee that there was no fucking way I was going to get killed a week before going on leave by some bullshit car bomb and that he should be prepared to immediately engage any vehicle I pointed out. I told him that if I saw a vehicle coming toward us driven by a nun and full of eight-year-old schoolgirls who I suspected might be sitting on piles of explosives, I was going to blow it up.

The engineers worked late into the day putting the barriers in place, and every time I saw a white or black car, my pulse would quicken. They finally finished work as the sun began to set. We returned to our base after a long, car bomb–free day.

December 2, 2004

"But I Haven't Seen Barbados, so I Must Get Out of This"

On my last day before going on leave, I was with CASEVAC and only had to make it to the end of my shift without getting killed. With only a few hours to go, we got a call that there had been an engagement on the highway and there was a wounded Iraqi national. An IED had exploded next to a convoy of civilian contractors, disabling one of their armored Ford Excursions. The Bradley unit from our base was in the area, and when they responded to the attack, a man with a cell phone was seen fleeing the area. After repeated commands to stop, he kept running and was shot by one of the soldiers. Despite being hit, the man continued to run, so one of the Bradleys shot him with its 7.62mm coaxial gun. This put him down. When they got to him, they saw he had been hit in the foot, leg, both forearms, and in the chest.

Knowing I was so close to being home free, I had switched into autopilot mode for the day, and I refused to be affected by anything short of a nuclear disaster or an Elvis sighting. When we got to the scene, the man was still alive and had already been given first aid for his wounds, but was still in need of help to be kept alive. The combat lifesavers who worked on him had done a good job, but the wound to his chest was still a serious concern. One of the 5.56mm rounds had struck him in the back and exited just below his collarbone. Matt took over and installed in the chest wound one of those snazzy one-way valve devices for treating sucking chest wounds. (I've always loved the term "sucking chest wound." During basic training, when we were taught how to treat them, I thought the drill sergeants were being funny and calling them that because getting shot in the chest really sucked. I later learned they were called this because as the wounded person continued to breathe, the chest cavity would fill up with air sucked in through the hole, eventually causing the lungs to collapse.)

As I stood over the wounded man, it occurred to me that I had lost count of how many times we'd encountered wounded Iraqis. There was a time when seeing something like this would have been trauma- tizing, but all I wanted now was to see the wounded guy get loaded into the ambulance and driven back to our base so I could go on leave. I had no idea if this guy was innocent or not, but either way I had a hard time feeling much sympathy for him. If he was involved in the attack, his current condition was part of the territory that comes with being a combatant. Or maybe he was an innocent bystander who had taken out his cell phone to call his wife to let her know he might be a little late for dinner because the U.S. Army had stopped traffic on the highway again, but instead of calling her he found him- self inexplicably drawn to the stopwatch function in his phone and on an impulse decided to time how fast he could run the hundred-yard dash. I'm a solid believer in civil liberties, and a person should have the right to wield a cell phone during spontaneous solo track events, but a person should also have enough common sense to realize that suspicious furtive behavior while using a cell phone in a combat zone is an unsafe combination.

There was a young man kneeling down at the side of the wounded man, holding his hand and praying softly. No one seemed to know where this guy had come from, but he wasn't in our way, so we left him alone. I tried to imagine how the man who was praying might have been feeling at that moment. If you were with someone you loved who was shot and dying, how would you remember that day? I wondered what it would feel like for this otherwise nondescript place to be part of an indelible mark left on me emotionally. It seemed strange to be near someone who was probably going through one of the most emotionally painful experiences of his life while I felt almost nothing at all.

About a month earlier, I was on a mission with the QRF where two local men were killed. Another unit from our base was visiting the home of an informant who had regularly provided them with valuable information. As a show of gratitude for his help, the unit came by his home to drop off shoes and clothes for his children. The informant had a brother who was not pleased to learn that his sibling had been giving information about the insurgency to the Americans, so during the visit, while the two of them were in the house together, the brother shouted "traitor" and threw a hand grenade. It was not clear if the grenade was meant to be thrown out the window toward the troops or meant to kill his brother, but the fact remained that the grenade didn't leave the house, and the blast wounded both men. Perceiving this as an attack, one of the soldiers shot and killed both brothers. A second grenade was found on the assailant's body.

By the time we got to the house, there wasn't much left to do.

There were no further attacks, and a search of the area yielded nothing significant. Normally when a civilian is killed or found dead, the body is transported to the police station to be identified so the police can inform the family. In this case, we were already at the family's house, so there was no need to identify the bodies. After our battalion commander (who had tagged along with the QRF) had his photograph taken, posing like a hunter over one of the dead men, we asked the father what he wanted us to do with the bodies of his sons. He asked us to move the bodies to the middle of the backyard, and the family would take care of it from there.

The rest of the family and some of the neighbors were in a group in the backyard and in a state of agony. As the bodies were carried into the yard, the group became hysterical. Most of the adult women performed the grief routine of shrieking, tearing the necks of their dresses open, beating themselves on the face and chest, then clawing the ground and throwing dirt over themselves. The pain and despair of the women was difficult to witness, but I found the cultural method in which they expressed it interesting. I had never in my life seen anything like this. What got to me the most was seeing the men cry. No dramatics, just simple weeping. It only got worse when the family got a closer look at the bodies. To have someone you love die is one thing, but to see their dead body, still warm and torn apart by grenade shrapnel and bullets, is something I can't even begin to fathom. It seemed, in a way, an important event in *my* life, to witness something like this. I felt that maybe I should have taken a photograph of the grieving family, but I couldn't bring myself to do it. There was nothing I could do to comfort them, and I felt I was getting too emotionally involved in the situation. So I stopped worrying about the crying women and switched my focus to the men. I figured our presence was no longer welcome, and I was worried there might be a grief-driven attack of retaliation. I wanted to get out of there before someone had the chance to get their hands on an AK-47, giving us cause to kill more of the family. When we left, I felt so strange. What do you say in a situation like this when you leave? "Um, sorry about killing part of your family. We'll just leave the clothes and shoes for your kids right here. See ya later, I guess."

The man with the sucking chest wound lay next to the Bradley that had shot him. When I looked up in the turret, I saw Karl in the gunner's seat, the guy I went to Qatar with. I rarely ran into him, so I gave him a cheery hello. When he looked back at me, he put his hands up and shrugged. This seemed like a strange response to my greeting. Then I realized that he was probably the one who had shot the man. I remember a conversation I had with him in Qatar where he told me how little action the guys in Bradleys see. They have too much fire-power to be useful for most of the missions in our area, and I'd venture a guess that this was the first time he'd fired in combat. It was still unclear if the man who was shot was innocent, and Karl probably wasn't feeling great about having to sit there and watch him suffer.

The wounded man was stabilized and transported back to our base, where one of the head medics decided to pour a clotting agent into his chest wound, which killed him.

I decided to go to Barbados for my leave. The thought of going back to the States really didn't appeal to me. More than anything, I wanted to relax and spend my leave doing absolutely nothing, and I knew if I went home I'd spend the entire time visiting everyone I knew. Endless social engagements for two weeks would have been fun and probably would have entailed a lot of sex, but it sounded like more trouble than it was worth. Besides, I didn't want to go home until I was completely done with my deployment. With how often we were given time off while we were at Fort Drum, I felt like I had had a hundred "going away" parties and nights of drinking. I didn't want to repeat this sort of thing with multiple homecomings.

When I was trying to decide where to go for leave, my primary criterion was to go somewhere warm and quiet, and the Caribbean seemed like the logical choice. I'd never done much traveling, and I knew nothing about the islands, so I had to arbitrate a destination. I didn't want to go anywhere named after a saint, and I didn't want to go anywhere with a weird name like Anguilla or Nevis, so I chose Barbados because it seemed exotic and utterly random. In retrospect, I think subconsciously I chose it because of the Tori Amos song "Me and a Gun," where she sings, "But I haven't seen Barbados so I must get out of this."

The process for going on leave is a tremendous pain in the ass; it takes days of briefings and out-processing before you actually leave the Middle East. But the coolest thing I've ever seen the Army do was fly me to any destination I chose without asking any questions.

For three days I was a zombie who got on and off flights. I wanted to close my eyes, curl into the fetal position, bleed pinesap from every pore, and form a hardened cocoon around myself in which I could hibernate until I was in Barbados. I got as close to that as possible. For three days I didn't open my eyes or mouth unless I absolutely had to. I had connecting flights in Georgia and Texas, where I was respectfully ushered to the front of every line.

It was so fucking weird to suddenly be back in America. And there were so many people thanking me, telling me they respected me and appreciated what I was doing, patting me on the back, paying for my coffee, paying for my bagel, paying for my gum and magazines. It wasn't uncommon for people to tell me in some form, "I don't support the war, but I support you." The appreciation was a bit overwhelming, but it felt great. I was impressed by the respect and candor of the people and it made me proud.

I had arranged online to rent a room in a guest house in a quiet residential area in Barbados. It was around 11:00 p.m. when I arrived at the house, where I was greeted by the middle-aged German woman who owned it along with her young Turkish husband. Her husband didn't speak any English, and he seemed a little intimidated by my uniform, so his wife told me he wanted to know if I had flown through Turkey or if I had ever had the chance to work with Turks. I answered that I hadn't. It was late, and none of us were much interested in chatting, so after they showed me my room, they went to their own home across the street and I sat on the porch and drank a warm freedom beer and listened to the waves. When I first noticed the crash of the waves, I thought it was a gunshot. So typical. A soldier leaves combat and thinks everything sounds like a gunshot.

The next morning I met the two Jamaican guys who were also renting rooms at the house. The younger of the two was quiet and reserved and probably no older than twenty. The older one was loud and outgoing and in his thirties. They had jobs working at a construction site in the area and were staying at the house for a few months. In the evening, when they were back from work, we would sometimes drink beer on the porch together. Both were nice enough guys and we got along well, but they were a little shady. The older one was dealing drugs out of the house and would get strange visitors at all hours. The younger one told me he had stolen a lot of money from a drug dealer in Kingston, Jamaica, and could never go back. When he got back from work, he'd roll two joints, smoke both of them by himself, then pass out on the couch with his thumb in his mouth.

I spent a few days at the beach and visiting different sights, but what I was most concerned with was eating at every chance I got. I ate like a pig king. The room was cheap, so I thought this would justify spending a ridiculous amount of money on food.

The island was beautiful, and the people were nice, but I didn't feel like I was getting what I needed. Everyone spoke English, which was convenient, but I couldn't get over how I felt like I was in Brooklyn.

This wasn't a bad thing, but it wasn't the carefree paradise I had hoped it would be. I never slept deeply in Iraq, but I always slept well. Now I was getting horrible sleep. I had dreams about guns and Humvees and helicopters and explosions. I would wake up every hour. I would grind my teeth and sometimes wake up with cramps in my calves from flexing my feet all night. The humidity and lack of air conditioning made me sweat, and my sleep seemed feverish. There was a political rally one night at the fish market where a man yelled over loudspeakers about misspent tax money and the corruption of the government. Another night it rained so much the roads turned into rivers. None of this would normally have bothered me, but I couldn't get away from this nagging feeling of anxiety and dread. I was unarmed, and it made me feel insecure. What if someone attacked me? I didn't even have a pocketknife. I didn't want to see people, I wanted to be alone, I wanted to escape. I didn't want to have to worry about locking my room because of sketchy housemates. I didn't want to be a tourist, I didn't want to be a soldier, I didn't want to be American, I didn't want to be white, I wanted to be nobody, invisible, a spirit.

The escapist impulse in me was strong when I was in Iraq. I wanted so badly to just get fucked up and leave my mind and body behind. I would daydream about this bar in New Paltz that plays eighties music on Thursday nights, and I wanted more than anything to be drunk on cheap beer and nostalgia. I fantasized about going to Amsterdam for my leave and spending two weeks in a state of perpetual intoxication from various combinations of absinthe, hash, vodka, mushrooms, mescaline, and ecstasy.

Speaking of which, my second day in Barbados, I spent the afternoon at the beach with my ex, Stasy. I thought it would be fun. The few times I'd hung out with her in the past were always really good experiences, but this time it went all sideways. I was a mess of repressed anxiety, and she brought it out. The beach was near the flight path for the airport, and every time a plane approached the island, I was certain it was going to explode and bloody bodies and aluminum would rain into the ocean. People at the beach looked soft and fleshy and delicate in their bathing suits, and I couldn't stop wondering what their guts looked like. I wanted them all to be torn apart where they stood, each rendered into a bloody mound of flesh and bone. Would the woman in the bikini still seem beautiful if she were split apart so you could see exactly how much of her appeal was a yellow layer of fat or the deep red color of muscle tissue? I've always wondered if I could recognize someone by their skull. If someone you loved was killed, do you think you know their face and body well enough that you could identify their skeleton? It wasn't fear that I felt; it was a desire for there to be no fear. I didn't want to worry about the people or the planes. I just wanted to see them all dead and everything destroyed. I couldn't take the anticipation, I just wanted the beach to be littered with entrails and carrion and everything on fire. I was covered in a cold sweat and I thought I was going to implode or at least spontaneously combust. I couldn't talk, I couldn't move, and I was certain everyone around me knew I was seething. There was a Rastafarian speed-walking back and forth across the beach in front of me. I couldn't stop staring at him. He was happily speed-walking through my nightmare, completely unaffected by the horrors of life on earth. He smiled at me and put his arms in the air like he was cheering for having won an award. This cheered me up. I learned something that day: it's not a good idea to hang out with your ex, Stasy, right after having been in a combat zone.

I was flipping through the Lonely Planet guide to the Eastern Caribbean when I read about Saba. It is a tiny island, only five square miles, with a population of about twelve hundred. It has no beaches and little tourism. It sounded gorgeous and quiet. The more I read, the more I liked the sound of it. I decided to spend my last week there. I immediately called a travel agent and arranged tickets.

I had paid for my room at the guest house in advance, and I hoped the woman who ran it would refund me the rest. When I went to her house that night to talk to her, her husband answered the door. He wasn't wearing a shirt. He didn't wear shirts *ever*. I had seen him on various occasions during the week, working in the yard or washing the car, and not once was he wearing a shirt. He was a good-looking guy with long, dark, wavy hair, a hairy chest, a perfect tan, and a great physique. He belonged on the cover of a romance novel. The fact that he never wore a shirt, didn't speak English, and was always doing chores screamed eighties porn. He was the gardener, the pool cleaner, and the cable guy all rolled into one. His aging wife was not exactly a catch and had to be at least twenty years his senior. She was old and sagging, but she had money and a beautiful house on the beach. And a pet husband. It's fucking hilarious that people like this actually exist. She denied my request for a refund.

The ticket agent at the Barbados airport told me I couldn't fly to Saba without a passport. I should never have been allowed in the country without one, or at least not without my birth certificate to prove that I was an American, but now leaving for anywhere other than the United States was not going to happen. I'd never bothered getting a passport because I'm not exactly the world traveler type. The ticket agent advised me that I'd need to go to the United States embassy to get a passport or emergency travel orders if I was to be allowed to go to Saba.

The embassy in Barbados was an interesting experience. With my military ID in hand, I was treated like a VIP. The waiting area inside was packed to capacity with people sitting silently on wooden benches. The room resonated with anxiety, and it was as quiet as a church. I suppose everyone there was waiting to speak to an agent about a visa permitting them to travel to America. The rules of conduct in the waiting area were strict. You couldn't talk, stand, or sit anywhere other than on a bench. Everyone was dressed, groomed, and behaving as though they were waiting to interview for the most important jobs of their lives.

When it was my turn to speak to an agent, my status was immediately changed from VIP to shithead. The agent was a fairly attractive young woman, younger than I was, and full of skepticism and distrust. She looked like she was a recent college graduate, probably full of ambitions in international relations, thinking it would be a good first step for her career to work at an embassy in an exotic Caribbean country.

"How exactly did you get into the country without a passport?" she asked, eyeing me suspiciously.

"I dunno. The guy at the airport just let me in. He told me there was a time when you could enter the country with only a military ID, but now you need a passport or your birth certificate. Then he let me in anyway. I wasn't going to argue with him."

She then looked at my military ID, which I had passed her under the slot in the bulletproof glass and laughed. "Is this supposed to be real?"

The IDs the Army gave us in Iraq were a joke. Our personal information was handwritten on antiquated blank ID cards and cheaply laminated. My military ID is usually the only form of ID that I carry, and I didn't want anyone to think it was fake, so while I was on pass at the base in Qatar several months ago, I had a new one made. The new ID they gave me was the modern version, but the machine used for laminating the face of it had been broken, so the kid who made it for me put a piece of clear packing tape over it instead. It was a lot better than the one it replaced, but it still looked half-bogus. I told all of this to the agent and that if she thought this one looked fake, she should have seen the other one.

She looked at me like I was an idiot. "So you're basically telling me that the Army isn't organized enough to give you a proper ID card."

"That's exactly what I'm telling you. Everyone thinks the U.S. military is this well-oiled machine. The truth is you would be shocked if you knew how *dis*organized it is. There are times I'm amazed anything ever gets done." This was my attempt at humor, hoping to get her to relax a little.

"Regardless, you know your military ID doesn't prove citizenship, right?"

"Yes, I realize there are resident aliens in the U.S. military." Ha! I beat her to her punch line.

"Therefore you should know that you need a passport to fly internationally. To get to Iraq you had to fly there, right? This means you must have flown through other countries." She looked exasperated and shook her head in disbelief. "This doesn't make any sense. How could you possibly fly all the way to the Middle East without a passport?"

I told her, "How could the United States invade a sovereign nation without the blessing of the United Nations? The U.S. Army does pretty much whatever it wants. That's how."

About an hour later, I left the embassy with a temporary passport, good for one year. Score one for the Sarcrastic Method!

The landing strip at the airport in Saba is the shortest in the world for an international airport. The island is a dormant volcano, and the airport is located on a small flat area at the base of the island, once a pool of lava runoff. The fifteen-minute flight in a tiny plane to the island originates only from St. Maarten. The landing was the most intense experience I'd had on a plane without a parachute. You fly shockingly close to a set of cliffs, and just when you think you're going to crash into them as the plane's proximity alarm starts blaring and the red light in the cockpit flashes, the plane drops onto the runway that has suddenly materialized. Women cry, men curse, everyone claps.

Saba was everything that I'd hoped it to be, and more. Since the island is so steep, no matter where you are you always have a suicide-inducing view of everything. Because of the Dutch influence, every building is white and ridiculously cute with its red roof and green shutters. The roads are narrow, and so steep and winding they'd make San Franciscans nervous. The humidity is completely bearable, and the temperature is seventy degrees, twenty-four hours a day, all year. There was always a lonely cloud at the peak of the mountain, just to make sure you got the point about the island being a magical fairy-tale land. I would not have been surprised to see a unicorn. Everything was a lush green, and the air smelled so good. Iraq smells horrible. The whole fucking country stinks. It's like one big landfill. God, I hated Iraq. I hated everything. This place was so heartbreakingly beautiful, my entire life before this moment instantly seemed shitty. I wanted to buy a house and live here for the rest of eternity. This place wasn't actually a part of mortality. Combat was something that happened on that crappy little planet called Earth. I was somewhere else.

The small hotel where I stayed was in an area called Hell's Gate. This made me love the place even more. The hotel was run by a French couple; he was a chef, and she a wine connoisseur. My room was small and sunny, and the view from my window made me want to kill myself, it was so perfect. I wasn't given a key to my room because there was no need for one. There isn't crime in Paradise! It was quiet and secluded, tourist-free, and I saw almost no people. Exactly what I needed. But the best part was the food. I would wake up with the sun, stare at my watch until it was breakfast, have eggs, coffee, a fresh chocolate croissant, and a freshly squeezed glass of orange juice, then stare at my watch all morning until it was lunchtime. My favorite lunch dish was a seafood couscous thing. I ate it almost every day. Then I would stare at my watch all afternoon until dinner. I ate lamb, lobster, venison, duck, foie gras, escargot, and drank wine so good I wanted to cry. With a gut full of food and wine, I would pass out immediately after dinner and repeat the process again when the sun came up the next day. I had found heaven at Hell's Gate.

I wasn't apprehensive about returning to Iraq. I enjoyed every moment I was in Saba without thinking about the next, and I was prepared for it to end. When that day came, I packed, paid, waved goodbye, and got on the plane.

December 28, 2004

ONLY SLAVES ARE HAPPY

A few days before I went on leave, Matt and I were sitting at the table we shared between our bunks. We were both on our laptops—I was writing, he was watching *Alias* DVDs, and together we were clandestinely imbibing smuggled Jim Beam. I love the Jim.

We were at the chatty level of intoxication when Matt asked me if I was ever going to put the blog back online. I told him I was thinking about putting it back up just before the end of our deployment, or maybe just after, if I wanted to play it safe. Then I figured, Fuck it, why wait? I said, "Whaddaya say I put it back up right now?" Matt was always the rational one and any harebrained idea he didn't put the kibosh on could be considered copasetic. "Fuck it man, do it," he permissed. The blog was already technically online, but hidden and therefore not publicly accessible. Putting it online was basically just a matter of flipping a switch—or twiddling a bit, as programmers like to say. A few clicks and keystrokes later, www.justanothersoldier.com silently went online. I was in the Caribbean a few days later.

The D.I.E. Decision Making Process:
Drink Jim Beam
Intone "Fuck It"
Execute Decision

I didn't dread returning to Iraq as much as I thought I would. In a perverse way, it kinda felt like coming home. Everything was so familiar: my platoon's Humvees lined up the way they always were; the noisy door to our bunker; the stupid tail of an old Iraqi bomb stuck in the dirt we used as a urinal. I had missed Wazina. It felt good to hold her again. I loved how she looked, I loved how she smelled. It's funny how attached you can get to a weapon. I wanted to keep her after we returned to the States. I wanted to put her on the wall over my bed. An assault rifle is the ultimate security blanket. The Marines acknowledge this the best with their "Without me, my rifle is useless. Without my rifle, *I* am useless" thing.

I knew we were a month away from returning home, and I figured it would be easy to coast through the rest of our time in Iraq. There was a time when I was considering asking to stay for another tour, but I had ditched that idea long ago. I'm not one to get homesick and I don't usually miss people, but I was getting excited at the idea of returning home. Being on leave gave me a much-needed taste of freedom. I was ready to dispense with my duty as Uncle Sam's killbot and I was eager to return to a place with fewer explosions and more college girls.

It was late when I walked into our bunker, and most everyone was asleep. I dropped my bags next to my bunk and saw that there was a stack of stapled papers on my bed. It was a printout of my most recent blog entry. My stomach sank. On the back, in handwriting, it read, "I need to talk to you ASAP—Jeff" Fuck. Oh well. I knew this could happen, but this was fast.

I didn't have a chance to talk to Jeff, who was now our platoon sergeant, until the following morning. He didn't seem overly upset but he told me the captain wanted to talk to me immediately. When I reported to our company's headquarters bunker, my first sergeant told me he wanted to talk to me before I saw the commander. He pulled me into his room and sat me down. He seemed really uncomfortable. He told me he didn't know why the captain wanted him to do this, but he asked me to explain why I'd done what I did.

I asked, "You mean put the blog back online?"

"Yes, why you put it on the internet again," he confirmed.

This was a good question. First off, I never felt as though I should have had to take it down at all, but an argument about this would have been a waste of time. He didn't want to be having this conversation and he didn't want to be involved. He wanted me to say something so he could scribble it down on the stupid counseling statement he had in front of him. Then his job would be done.

The way I remember it, taking the blog down was a "favor," and, at worst, I was a dick for retracting this favor. Back at Fort Drum almost a year earlier, when my commander first caught wind of the blog, I was escorted that night to his quarters by my platoon sergeant. When I entered his room, he was getting ready to go to bed. He was barefoot, in a T-shirt, and not wearing any pants. As I stood at attention, he approached me and stood in front of me, toe to toe. I never realized how short he was until he stood in front of me without his boots on. With little daggers shooting out of his eyes, he looked up at me and asked in a voice louder than was necessary, "ARE YOU OUT OF YOUR FUCKING MIND?!" Whenever he spoke, he would punctuate the end of each sentence by thrusting his head forward and tightly pursing his lips, his mouth a bulging floodgate forever on the verge of bursting. He berated me at length about the contents of what he had read online. The acidic spittle that flew from his mouth was burning tiny holes into the front of my uniform and plumes of sulfur smoke rose from his ears as he furiously listed transgression after transgression. To hear him tell it, my hands were holding the spear that had pierced the side of Christ. He told me he hadn't told his superiors yet and that I needed to decide right then if I was going to take the blog down or not. I thought about this for a second, then responded, "In that case I choose to *not* take it down." My first sergeant and platoon sergeant were present for this conversation, and when I said this, they both looked like they were going to faint. I think my commander was also taken aback, so he said, "I'm going to leave the room now, and these two men are going to convince you of why you should take it down." With my commander out of the room, my platoon sergeant told me, "Look, Jason. Just take it down. Do it as a favor to us. Do it as a favor to me." I didn't feel as though I should have to take it down, but I respected him a lot and this request was enough for me. My commander was called back into the room, and I told him I would take the blog down, but I would do so under protest, clearly reiterating that I was doing it as a favor to my platoon sergeant and first sergeant. My commander could have said, "Sergeant Hartley, I order you to take the blog offline," but he didn't. He wanted me to take it down, but for whatever reason he didn't explicitly order me to do it. He *kinda* ordered me. And I kinda complied.

I'll admit, I thought I'd be slick by putting it back online at the very end of our deployment. I had hoped that should it be found, no one would really care or want to bother making a big deal about it. But I know this was a lame thing to think. So you wanna know why I did it? Because I wanted to. And in my heart of hearts, I wanted to press the issue. I wasn't violating OPSEC and I wasn't smearing the

Army. These writings were the things I saw and felt. This was my life, and it was something worth sharing. That's why I put it back online. Because I felt compelled to. What more reason did I need?

I told my first sergeant the reason I put the blog back online was that since we were at the end of our deployment, I didn't think it would matter if I put it back up. I told him I understood that my commander probably wouldn't care if I put everything back online at the end, and I thought I had basically complied with this. I really wanted to remind him that taking it down in the first place had been a favor, that I had voluntarily agreed to stifle my own right to freedom of expression, and that I had decided I was ready to start exercising that right again. But this wasn't the time or place to make that argument, so I kept it simple. Given that I was an infantryman in a combat zone being counseled by one of my superiors, I found it not only absurd but physically impossible to utter any sentence that might contain the words "freedom of expression" in defense of my actions.

I signed a sworn statement where I explained briefly what I did and why. Then I met with my commander. He told me he wanted to say a few things and that he didn't want to hear what I had to say; in fact he didn't want me to say anything at all—it was not to be a discussion. He was relatively calm this time as he explicated in great detail how I was the world's biggest piece of shit. This was the second time I had listened to him insult me at great length. Once he was finished with the insults, he told me he was going to give me a freebie—without asking any questions, he would allow me to revise my sworn statement before he submitted it to the battalion. This was probably the biggest insult of all. I don't know if he actually thought I was hiding some huge secret or if he just wanted to see how I'd react, but I graciously declined the offer. Before I left, my first sergeant asked the commander if he wanted me to take the blog offline. He thought about this for a moment, then said he wanted me to keep it online so battalion could investigate it. This seemed a little strange but, what-ever, the irony that I was now being ordered to keep the blog *online* was humorous.

I was a little surprised at how well my commander was taking the news about the blog's being up again. He was mad, but not like he was the first time. When he came back to my bunker later that night, I un-derstood why. The printed-out pages he'd read earlier were only the most recent entry I had posted. He assumed this was the only thing online and nothing else. *I* assumed he knew there was an archive of the entire fucking blog online. Now he was back, after battalion had done a little further reading, and he was incensed. I had thought I'd al-ready witnessed the most livid my commander could get, but I learned there were several more levels he was capable of reaching. He was now using words like "lied" and "deceived" when he referred to me. He commanded that my laptop be seized, along with my exter-nal hard drive and anything that looked computery that might have aided in this perpetration. I was to be immediately relocated to the headquarters bunker, so I packed my bedding, shaving kit, weapon, and some other items into a sort of overnight kit until I could move the rest of my belongings. He did his best to do this with a minimal amount of lights and sirens, but when you have your platoon sergeant, platoon leader, first sergeant, and company commander all standing next to your bunk as you pack up your shit, it's going to attract a lot of attention. I was treated like a perp.

The next day, I was called to the battalion TOC, where I signed a statement they had prewritten for me; it read that I would agree, without being coerced, to voluntarily remove the blog from the inter-net. Our battalion intelligence section had already printed out a copy of the entire blog to conduct their investigation.

For the next month, until we left Iraq, I did almost nothing. My commander told me I was never to go on another mission, and the next time I left the base would be when we all left for good. I pulled some late-night shifts where I manned the company's radio, but that was it for work. Typically when a soldier is punished, he is given extra duty. This was horrible. The worst thing you can do to a soldier is to *not* let him work.

I was living in the same bunker as my commander, and my bed was next to the main meeting room, so getting sleep was virtually impossible. And it was humiliating when there were operations briefings going on in that room well within view of me in my pajamas lying on my bed reading a book or trying to sleep. And without a computer, I was bored out of my mind. I had only a few books left I hadn't shipped home and I spent most my time reading them. I borrowed a CD player from Matt and listened to CDs John had burned for me from his mp3 collection. It was miserable.

I had no idea what was going to happen to me. After a week of wondering, my commander sat me down and explained to me what would come next. He told me he had requested that I be given a court-martial. But he said that after seeing the story in the news about the soldiers who had refused to go on a fuel convoy mission and how they were not convicted in their courts martial, he changed the request to a field-grade Article 15 to be sure he could "see me punished." He also told me that if I fought the Article 15, he'd "make it his business" to see that I got convicted. Along with all this advice, he gave me another extensive serving of insults with regard to me and my writing. This insult business was really starting to wear on me. He was passionate, emotional, creative, and comprehensive with the insults. I have never in my life eaten so much shit. There was nothing professional about it anymore. Including the first tongue-lashing he gave me at Fort Drum, this was the fourth time I had to listen to a variation of the same scolding. (He seemed obsessed with the photograph I'd posted, taken of me and Willy one freezing day back at Fort Drum, where we both had our pants pulled down and were sitting on shitters in a latrine at one of the ranges; he brought it up every time.) All I could do was stare into his eyes while he delivered his screed. I took it all without saying a word until he said, "You know why you do this? Because you just don't care. You just don't give a fuck," his head thrust forward, lips tightly pursed. I had had enough. My blood was boiling. I interrupted him and said, "I don't like it when I'm told I don't care." I would have continued by saying the entire fucking reason I write is *because* I care, but before I could say any more he fired back with, "I don't give a fuck what you don't like!" From this point on, I ignored everything he said.

The unit replacing us was on our base now and they were put in the bunkers our platoons were living in. Some bunkers that weren't being used at the far end of our base were cleaned out, and most everyone from my company was moved into them. Space was tight, and the temporary bunkers were filled with soldiers. I was moved from headquarters into one of these crammed bunkers. Not having anything to do and not knowing exactly what was going to happen to me next was taking its toll on me. I was in a perpetual state of anxiety and I had a pain in my stomach that wouldn't go away. My laptop had been returned to me, but I couldn't concentrate on anything for more than three seconds, and it was impossible for me to write. After sixteen days of doing nothing but smoking, chewing gum, listening to CDs, and watching DVDs, I was called to the battalion TOC to be read the results of the investigation.

It's pretty pathetic when you actually look forward to being punished. I had started to wonder if anything was going to happen at all. I was eager to get the show on the road. The officer assigned to the investigation was a captain and coincidentally was Johnny-O's brother. When we sat down, he asked if he could get me some coffee. I appreciated the gesture but felt supremely uncomfortable with the idea of my investigating officer serving me coffee. He was friendly, and the first thing he told me was that he really enjoyed reading my writings. He was professional and polite. He told me that everyone steps in shit at least once in his military career. And that I had really stepped in some shit. He explained to me the issues he found with what I had written. The biggest concern he saw was that some of the things I had written could be seen as violating operational security. He wanted to know what I thought about this. This was the first time I was actually given the opportunity to speak. I told him I knew that OPSEC was a concern, and explained what I had done to protect it. I didn't want anything I wrote to be "news," so the stories I wrote about Iraq were two to three months old before I emailed them out. I didn't write anything you wouldn't find in a newspaper. I never used last names, I never divulged what company or battalion we were a part of or the name of the town where we worked. But he had a counterargument for everything I said. His logic was sound, but the response I wanted to give to each of the items he listed was "So?"

"You wrote that the last round in each of your magazines was a tracer."

"You wrote, 'Tomorrow we leave for Louisiana.'"

"You wrote, 'We flew to Kuwait by way of Shannon, Ireland, and Sicily.'"

"You divulged the name of Operation Salt Lick."

In addition to violating OPSEC, he determined I had violated the Geneva Convention by posting photographs of detainees and that my conduct was unbecoming a noncommissioned officer for posting a photograph of myself sitting on a shitter. I then signed the "Rights Warning Procedure" document, which stated that I had been questioned about "offenses of which I am suspected/accused: OPSEC violations, conduct unbecoming an NCO, Geneva Violations." I verified with him that these were the three things I was being accused of, and he agreed. Then he added, "Your commander probably feels you violated a direct order as well," but this was not listed in his investigation.

He explained that the next step was to meet with the battalion commander, who would decide what my punishment would be. The information my battalion commander would use to base his decision on the appropriate punishment would come from this investigation. This did not paint a very flattering picture of me, so he asked me if I wanted to make a sworn statement to better explain my side of it. I wrote out a statement reiterating how much "I love soldiering," why I felt my writings were a positive thing, and that what I had done "may not have been appropriate or legal" and that for this I was "remorseful." I felt good about everything I wrote in my statement, except for stating that what I did "may not" have been right. "May" was the most important word there. I was hedging my bets at this point. I knew the battalion commander was a fan of patriotic writing, and it was a well-known fact that he didn't get along with my company commander. I was hoping to use this to my advantage. I felt shady and manipulative for thinking like this, but I had little else to work with.

I had hoped that my meeting with the battalion commander would happen in the next few days, but it didn't. At least I knew what I was being charged with now, but I still hadn't met with JAG (Judge Advocate General) and I had no idea how the Article 15 hearing worked.

I always tell people that if there is only one thing they remember about me, remember this phrase: *Only slaves are happy*. Keith Wood, my tenth-grade English teacher, told me this, paraphrasing Tolstoy or Dostoevsky—I forget which. I know that this may seem like a cynical and depressing thing to tell people, but it's an idea I ponder regularly. This corporeal dispensation we call mortality is all about choice, about volition. This is how we define freedom: the ability to have choice. But there are times, oddly, when choice is what causes us so much pain, and the release from choice a relief. How often have you heard someone explain their actions by saying, "I had no choice," expressing an apparent release from accountability? It's often that only once circumstance dictates how we must choose do we seem to be happy. We spend so much time passively making decisions, listlessly wandering down the path of least resistance, until we no longer have any meaningful choice other than survival.

For years I've wondered if the idea would be better described by changing the word "slave" to "prisoner." If lack of choice is what creates this false happiness, then "prisoner" may be a more precise word to describe it.

Being a soldier is like being a happy slave. You always have something to do—a purpose, a duty—and little choice as to whether you should be doing it or not. In addition, this purpose is often considered righteous and noble. (The soldier: a noble slave?) And in combat, where the importance of survival is a very literal reality and not just some philosophical exercise, being a slave hardly seems like slavery at all because survival is the most basic of necessities. But after spending a month as a virtual prisoner, under house arrest and confined to my base, I was no longer allowed to perform the tasks of the noble slave. This taught me that prisoners are miserable. Without any doubt, I now knew that "only slaves are happy" was the correct wording. Resolving this question of which word was more correct ended something I had been philosophically struggling with for years. It was the only positive thing that came from my final month in Iraq.

I had been psychologically prepared for combat. But I was in no way prepared for this house arrest bullshit. What made it truly horrible was not knowing when I would be released from active duty. I was confident that if I refused to accept the Article 15 and demanded a court-martial, I could win. But this meant I would be kept on active duty, possibly for months. I was so utterly burned out now that the idea of spending an indefinite period of time at Fort Drum through a court-martial hearing was killing me. There was also the possibility that I could be kept in Iraq for the court-martial. I had permanent butterflies in my stomach. Eating made me nauseated. Then smoking started making me nauseated. I constantly felt the urge to gag, like having an itch I had to scratch. I wasn't nauseated, there was no need to gag, but the physical impulse itself was almost impossible to suppress. Then the butterflies turned into something worse. I felt like my body was digesting itself from the inside out. Every day I woke up wondering if this would be the day when I'd be called to the battalion commander's office to begin the Article 15 hearing. I doubt the delay in execution was being done spitefully, but if it was, it worked. I was a fucking wreck.

Since the new guys were taking over our missions, everyone had a lot of time on their hands. Our leaders were gone most the time, riding with the new guys on the missions, helping them get familiarized with the operations. This meant there were a lot of bored soldiers without much supervision. If it could be smashed, burned, run over with a Humvee, used as a sled, or used to get drunk or high, it was. It was pretty bad. But I was being accused of violating the Geneva Convention for chrissakes. As long as there were no crimes being committed against humanity, who was I to judge how guys chose to blow off steam?

Every new day was just as miserable as the one before. One of them was Christmas. Then I was informed that my Article 15 would be handled at Fort Drum, when we got back to the States. A few days later, after my stomach had successfully digested several years of life, we finally left FOB Orion via Chinook helicopters.

Home

January 8, 2005

"Awesome!"

Our first stop was Kuwait, and after a few days of out-processing and briefings, we went through customs and were put in a holding area awaiting our flight out of the Middle East. This small holding area, which you cannot leave for any reason, is called the "freedom area."

The flights back home were long. I took sleeping pills. There was a pillow fight in the cabin of the plane at one point. I threw pillows at my commander and first sergeant when they weren't looking. This made me feel better.

We landed at an airport in Maine, fifteen minutes into the new year. As we got off the plane, we were greeted by dozens of people who live in the area who regularly come out to greet the returning troops. The majority of these people were vets themselves. It was touching that they had chosen to spend the new year shaking my hand. Some of the people had done this hundreds of times. I wondered how they knew in advance the exact flight we were on.

The layover was short. Willy and I and several other guys clandestinely maneuvered on the hotel that was connected to the airport, found the bar, had a few quick beers (against the express wishes of our first sergeant), then got on the flight to Fort Drum. For a week we went through briefings, medical screenings, and an insane amount of paperwork. In the evening almost everyone would get drunk. My anxiety was at an epic level. My birthday was in a few days. I had decided I would demand a court-martial. I knew I hadn't done anything wrong, and as much as I didn't want to spend another birthday in uniform, I hated that I was being bullied. I knew that demanding a court-martial would keep me at Fort Drum while the rest of my unit would return to their homes.

Violating OPSEC wasn't the real issue. Everyone has a vision of how they want to remember their combat experience, and particularly how they want others to view their combat service. Most soldiers, and especially infantrymen, want to realize all their Jerry Bruckheimer–fueled fantasies with macho military fervor. In my writing, all I did was include some details in hopes of providing a more honest and humorous perspective on what soldiering is typically like. I could have written something like "We went on a raid tonight. We smashed the gate down and cleared the house, but the guy we were looking for wasn't home," and I probably wouldn't have gotten into any trouble. But instead I'd written something like "Tonight we went on a raid. It wasn't till 3:00 a.m., and I couldn't sleep, so I masturbated before we left. On the way to the raid we got lost, but after driving around for a while we finally found the house. We tried to breach the gate of the outer wall, but in the process accidentally ended up knocking the entire wall over. After clearing the house, we realized it was the wrong house. Actually, we hit the house we were supposed to, it was our intel that must have been bad. We asked the man of this house where the guy we were looking for lived, and he pointed out another house. We then raided that house, but the guy we were looking for wasn't home. He was at work—at a U.S. base. As I was pulling security on an alley, I realized that the chow we had for dinner wasn't agreeing with me and when I tried to fart, I ended up shitting my pants a little. Once we finished searching the house, we hopped back in our Humvees and took what we thought was our planned egress route, but instead found ourselves on a dead-end canal road. While turning around, one of the Humvees got stuck in the mud. Most raids do not go this badly. We eventually made it back to our base safe and sound. My ass had started to chafe from when I "sharted," so I took a shower, masturbated, and went to bed." (This, by the way, is a true story.)

If I had written a story like this, my commander would likely have berated me for smearing the Army by portraying our unit as incompetent, and condemned my scatological admissions as unbecoming and unprofessional, but in his report he'd likely have accused me of violating OPSEC because I'd disclosed tactical details on how we perform breaches.

A homecoming ceremony was held that week on the basketball court in the gym at Fort Drum, the same one where our deployment ceremony had been held. My parents and youngest sister came in from Salt Lake City for it. Matt's brother had dropped Matt's car off to him a few days earlier. Since Matt had a vehicle (against the express wishes of our first sergeant), we were able to get around post on our own now. Sean and I rode with Matt in his car to the ceremony. The families had started showing up, and everyone was making their way into the gym. As we were walking through the parking lot, Sean said, "That girl's got a nice ass." I looked at the people walking in front of us and at the ass in question, and I realized I knew who it belonged to. I said, "Dude! That's my little sister! She's, like, sixteen! Jesus!"

I crept up behind my mom and surprised her. She was ecstatic to see me. She hugged me, started crying, hugged me some more, cried some more, then hugged me longer than she ever had. It was great to see her. I was happy she didn't have to worry about me anymore.

The ceremony was awesome. "Awesome" was a word we used a lot in Iraq.

How to Use "Awesome!"

If someone says, "Dude, it's your turn again to do shit-burning detail," you say: "Awesome!"

"Holy shit, those idiots in Delta company shot at second platoon": "Awesome!"

"An entire busload of Iraqi Police graduates got killed by insurgents today": "Awesome!"

The bleachers in the gymnasium were packed with everyone's families and friends. Every soldier from our battalion filed into the gym, forming one huge mass formation. As we marched in, some awesome music was playing over the loudspeakers: "Bad Company," "The Boys Are Back in Town," and "Welcome to the Jungle," among a few other awesome songs.

I think it's a tradition in the Army for public-address systems to never work properly. The prayer the chaplain gave was mostly inaudible because of the crappy PA system. As he prayed, people in the audience kept yelling, "We can't hear you!" Someone finally fixed the speakers mid-prayer, making the second half of the invocation loud as hell. After the ceremony, Willy, Matt, and I went to dinner with my family.

My Article 15 was formally presented to me the morning of January 5, 2004, by the garrison support commander at Fort Drum. It read that I had violated a direct order and that I had violated operational security. The charges of having violated the Geneva Convention and of conduct unbecoming a noncommissioned officer were not included, but the accusation of having willfully disobeyed a direct order was new.

After the reading of the Article 15, I elected to meet with a JAG lawyer. Before meeting with the lawyer, I was put in a waiting room at the legal assistance center. It was full of soldiers who had also chosen to meet with a lawyer concerning the Article 15s they had been given. I noticed there were a lot of soldiers with black eyes in the room. When it was my turn, I sat down in a chair across the desk from one of the JAG lawyers in his office. He was a captain. He opened the folder to my Article 15, which contained a stack of papers easily four inches thick—it included the entire blog, photographs and all. He started reading the first page, then the second. I asked him if he was familiar with my case. He told me this was the first time he'd seen it in his life. I asked him if he'd like me to summarize it for him, and I did.

After I was done briefing him, he explained to me that I would almost certainly lose a court-martial. What I didn't know until now was that being convicted in a court-martial is a federal conviction, not unlike a felony. He rambled on at length, and I could barely get a word in edgewise. He told me he believed in fighting a good fight more than anyone, but that my case couldn't be won. His "advice" wasn't of much help. He told me I should say that I was a good soldier and that writing the blog was something I had done in the heat of the moment, to cope with the stress of combat. This guy was obviously used to dealing with soldiers who got into trouble for stuff they did when they were drunk. To argue that fifteen months' worth of writing was something I had done in the "heat of the moment" was ludicrous.

After the useless meeting with the lawyer, I reviewed the contents of the Article 15 on my own. It was documented that the meeting I had with the investigating officer back in Iraq had ended at 1:00 a.m., on December 20. This meeting was to discuss the charges against me, and violating a direct order was not a conclusion of the investigation at that time. At the end of the meeting, I signed that document. At 11:00 p.m., on December 19 (while I was in the meeting with the investigating officer), a sworn statement was signed by one of my leaders stating that I had been given a direct order eleven months earlier at Fort Drum. There was another sworn statement, similar in effect and from another one of my leaders, signed and dated December 20, at 7:00 a.m. The investigation was then concluded and signed off on by the investigating officer an hour later, at 8:00 a.m.—and it now included that I *had* violated a direct order.

I had a day and a half before the final part of the Article 15 hearing to decide what I wanted to do. I felt I could beat the OPSEC charge, but I had no chance beating a charge of having violated a direct order. With my commander saying he had given me an order, I was fucked. And with multiple sworn statements to back this up, I had no chance. I could still demand a court-martial to prove a point, but I wasn't going to risk becoming a felon on account of some stupid blog. Regardless, even if I was *certain* to win a court-martial, this still meant that everyone involved (company commander, first sergeant, platoon leader, former and current platoon sergeants, investigating officer, everyone who signed sworn statements, etc.) would also likely be kept on active duty throughout the proceedings. How was I supposed to make a decision that would have prevented that many of my fellow soldiers from returning to civilian life?

I decided I would fold and accept the Article 15. Now I had to decide how I was going to go out. At the hearing I would be given an opportunity to present matters of defense, mitigation, and/or extenuation—in other words, I could beg for mercy. Once I finished presenting a defense for myself, the commander in charge of the hearing would decide my punishment, which could include any of the following: forfeiture of pay for up to one month, loss of one grade in rank, up to forty-five days extra duty, and up to forty-five days restriction.

I had expected to lose pay, but I wasn't in the Army for the money, so I wasn't worried about that. I had also expected to be demoted. I had to ask myself if trying to keep my stripes was a priority. I could beg to not be demoted, but there was no way in hell I was going to give my commander that satisfaction. And when it came down to it, I knew I wasn't in the Army for the rank, either. Being given extra duty and restriction would have prevented me from being released from active duty, and I couldn't see the colonel being that vindictive. I wasn't worried about that either. So all I had to decide was what to say at the hearing.

The Article 15 hearing was held on January 6, 2004, and started just before 10:00 p.m. I stood at attention in the office of Colonel David Gray, in front of the large oak desk where he sat. Present were my company commander, my platoon leader, my platoon sergeant, my former platoon sergeant, and my first sergeant. There was no reason for any of them except my commander to be present for the hearing but, whatever; my commander had dragged them along for some reason. After I saluted the colonel, he began to read the charges against me. As he read, I wondered if he knew about the singer named David Gray. I loved David Gray. It didn't seem right to be getting an Article 15 from someone with that name. Then the oak grandfather clock behind him, which matched his oak desk, started to chime ominously. What the hell was a grandfather clock doing in his office? And how many times had this happened before? I wondered if he usually tried to schedule Article 15 hearings at high noon. After the tenth chime, he continued reading.

"In that you, having received a lawful command to dismantle your website www.justanothersoldier.com . . ."—was what he was saying, but I think it would have been much funnier if he had sang it to the tune of "Babylon," seeing as how he was David Gray—". . . were derelict in those duties in that you willfully failed to practice operational security, as it was your duty to do. This is a violation of Article Ninety-two, UCMJ."

Once he was finished reading, he asked me if I wanted to demand a court-martial. I said I didn't. He asked if I wanted the hearing to be open or closed. I had the option of deciding if I wanted witnesses present, which I saw no need for, so I chose closed. He then told my commander that his entourage would have to leave. They all stood up in unison from the tan leather couch they were sitting on. Then the colonel asked me, "It's up to you, really, if you want them to stay or not." I told him, "I don't mind if they stay, sir." They all promptly sat back down in unison. The colonel then asked me if I wished to present matters in defense, mitigation, and/or extenuation. I told him I did not. He seemed a little disappointed that I chose not to say anything in my own defense, so he asked, "Do you have anything else you'd like to say at this time?"

I told him, "Sir, everything I wish to say I've already stated in the two sworn statements I signed."

I knew there was nothing I could say that would do me any good. Anything I said would just make me look like an asshole. My response didn't satisfy the colonel. He asked me, "So why did you disobey the order?" My commander was standing for the hearing, off to the side of the colonel's desk, and as soon as the colonel asked this question, he started to fidget. He shuffled his feet a little, bent over and looked down at his boots, then stood upright again.

I answered, "What order? If I had been given an order, I would have obeyed it. What can I do to make this more clear to you, sir? I WAS NEVER GIVEN A FUCKING ORDER!"

I didn't say this, but it would have been cool if I had. God knows it's what I was thinking. So I compromised. I said, "I misinterpreted the order my commander gave me."

Thankfully the colonel didn't press the issue about the order any further. Then he dispassionately lectured me about operational security and how anything I wrote didn't have to directly violate OPSEC to give the insurgents an advantage over us because all it would take was one piece of seemingly harmless information to complete a puzzle for the enemy. I had heard this reasoning before. It's true. Just because I can't imagine how a piece of information could be used against me doesn't mean it's not useful to the enemy. I guess this means the only way to be completely safe is to never communicate anything ever.

Once the colonel finished with the lesson, he announced my punishment: reduction to the grade of specialist and forfeiture of five hundred dollars pay per month for two months. I saluted the colonel, signed the Article 15, muttered "Awesome!" under my breath, then exited the office.

We were released from active duty the following afternoon.

January 21, 2005

THE ALAMO, THE GAP, AND HOOTERS

Half the guys from my original company in Manhattan weren't deployed at the time I was but were deployed with another battalion less than a year later. This battalion was sent to Baghdad. Felix Vargas, a very close friend of mine and Willy's, was part of this battalion. Felix hadn't even been in Iraq for two months when his Humvee was hit with an IED. He survived the blast, but his leg was broken badly and he was recovering in a hospital at Fort Sam Houston, in Texas.

His birthday was coming up, so Willy and I decided we'd surprise him with a visit.

I was on leave in Saba when a friend sent me an instant message telling me that Felix had been injured. I nearly had a heart attack when I got the news. For a while, he was in danger of losing his leg. Felix was a fitness nut, and losing one of those athletic legs of his would have been devastating. For guys like me who spend more than twelve hours a day in front of a computer, losing a leg wouldn't nearly have affected our lives as much as it would have Felix's.

I booked a flight and a hotel room, and Willy and I left on Felix's birthday. Our flight arrived late in the evening, and I was worried that we'd be too late to make it before visiting hours at the hospital were over, but just when we got to the hospital, I learned that their visiting hours were incredibly liberal. I was almost disappointed. I had been looking forward to the scene I know Willy would have made if they had denied us entrance.

The hospital was immaculate. Hospitals are usually pretty clean places, but this one was impressive. We got our visitor IDs and took the elevator to the floor where Felix was staying. The staffperson on duty pointed out his room and advised us that he had a "no touch" status. I asked him what this meant. He said it meant we couldn't touch him—to prevent any infections. I laughed. Are you fucking kidding me? I haven't seen this guy in a year and a half, he's one of my closest friends, he almost got killed, it's his birthday, and you're telling me I can't hug him because he might get my cooties?

Felix's favorite thing to say is "What the hell?" It's his trademark phrase. He likes it so much, in fact, it's usually how he greets me and Willy. So when we burst into Felix's room, Willy yelled, "What the hell?" Felix was lying in his bed talking on his cell phone. He looked shocked and confused. It was priceless. He sat up in his bed and told us how good it was to see us, then gave us both a huge hug and a kiss.

(Felix isn't gay, he's just Latin.) He hadn't hung up his phone yet, so he said into it, "Ma. Ma. I gotta go. Some jerks just showed up. I'll talk to you later. Love you." After he hung up, he said, "So what do you fags want?" Another thing that Felix always does whenever he sees me is he sings this little song that goes, "Hartley is an asshole, he takes it in the butt," which he sang for me again. I know you probably think that soldiers only say cool macho things to each other, like in *Top Gun*, but in reality, saying ridiculously stupid shit like this to one another is more the norm.

Willy and I hung out in Felix's room for hours. He showed us his leg. When he unwrapped the bandage, I almost threw up. It looked like Dr. Frankenstein's monster. Willy is excellent at downplaying things that are fucked up. He said, "That's not that bad. It looks pretty good, actually."

I told Felix, "Fuck that man. Your shit is fucked UP! Why the hell does it look like that?" There was this bulging diamond-shaped slab of flesh that looked like it had been sewn onto his shin. He explained that the wound had gotten infected and the surgeons had had to remove a large chunk of flesh from the back of his calf and graft it onto his shin to replace all the gangrenous flesh that had to be removed. All I could think was, Damn!

Felix told us that he was in the last Humvee in the convoy when they got hit. A 250-pound bomb had been buried in the road, and when it exploded the last thing he remembered seeing was a huge wave of dirt created by the shock wave. The blast was so powerful that the Humvee flew into the air and landed upside down. The bomb tore the Humvee apart, and Felix was ejected from the vehicle before it hit the ground. He caught his leg on the Humvee as he was thrown from it, nearly tearing his leg off at the shin. When he was found, his leg was only partially attached.

Everyone from our original company has always made fun of

Felix for his chin. It's superhero sized. When he regained consciousness, one of his platoon mates who was standing over him said, "You're gonna be okay. Your chin saved you."

Two of the soldiers in the Humvee were killed: Wilfredo Urbina and Christian Engeldrum. Urbina was twenty-nine years old and a volunteer firefighter from Baldwin, Long Island. Engeldrum, age thirty-nine, was a New York City firefighter from the Bronx, and the first city employee killed in Iraq. I had known both of them. They were great guys.

The next day, Willy and I decided we would do what every American is supposed to do at least once in his life: visit the Alamo. For some reason I always figured the Alamo was a rundown building in the middle of the desert. But in reality, it was only a few blocks away from our hotel, right in the middle of San Antonio.

We wandered around the building, the grounds, and the souvenir shop for a bit, then sat down and listened to a historical presentation about the history of the Alamo. The Alamo does not have a basement.

Located adjacent to the Alamo was . . . a huge mall! Like good Americans, we knew if we didn't go buy some shit, the terrorists would win. Nothing is more American than the Gap, so we purchased tastefully boring clothing at affordable prices. Then we had lunch at Hooters, where we ordered food from a predictable menu and drank light beer served from a plastic pitcher. We had horrible service from a semi-hot girl. This is what America is all about. This is what we fought for, right?

Glossary

.50-cal. Used to refer to the M2 Browning .50-caliber machine gun

155mm artillery rounds. Very common charge used to make improvised explosive devices

40mm grenade. Ammunition fired by the M203 grenade launcher, typically high explosive, illumination (flare suspended by a parachute), or smoke

550 cord. Nylon cord capable of holding up to 550 pounds, used in parachute rigging

AAFES. Army and Air Force Exchange Service; the company that runs all the PXs

Abrams. M1 main battle tank, armed with a 120mm main gun, M2 .50-caliber machine gun, and M240 machine gun

ACLU. American Civil Liberties Union

ACOG. Advanced Compact Optical Gunsight

ACT. Standardized college entrance assessment test, similar to the SAT

Aimpoint. Manufacturer of the non-magnifying red-dot sight used by the U.S. Army

AK-47. Russian-made 7.62mm assault rifle

al-Sadr, Muqtada (born c. 1974). De facto ruler of the Sadr City section of Baghdad and leader of the Mahdi Army militia

AO. Area of operations

Apache. AH-64 twin-engine, four-bladed, single-rotor attack helicopter with a tandem-seated crew consisting of the pilot, located in the rear cockpit position, and the co-pilot gunner, located in the front position. AH-64D Longbow is the upgraded version.

battalion. 300 to 1,000 soldiers, usually four to six companies, commanded by a lieutenant colonel and a sergeant major

BC. Battalion commander

blog. Online journal, from "web log"

Bradley. M2 fully armored, fully tracked fighting vehicle, armed with a 25mm chain gun, M240C 7.62mm machine gun, and two TOW anti-tank missiles, and used to transport six dismounted infantrymen

brigade. 3,000 to 5,000 soldiers, usually two to five battalions, commanded by a colonel and command sergeant major

C-130. Hercules four-turboprop-engine cargo transport plane

C-17. Globemaster four-jet-engine cargo-transport plane

C4. Plastic explosive with a consistency similar to clay

CASEVAC. Casualty evacuation, usually via field litter ambulance

Chinook. CH-47 twin-engine, dual-rotor cargo-transport helicopter

CO. Commanding officer, usually used to refer to a company commander

company. 62 to 190 soldiers, usually three to five platoons, commanded by a captain and a first sergeant

CQ. Charge of Quarters

CQB. Close-quarters battle

CS gas. Chemical irritant commonly referred to as "tear gas"; it is actually a white solid powder, usually mixed with a dispersal agent that carries the particles through the air.

DCU. Desert camouflage uniform

defilade. Protection of a position, vehicle, or troops against enemy observation or gunfire; typically used to describe a terrain depression

division. 10,000 to 15,000 soldiers, usually consisting of three brigades, commanded by a major general

E-1, E-2, etc. Enlisted ranks (as opposed to officer ranks)

egress. To leave, retreat, escape, or exit a place

EOD. Explosive ordnance disposal

exfil. Exfiltrate

FDNY. Fire Department, City of New York

FLA. Field litter ambulance

FOB. Forward operating base ("forward" means "in a combat zone")

ghillie suit. Camouflage suit, commonly made from strips of burlap, meant to simulate the appearance of bushes and foliage

GPS. Global positioning system

HEDP. High explosive dual purpose (armor-piercing, anti-personnel) also referred to as *HE*.

Humvee. From "HMMWV," meaning high-mobility multipurpose wheeled vehicle; never called a "Hummer" in the military (a hummer is a blowjob).

IBA. Interceptor body armor

ICDC. Iraqi Civil Defense Corps, preceded the ING

IED. Improvised explosive device, commonly in the form of a "roadside bomb"

illum. Illumination

infil. Infiltrate

ING. Iraqi National Guard

intel. Intelligence

IR. Infrared

JRTC. Joint Readiness Training Center, a training course at Fort Polk, Louisiana

KBR. Kellog Brown & Root, a construction, engineering, and services subsidiary of Halliburton

KIA. Killed in action

Kiowa. OH-58 two-seat, single-engine, four-bladed single-rotor light observation/attack helicopter

LT. Lieutenant

M14. 7.62mm semi-automatic rifle, typically used by snipers and marksmen

M16. 5.56mm assault rifle, standard service weapon used by most soldiers

M2. Browning .50-caliber belt-fed machine gun

M203. 40mm grenade launcher, attached to either an M16 or an M4

M24. 7.62mm bolt-action sniper rifle

M240B. 7.62mm belt-fed machine gun

M249. 5.56mm magazine- or belt-fed light machine gun (a.k.a. SAW)

M4. 5.56mm assault rifle; essentially an M16 with a shorter barrel and butt stock

M60. 7.62mm belt-fed machine gun, preceded the M240B

M9. Beretta 9mm semi-automatic handgun

medevac. Medical evacuation, usually via helicopter

MILES. Multiple Integrated Laser Engagement System (military laser-tag equipment)

MK19. Belt-fed automatic 40mm grenade launcher

MOI. Monastic Order of Infantrymen

mortar. Weapon that consists of a tube mounted on a baseplate and bipod that fires a round with a high-arching trajectory, commonly used to fire illumination and high-explosive rounds

MP. Military Police

MRE. Meal, ready to eat

MWR. Morale, welfare, recreation

NAI. Named area of interest

NBC. Nuclear, biological, and chemical

NCO. Non-commissioned officer

nine-line report. Radio procedure consisting of nine parts used for reporting a casualty

NVG. Night-vision goggles

NYPD. New York City Police Department

PAQ4. Weapon-mounted infrared laser, invisible to the naked eye but visible through night-vision goggles

PEQ2. Weapon-mounted infrared laser with infrared spotlight

PETA. People for the Ethical Treatment of Animals, a nonprofit animal-rights organization

platoon. Four squads, usually led by a sergeant first class and a lieutenant

pogue. a non-combat arms soldier

poleless litter. Lightweight nonrigid (no poles) fabric stretcher used to carry wounded soldiers

PX. Post Exchange (military post department store)

QRF. Quick reaction force

RPG. Rocket-propelled grenade

RPK. Russian-made 7.62mm machine gun

RTO. Radio telephone operator

SAW. Squad automatic weapon, M249 light machine gun

squad. nine men, usually two teams, led by a staff-sergeant

T&E. traverse and elevation; a device mounted on a machine gun tripod used to limit the vertical and horizontal pivoting movement of the gun

TC. Truck/tank commander

team. Usually four men, led by a sergeant

TOC. Tactical operations center

TOW. Tube-launched, optically tracked, wire-guided missile system; a 50-pound anti-tank rocket that can be mounted on and fired from

Humvees, tanks, helicopters, or other vehicles, or from a tripod on the ground

UCMJ. Uniform code of military justice; military legal system

USO. United Service Organization; a nonprofit, congressionally chartered, private organization that provides comfort, morale, and recreational services to military service members and their families

UXO. Unexploded ordnance

WIA. Wounded in action

WTF. "What the fuck"

XO. Executive officer, second in command to the commanding officer (CO)

Acknowledgments

It was my friend and fellow geek Mike Fayer who suggested I create a blog to chronicle my deployment. At the time, I could find only one infantryman in Iraq who had a blog, and writing about my Army misadventures sounded like fun. Once I started writing, my friend Ernie Hilbert (a.k.a. "My friend with a Ph.D. in English from Oxford") would occasionally plug my blog in his daily literary newsletter, E-verseRadio. One of Ernie's readers, the novelist Dave King, was kind enough to mention me to his agent, Kim Goldstein, for which I cannot thank him enough. Expecting nothing in return, Kim worked hard to help put me in touch with Paul Bresnick, who is now my agent. Paul's experience as an editor and agent was invaluable in helping me get a contract quickly and with little fuss from HarperCollins. I would like to give love and special thanks to my editor, Marjorie Braman, for being an excellent therapist and friend. She's also an outstanding editor whose talents made it possible to both clarify and preserve the voice in my stories.

I want also to thank:

Our platoon sergeant, Mike O'Brien, who was our anchor through this deployment. There cannot be enough good things said about him as a leader and as a man. His craft as a soldier was invaluable to our platoon, but his even temper and commonsense approach to operations are what kept our platoon safe and sane.

John Therrien, for being the best first sergeant I've ever had, for being an all-around bad-ass, and for all the ways he's been a heartening example to me. I wish he could have been with us for this deployment.

Katie Gostinger, my manager, my lawyer, and my friend, for her inexhaustible support and encouragement for the duration of my deployment and the development of this book.

And my parents, Jim and Linda Hartley, for being supportive and understanding of my writing and my career in the Army, both of which, I'm certain, cause them great distress at times. I love you both.